Caliban's Voice

In Shakespeare's *Tempest*, Caliban says to Miranda and Prospero:

> "… you taught me language, and my profit on't
> Is, I know how to curse."

With this statement, he gives voice to an issue that lies at the centre of post-colonial studies. Can Caliban own Prospero's language? Can he use it to do more than curse?

Caliban's Voice examines the ways in which post-colonial literatures have transformed English to redefine what we understand to be 'English literature'. It investigates the importance of language learning in the imperial mission, the function of language in ideas of race and place, the link between language and identity, the move from orature to literature and the significance of translation. By demonstrating the dialogue that occurs between writers and readers in literature, Bill Ashcroft argues that cultural identity is not locked up in language, but that language, even a dominant colonial language, can be transformed to convey the realities of many different cultures.

Using the figure of Caliban, Ashcroft weaves a consistent and resonant thread through his discussion of the post-colonial experience of life in the English language, and the power of its transformation into new and creative forms.

Bill Ashcroft is a founding exponent of post-colonial theory, co-author of *The Empire Writes Back*, the first text to examine systematically the field of post-colonial studies. He is author and co-author of twelve books including *Post-Colonial Transformation* and *On Post-Colonial Futures*. He is Chair of the School of English at the University of Hong Kong, on leave from the University of New South Wales.

Caliban's Voice

The transformation of English in post-colonial literatures

Bill Ashcroft

Routledge
Taylor & Francis Group

LONDON AND NEW YORK

First published 2009
by Routledge
2 Park Square, Milton Park, Abingdon OX14 4RN

Simultaneously published in the USA and Canada
by Routledge
270 Madison Ave, New York, NY 10016

Routledge is an imprint of the Taylor & Francis Group, an informa business

Typeset in Baskerville by
Book Now Ltd, London
Printed and bound in Great Britain by
TJ International, Padstow, Cornwall

British Library Cataloguing in Publication Data
A catalogue record for this book is available from the British Library

Library of Congress Cataloging in Publication Data
Aschcroft, Bill, 1946–
Caliban's voice: the transformation of English in post-colonial
literatures/Bill Ashcroft.
        p. cm.
1. Commonwealth literatures (English—History and criticism. 2. English
literature—History and criticism. 3. English language—Political aspects—
Commonwealth countries 4. English language—Discourse analysis.
5. Postcolonialism—English-speaking countries. 6. Postcolonialism—
Commonwealth countries. 7. Great Britain—Colonies—Languages.
8. Postcolonialism in literature. 9. Colonies in literature. I. Title
PR9080.A75 2008
820.9'3581—dc22   2008006846

ISBN10: 0–415–47043–9 (hbk)
ISBN10: 0–415–47044–7 (pbk)
ISBN10: 0–203–09105–1 (ebk)

ISBN13: 978–0–415–47043–8 (hbk)
ISBN13: 978–0–415–47044–5 (pbk)
ISBN13: 978–0–203–09105–0 (ebk)

Contents

Acknowledgements

The publisher and author would like to thank the following for permission to reprint material under copyright:

'Prospero Caliban Cricket' by John Agard from *New Writings 2*, ed. Malcolm Bradbury & Andrew Motion, Minerva, 1993. © John Agard. Reprinted by permission of John Agard care of Caroline Sheldon Literary Agents.

'Naming' from *Arrivants: A New World Trilogy* by Edward Kamau Brathwaite, OUP. © 1973 by Edward Kamau Brathwaite. Reprinted by permission of the author and Oxford University Press.

Extract from 'Caliban' from *Arrivants: A New World Trilogy* by Edward Kamau Brathwaite, OUP. © 1973 by Edward Kamau Brathwaite. Reprinted by permission of the author and Oxford University Press.

Extract from 'Translations' by Brian Friel, © 1986 The Catholic University of America Press and © 1981 Faber and Faber. Used with permission: The Catholic University of America Press. Washington, DC and Faber and Faber.

Extract from 'Dan is the Man' by Slinger Francisco. © Slinger Francisco. Reproduced by permission of Slinger Francisco, DLitt, O.C.C.

Extract from 'Very Indian Poems in Indian English' in *Collected Poems 1952–1988* by Nissim Ezekiel, Delhi, OUP. © Nissim Ezekiel 1989. Reprinted by permission of Oxford University Press India.

Extracts from 'Caribbean Proverb Poems' by James Berry from *News for Babylon* ed. James Berry, Chatto and Windus, 1984. © James Berry. Reproduced by permission of James Berry.

Extract from 'In My Name' from *I is a long memoried woman* by Grace Nichols, published by and © Karnak House 1983/2008. Reproduced by permission of Karnak House.

Extracts from 'Street 66' and 'Reggae fi Dada' by Linton Kwesi Johnson. © LKJ Records and Linton Kwesi Johnson. Reproduced by permission of the author.

Extract from '*First Language*' by Sanjukta Dasgupta, Kolkatta: Dasgupta and Co., 2004. © 2004 Sanjunkta Dasgupta. Reproduced by permission of the author and publisher.

Excerpt from 'Shabine Leaves the Republic' from 'The Schooner *Flight*' from *The Star-Apple Kingdom* by Derek Walcott. Copyright © 1979 by Derek Walcott. Reprinted by permission of Farrar, Straus and Giroux, LLC.

Every effort has been made to trace and contact copyright holders. The publishers would be pleased to hear from any copyright holders not acknowledged here, so that this acknowledgement page may be amended at the earliest opportunity.

"Prospero Caliban Cricket"

John Agard

Prospero batting
Caliban bowling
and is cricket is cricket in yuh
ricketics
but from far it look like politics
Caliban running up
from beyond de boundary
because he come
from beyond de boundary
if you know yuh history
Prospero standing
bat and pad
thinking Caliban is a mere lad
from a new-world archipelago
and new to the game
But not taking chances
Prospero invoking de name
of W. G. Grace
to preserve him
from a bouncer to the face
Caliban if he want
could invoke duppy jumbie

zemi baccoo douen all kinda
ting,
but instead he relying
just pon pace and swing
Caliban arcing de ball
like an unpredictable whip.
Prospero foot like it chain to de
ground.
Before he could mek a move
de ball gone thru to de slip,
and de way de crowd rocking
you would think dey crossing
de atlantic
Is cricket is cricket in yuh
ricketics
but from far it look like politics.
Prospero remembering
how Caliban used to call him
master.
Now Caliban agitating de ball
faster
and de crowd shouting

POWER

Caliban remembering
how Prospero used to call him
knave and serf
Now Caliban striding de cricket
turf
like he breathing a nation,
and de ball swinging it own
way
like it hear bout self-
determination
Is cricket is cricket in yuh
ricketics
but from far it look like politics.
Prospero wishing
Shakespeare was the umpire,
Caliban see a red ball

and he see fire
rising with glorious uncertainty.
Prospero front pad forward with
diplomacy.
Is cricket is cricket in yuh
ricketics
but from far it look like politics.
Prospero invoking
de god of snow,
wishing a shower of flakes
would stop all play,
but de sky so bright with carib
glow
you can't even appeal for light
much less ask for snow.
Is cricket is cricket in yuh
ricketics
but from far it look like politics

Introduction

to you, my holy language
to you, the one I adore
more than all the silver
and more than all the gold
    (Haim Vidal Sephiha)

Why is language so sacred? What is it that can send people onto the streets, or to war, to demand the protection or victory of their mother tongue? What is it about language that seems to go right to the core of our perception of ourselves, of our understanding of our identity? The lines above were written about the Judeo-Spanish language spoken by Sephardic Jews when they were expelled from Spain in 1492 by Ferdinand and Isabella. Here was a people in exile, so of course one would expect the language to be sacred. But the language Sephiha is talking about, 'Ladino' – or 'Judezmo' in its spoken form – is simply Spanish with Hebrew syntax. It is utterly hybrid, yet it is as sacred as Sephardic identity itself. How did this strange mixture enter the essence of Sephardim?

Clearly the answer to this question has something to do with suffering and something to do with writing, and a similar operation of power comes about in the colonial relationship. The unshakeable link between 'our' language and *us* has made language not only the most emotional site for cultural identity but also one of the most critical techniques of colonization and of the subsequent transformation of colonial influence by post-colonized societies. The control over language by the imperial 'centre' – whether by displacing native languages, by installing the imperial language as a 'standard' against other variants denigrated as 'impurities', or by planting the language of empire in a new place – remains a potent instrument of cultural control.

Language has power. It provides the terms by which reality may be constituted, it provides the names by which the world may be 'known'. The system of values it conveys – the suppositions on which it appears to be based, the concepts of geography and history it articulates, the attitudes to difference inscribed in its words, the myriad gradations of distinction encompassed by its lexicon and grammar – becomes the system upon which social, economic and political discourse is grounded. Whether these characteristics are properties of the language *itself* rather than properties of its *use* becomes a crucial question in any discussion of discursive resistance to colonial power. But it is incontestable that language is the mode of a constant and pervasive extension of cultural dominance – through ideas, attitudes, histories and ways of seeing – that is central to imperial hegemony.

This book is concerned, then, with what colonized people do with language, in particular what they do with the colonial language, and this includes trying to understand how and why language works in post-colonial writing. For our purposes this means writing in English. To understand the remarkable transformation of English literature from post-colonized societies is to understand the remarkably malleable nature of language. As one colony after another gained independence after the Second World War the question of language became one on which a whole range of issues of self-determination and cultural empowerment seemed to hinge. This book pivots on a moment in Shakespeare's *The Tempest*, which has become the very symbol of the impact of a colonial language. When Caliban says to Miranda and Prospero:

> you taught me language, and my profit on't
> Is, I know how to curse. The red plague rid you
> For learning me your language

he gives voice to an issue that lies at the centre of post-colonial studies: is that language good for nothing but cursing, or can Caliban use that language to change the world? So much depends on this question, so easily does it slide into polemic and sloganeering, yet so enormous are its consequences that we need to examine it carefully and extensively.

The depth, comprehensiveness and bitterness of the linguistic struggle at the heart of colonialism have embedded some recalcitrant myths about the relationship between language and culture. The struggle between indigenous and global languages compels us to be very clear about what potential language might have for communication and self-expression. Leonard Bloomfield posited three levels of people's response to language: the 'primary' response of actual usage; 'secondary responses' which are people's views about language; and 'tertiary responses' that are the feelings that emerge when anyone questions these views (Crystal 1997: 2). The secondary and tertiary responses are so strong that they very often become conflated. What people think about and feel about language may become mistaken for language itself, and this is particularly so in discussion about language in the colonial context where language bears no less a burden than cultural survival itself.

This examination of the issues emerging from Caliban's bitter retort hinges on the simple distinction between what language actually does and what it stands for as a cultural and political discourse. Most of the battles fought over language in post-colonial theory stem from a confusion between language as a communicative tool and language as a cultural symbol. The reason for this is easy to see. Colonial languages were the vehicles of such a pervasive and intrusive cultural control that it was almost inevitable that many people in post-colonial societies assumed that the language itself was *inherently* the key to that control. Indeed, the colonizers themselves thought so. Because colonization occurs most subtly and comprehensively in language, because language itself is so manifestly connected to power, it seemed natural to see that language somehow embodied the "thought processes and values" of the imperial culture (Ngũgĩ 1981: 10). The English language was imposed on colonized peoples by a conscious strategy of cultural hegemony. Colonialism imposed a way of talking about the world that privileged certain kinds of distinctions and representations and debased others. This way of talking became so connected with the power of the colonial society that it often became confused with a way of being.

However, if a way of talking can be a way of being it is not the only one available to speakers. Colonial languages can, and have, been taken and used in ways that privileged the local culture. The most powerful discovery made by an examination of post-colonial language use is that language is *used* by people. Although it *can* be an ontological prison it *need* not be, for the key to post-colonial resistance is that speakers have agency in the ways they employ language to fashion their identity. The underlying assertion of this book is that colonial languages have been not only instruments of oppression but also instruments of radical resistance and transformation.

The critical discovery we make here is that any time people assume that some characteristic cultural feature or other is a property of language, any time they assume that a way of life or belief is embodied in the language itself, we may track it down to some habitual way in which the language is used. There is something very bewitching about the assumption that our cultural identity is somehow locked up inside our language, that there is some natural and organic relation between language and culture. But this is really an extension of a simpler assumption, which Saussure disproved: that signifieds and signifiers are naturally linked. There is nothing, for instance, in the signifier 'dog' which is naturally connected to that four-legged animal known as 'man's best friend' any more than it is for the word '*chien*'. The link between signifiers and signifieds is arbitrary. So too is the link between language and that range of signifiers which go to make up a culture. The claim that cultural experience is *inherent* in language would be a similar order of assertion as saying that the mental experiences of people who used that language were the same; that signifieds and signifiers were naturally linked. We will ponder this issue at length since the relationship between language and culture is the most persistently misunderstood in cultural theory. The key to this problem is that speakers very often conflate the *experience* of speaking a particular language, the experience of identification, belonging and location that it gives them, with the language itself, as though the act of speaking were a unique cultural event. What is at stake here is the validity and even the very existence of post-colonial writing.

Time after time, post-colonial writers have expressed their objections to a colonial language in terms of the way it *has been* used, the way it has been represented, and what it has stood for as an institution of power. There is ample evidence that speakers who have been forced to speak a colonial language have felt alienated by the experience, and alienated by the language. Yet the most exciting feature of post-colonial writing has been the constant and varied demonstration of the way English *can be* used. This appropriation of language, this capacity to make it do a different cultural work from that of the colonizers, is metonymic of post-colonial cultures themselves. The central argument here, therefore, is that language is not simply a repository of cultural contents, but a tool, and often a weapon, which can be employed for various purposes, a tool which is itself part of the cultural experience in which it is used. The meaning achieved through language is a social event negotiated by real people, not a simple function of its structure or grammar or lexicon. Language therefore can be made to change, to be used in different ways of talking about the world and in a metaphorical sense, to lead to changing the world itself.

This is not to assume that language is perfectly transparent, a simple mechanical tool for representing the world. The English language, for instance, is not only an historical composite of Anglo-Saxon, Norman French and Latin, but also a cultural palimpsest. Words themselves emerge as socio-cultural palimpsests built up over time. Words such as the obvious 'black' and 'white' come down to us with a deep and complex history of usage. The penumbra surrounding the word 'black' can indeed be a feature of the mental associations of an English speaker. But this does not mean that those associations are somehow *embedded* in the word, they are implicated in the word.

Inevitably, the politics of language *use* transfers to assumptions about particular languages themselves. Said points out that the conflation of language and culture is just one aspect of a process in which language itself is crucial.

> In everything I have been discussing, the language of Orientalism plays the dominant role. It brings opposites together as 'natural,' it presents human types in scholarly idioms and methodologies, it ascribes reality and reference to objects (other words) of its own making. Mythic language is discourse, that is, it cannot be anything but systematic; one does not really make discourse at will, or statements in it, without first belonging – in some cases unconsciously, but at any rate involuntarily – to the ideology of the institutions that guarantee its existence. These latter are always the institutions of an advanced society dealing with a less advanced society, a strong culture encountering a weak one.
>
> The principle feature of mythic discourse is that it conceals its own origins as well as those of what it describes. 'Arabs' are presented in the imagery of the static, almost ideal types, and neither as creatures with a potential in the process of being realized nor as history being made. The exaggerated value heaped upon Arabic as a language permits the Orientalist to make the language equivalent to mind, society, history, and nature. For the Orientalist the language *speaks* the Arab Oriental, not vice versa.
>
> (1978: 321)

Language becomes in this schema, a potent mode of representation and marginalization. Words themselves have a notorious capacity for limiting the referents, 'freezing' them into objects of terror or revulsion. By surrounding the language with an aura of difficulty, mystery, the Arab culture becomes constituted as 'difficult'.

Language and discourse

Of course, what Said is talking about when he refers to the language of Orientalism, is discourse. The term 'discourse' itself is used in many ways and is open to some confusion. 'Discourse' was originally used from about the sixteenth century to describe any kind of speaking, talk or conversation, but became increasingly used to describe a more formal speech, a narration or a treatment of any subject at length, a treatise, dissertation or sermon. But two major uses of the term are important to the operation of language. Language itself is intimately involved in discourse because it is a social practice: discourse in this sense means 'language as a social practice'. 'Discourse analysis' therefore, examines the ways in which language is used, the contexts and situations in which it is deployed and the ways in which social realities operate within it. This sense of discourse is important because it helps to resolve the tension between the idea of language as a *determining* force upon people's perception on one hand, and a *reflection* of social realities on the other. Language has meaning in people's ordinary lives as discourse because it is intimately involved in their social experience. Language is a part of those social processes and practices that go to make up that social experience, it neither *causes* that experience nor simply *reports* it.

However there is another use of the term 'discourse' which does not correspond directly to language. For Michel Foucault the term 'discourse' refers, rather, to firmly bounded areas of social knowledge, the statements that can be made about a particular topic at a particular time in a particular culture. Indeed in order to understand Foucault's use, we need to see it as a totally different concept from the term discourse that refers to speaking. For him, a discourse is a system of statements within which a particular aspect of the world can be known. The world is not simply 'there' to be talked about; rather, it is through discourse itself that the world is brought into being. In this formulation, discourse is that which determines that in any given historical period (or any given culture) we can write, think or speak about a given social object or practice (medicine for instance) in certain specific ways and not others. 'A discourse' would then be *whatever* constrains – but also enables – writing, speaking and thinking within specific historical and cultural limits (McHoul and Grace 1993: 31).

There are certain unspoken rules controlling which statements can be made and which cannot within the discourse, and these rules determine the nature of that discourse. Since a virtually limitless number of statements can be made within the rules of the system it is these rules that characterise the discourse and that interest Foucault. What are the rules that allow certain statements to be made and not others? What rules order these statements? What rules allow the development of a classificatory system? What rules allow us to identify certain individuals as authors? These rules concern such things as the classification, the ordering and the distribution of that knowledge of the world, which the discourse both enables and delimits. These are the unwritten but ubiquitous rules of the discourse of Orientalism.

The reason for making the distinction between discourse as the social practice of language, and discourse as a firmly bounded area of social knowledge, is that in discussion of colonial language the two become conflated in ways that negate the individual actions of speakers. The distinction between these definitions of discourse illuminates a confusion that lurks around all discussion of post-colonial language use. Many people speak of a colonial language *as though* it was an almost impenetrably bounded area of cultural knowledge, a discourse in which the social practice of speakers was entirely controlled by convention. This assumption emerges most often in assertions that to use a language one must think (or will inevitably think) like its native speakers, or that in using a language one is inescapably indoctrinated into a culturally based way of seeing. Derek Walcott once said that "to change your language you have to change your life" ("Codicil", Walcott 1965: 61). This does not mean however, that language *is* life. Bilingual speakers do not become different people when they talk, or at least do not *have* to. The social and political reasons for using one language rather than another are a different matter – a matter of performativity rather than ontology. Such assertions as 'changing your life when you speak' tend to refer to language as though it were a firmly bounded system of knowledge rather than a social practice in which discursive convention is always open to transformation. In fact, it is the employment and transformation of these conventions by post-colonial literatures that stand as the key to their power to unsettle colonial discourse. A global language such as English, inflected with locally produced variations, can become a key mode of empowerment.

Samuel Johnson's 1755 "Preface": Language and colonial contamination

Let us think for a minute about that English language that lies at the centre of these debates. What inherent instabilities are present in that tongue that has been so fundamental to the dominance of Empire? When we examine one of the most significant moments in the history of the English language, the moment when it became institutionalized, in Samuel Johnson's Dictionary, we find that even to the lexicographer it resists stability. Language is basically unstable because its potential uses are so varied.

Here in Johnson's "Preface", at the very beginning of the attempt to 'fix' the language, we discover an allusion to colonial relationships and imperial cultural contacts as tropes for the vulnerability of language to alien influences. Martin Wechselblatt says:

> Critics of Johnson's Plan and "Preface" have … never taken into account the metaphors of colonial conquest and settlement which Johnson habitually

employs as the melancholy examples of lexicography's failures: failures both to exemplify the professional authority of the lexicographer, and to demonstrate the transmission of national identity through examples of linguistic usage.

(1996: 389)

If this observation is correct, the remarkable fact is that almost before the English language had begun to be transported to British colonies, its vulnerability to change had already been described in terms of *the imagery of colonial contact*.

The great drama in the production of Samuel Johnson's 1755 Dictionary was the struggle between the attempt to 'fix' or stabilize the language and the recalcitrant impossibility of ever doing so. At the beginning of the "Preface" he says: "I found our speech copious without order, and energetick without rules: wherever I turned my view, there was perplexity to be disentangled, and confusion to be regulated" (1785: 2). His aim was to "pierce deep into every science, to enquire the nature of every substance of which I inserted the name". But he finds such goals to be "the dreams of a poet doomed to wake a lexicographer" (1785: 10). The authority sought for such an enterprise is thwarted by language itself. Near the end of the "Preface" he makes the melancholic observation:

> I saw that one enquiry only gave occasion to another, that book referred to book, that to search was not always to find, that to find was not always to be informed; and thus to pursue perfection was, like the first inhabitants of Arcadia, to chase the sun, which, when they had reached the hill where he seemed to rest, was still at the same distance from them.
>
> (1785: 10)

This is one of the most important observations made about the English language and indeed, about language in general. But it was an observation about which Johnson was remarkably ambivalent. He wanted to be a successful and history-making lexicographer, and to do that he saw the opportunity of recording the language for posterity. But his scrupulous observation of language could not avoid the admission that the attempt to make a monument of language is a futile and even derisory task:

> We laugh at the elixir that promises to prolong life to a thousand years; and with equal justice may the lexicographer be derided, who being able to produce no example of a nation that has preserved their words and phrases from mutability, shall imagine that his dictionary can embalm his language, and secure it from corruption and decay, that it is in his power to change sublunary nature, and clear the world at once from folly, vanity and affectation.
>
> With this hope, however, academies have been instituted, to guard the avenues of their languages, to retain fugitives, and repulse intruders; but their vigilance and activity have hitherto been vain.
>
> (1785: 11)

Despite his honesty about the futility of 'fixing' the language, such fixing is the very thing that a lexicographer most wants to do. Although he recognizes the impossibility of pursuing perfection, of "chasing the sun", like the Arcadians, and senses the futility of "repulsing intruders", Johnson is inclined to think that *some* effort should be expended to preserve the language: "tongues, like governments, have a natural tendency to degeneration; we have long preserved our constitution, let us make some struggles for our language" (1785: 13). Consequently, the conflict between cannily recognizing the fluidity of linguistic meaning on one hand and protecting those meanings sent down from posterity by the greatest of English writers on the other, resolves itself in the colonial imagery of contamination and miscegenation.

The fact that the lexicographer's task is not simply to record but to "struggle for" the language may explain why Johnson announces somewhat histrionically that "defects [in pronunciation] are not errors in orthography, but spots of barbarity impressed so deep in our language that criticism can never wash them away" (1785: 3). What he alludes to as contamination can be described from Caliban's point of view as transformation. But for the lexicographer such vulnerability to change and corruption is the sign of a failure in his struggle to preserve the best of English writing.

It is curious that Johnson uses colonial imagery as evidence of failure, because he was far ahead of his time in his sympathy for indigenous peoples. The "American dispute between the French and us is," he declares, "only the quarrel of two robbers for the spoil of a passenger", and that "no honest man can heartily wish success to either party" (1756, vol.10: 188, 186). But there is a bigger issue here that lies in the link between language and national identity. Such national identity has an interesting racial caste: "Our language, for almost a century, has … been gradually departing from its original *Teutonick* character, and deviating towards a *Gallick* structure and phraseology, from which it ought to be our endeavour to recall it (*Preface*: 9). "To colonize," says Wechselblatt, " – to reproduce English culture in others – is to (retroactively) produce a national 'common language' at home. Englishness, it seems, is crucially, perhaps necessarily dependent for its exemplarity upon the prior production of itself abroad, among other nations and peoples" (1996: 393).

While Johnson never actually mentions colonialism in his "Preface", the language of contamination is central to the imperial project. The continuous, "native" genealogies of national cultures are contaminated by linguistic contact in the same way that the English essence is contaminated by various kinds of commerce with aliens. "Total and sudden transformations of language seldom happen;" he says, "conquests and migrations are now very rare;" but there are other causes of change that come about simply by contact with aliens:

> Commerce, however necessary, however lucrative, as it depraves the manners, corrupts the language; they that have frequent intercourse with strangers, to whom they endeavour to accommodate themselves, must in time learn a mingled dialect. [That] will be communicated by degrees to other ranks of people, and be at last incorporated with the current speech.
> (1785: 12)

While a 'corrupted' or 'contaminated' English may reflect badly on the capacity of the English language to reflect the essential English national character, clearly its mutability, its vulnerability to change is, for Caliban, a powerful asset to the task of using it for post-colonial purposes.

Language sometimes goes native since it is "incident to words … to degenerate from their ancestors, and to change their manners when they change their country" (Brady and Wimsatt 1977: 282). "Single words may enter by thousands" (1785: 12) and a tight immigration control is needed to curb "the folly of naturalizing useless foreigners to the injury of the natives" (1785: 5); moreover, Johnson himself carefully examines words he suspects are "not genuine and regular offsprings of English roots" (1785: 5–6). "Johnson's *Preface*," says Wechselblatt, "enacts the dangers it seeks to 'retard,' by suggesting that the nation is already contaminated by foreigners who have consequently 'impressed' themselves, like those 'spots of barbarity,' on the lexicographer's own ability to exemplify" (1996: 390). Endogamy, inbreeding between "words of the same race" is, however, as much of a problem as exogamy, since "kindred senses may be so interwoven that the perplexity cannot be disentangled". Particularly productive of hybrids, translation's introduction of "new phraseology" poses a threat to English self-rule, which will "reduce us to babble a dialect of France" (1785: 12).

The "Preface" is a deeply ambivalent moment in the institutionalization of the English language. It is, for Johnson, a task of utmost importance for the preservation of the genius of English writers, and yet it is a task that will never be completed. "If the changes we fear are thus irresistible, what remains but to acquiesce with silence, as in the other insurmountable distresses of humanity? It remains that we retard what we cannot repel, that we palliate what we cannot cure" (12). The inability to ward off invasion (by those ironically, whom we invade) is an insurmountable distress. And it is so because the construction of a dictionary is a national task.

> In hope of giving longevity to that which its own nature forbids to be immortal, I have devoted this book, the labour of years, to the honour of my country, that we may no longer yield the palm of philology, without a contest, to the nations of the continent.
>
> (13)

"The chief glory of every people arises from its authors," (13) says Johnson, yet the task of seeing the language embodied in those authors is doomed to failure because of the encroachment and contamination of alien influences. What Johnson does not realize is that his sense of the vulnerability of language is a prophecy of the way the language will one day be transformed and used as capital by those the language has intended to dominate with "the English spirit". For that spirit will never reside in the language, and it will be the achievement of generations of post-colonial writers to show that the language will belong to those who use it.

Max Müller: Dialects and literary language

The great nineteenth-century philologist, Orientalist and translator of the Upanishads, Max Müller, uncovered the fluidity of language in an intervention as profound as Johnson's discovery of the elusiveness of meaning. He cites Waldeck's report of missionaries in Central America who attempted to write down the language of savage tribes, and who compiled with great care a dictionary of all the words they could lay hold of. Returning to the same tribe after the lapse of only ten years, they found that this dictionary had become antiquated and useless (1882: 58–9). In general, though, the issue for Müller was not a matter of the impermanence of definitions but a fluidity of living language best conceived in the struggle between 'dialects' and literary languages.

> What we are accustomed to call languages, the literary idioms of Greece, and Rome and India, of Italy, France and Spain, must be considered to be artificial, rather than as natural forms of speech. The real and natural life of language is in its dialects.
>
> (1882: 52)

This was quite contentious at the end of the nineteenth century, immersed as it was in the link between language and race, but it represented an early salvo in the debate between oratures and literary languages, a debate that could be said to represent the contending positions in the post-colonial linguistic struggle: local vs. colonial language; oral vs. literary language; dialect vs. Standard English. The contention is that literary languages have had their grammar, morphology and lexicon solidified by print, while the real life of language, its life of constant development and change, its 'reality', exists in the realm of dialect.

The term 'dialect' has become a confirmation of the myth of a standard language. But in Müller's formulation, a 'dialect' is where the life of language lies. With post-colonial writing this situation becomes dramatically confirmed. For the entry of 'dialect' into the literary form disrupts it. But it does so in a peculiar way. It leads to change in language very slowly, if at all, for there are too many contending influences. Rather, it expands the horizon of acceptable and identifiable language. This horizon itself disturbs the authority or solidity of the received literary language:

> Dialects have always been the feeders rather than the channels of a literary language ... they are parallel streams which existed long before the time when one of them was raised to that temporary eminence which is the result of literary culturation.
>
> (1882: 55)

If we see the word 'dialects' here as a term for 'local' or vernacular languages, the mother tongues of colonized people, we may see embedded in the relationship a model for post-colonial literary transformation. This is why, if we take

Müller's formulation, it might be useful to retain the concept of dialect (under the assumption that *all* languages are dialects) because dialects suggest the remarkable vitality that these vernacular languages may provide for the transformation of the 'literary language', English.

Müller goes on to say:

> Dialects exist prior to the formation of literary languages, for every literary language is but one of many dialects; nor does it all follow that, after one of them has thus been raised to the dignity of a literary language, the others should suddenly be silenced or strangled ... On the contrary, they live in full vigour, though in comparative obscurity, and unless the literary and courtly languages invigorate themselves by a constantly renewed intercourse with their former companions, the popular dialects will sooner or later assert their ascendancy.
>
> (1882: 56)

Orature as well may have a formalizing influence.

> It may not be a written or a classical literature to give an ascendancy to one out of many dialects ... Speeches at ... public meetings, popular ballads, national laws, religious oracles, exercise, though to a smaller extent, the same influence. They will arrest the natural flow of language in the countless rivulets of its dialects, and give a permanency to certain formations of speech, which, without these external influences, could have enjoyed but an ephemeral existence ... whatever the origin of language, its first tendency must have been towards an unbounded variety.
>
> (62)

We invariably put the oral in a binary relation to the literary and assume that variations emerging from appropriations are oral. But orature is itself a form of 'inscription', a form of literary language, which may standardize a certain dialect form. The language variation operating in the post-colonial is potentially unbounded, except that it operates, whether consciously or not, under the constraints of a purpose that is essentially political. Müller might be said to have pre-empted Derrida.

One common way in which colonization may "arrest the flow" of languages is by putting them into written form. This was often the case as missionaries and administrators transcribed and codified a language to become a medium of education. This led sometimes to unfortunate consequences. Bauan was the dialect of the island of Bau, in Fiji, home to the highest chief of the land at the time of the Deed of Cession. Methodist missionaries decided, for political and economic reasons, to codify this dialect and use it for publishing purposes (Geraghty 1984). However, as the missionaries were under pressure to learn the language and make translations quickly, both from their supervisors and their Fijian converts, what they objectified was their imperfect understanding of the language. In this way, missionary codification of badly spoken Bauan became the classic literary standard of Fijian (Geraghty 1984, cited in Lotherington 1998).

Literary dialects, or what are commonly called classical languages, according to Müller, pay for their temporary greatness by inevitable decay. They are like artificial lakes at the side of great rivers (1882: 65). Sometimes it seems

> that the whole stream of language was absorbed by these lakes. But there are rivulets that run on and further lakes are formed by these rivulets. As soon as language loses its unbounded capability of change ... its natural life is changed into a merely artificial existence.
>
> (66)

Rather than a leading shoot, it is a "broken and a withering branch" (67). What Müller sees as the innate fluidity and fecundity of living language, a fecundity that may become ossified in writing, we may see as the depiction of the ways in which post-colonial literary languages have regenerated and transformed English. Ironically, the 'life' of the language, which for Müller existed outside the literary language in the range of dialects that preceded it, is now imbued in the literary language through the power of those 'dialects' to transform it.

If we see this struggle between 'dialects', and 'literary languages', as a model for the engagement between English and the vernacular languages, we can see that the struggle of post-colonial writing is manifestly a power struggle. One of Foucault's most influential insights was that power *produces* rather than simply oppresses. This productive power is nowhere more in evidence than in the colonial language. The paradoxical nature of language's productive power can be seen in most clearly in the power of literary production itself. In *Imaginary Homelands* Salman Rushdie tells of his visit to his father's Bombay home, which he had only ever seen as a black and white photograph:

> The colours of my history had seeped out of my mind's eye; now my other two eyes were assaulted by colours, by the vividness of the red tiles, the yellow-edged green of the cactus leaves, the brilliance of bougainvillea creeper. It is probably not too romantic to say that was when my novel *Midnight's Children* was really born; when I realized how much I wanted to restore the past to myself, not in the faded greys of old family-album snapshots, but whole, in CinemaScope and glorious Technicolor.
>
> (1991: 9–10)

The past, which is so much the fixed point of his memory, is open to renewal and revivification in language. But "we will not be capable of reclaiming precisely the thing that was lost; ... we will, in short, create fictions, not actual cities or villages, but invisible ones, imaginary homelands, Indias of the mind" (1991: 10). This addresses one of the most persistent myths of anti-colonial rhetoric, the need to regain the paradisal state of a lost cultural past, the belief that Caliban can regain his island as it was before Prospero. That past "is a country from which we have all emigrated", says Rushdie (12). But although that past is incapable of reclamation, its reproduction in literature, the creation of an "imaginary home-land", offers a virtually boundless horizon to the identity that seemed enclosed by the past. That which was taken away by colonization, and thus, in a sense, robbed by the imperial language, is capable of vivid restitution within that language. "The broken mirror may actually be as valuable as the one which is supposedly unflawed" (11). The creation of an imaginary homeland is an evocative description of the way in which linguistic power "comes from below", so to speak. Literary writing appropriates, perhaps more forcefully than any other form of language use, the representational and re-creative power of language. This power is crucial to ideas of identity, whether personal, national or cultural, because identity is neither 'revealed' nor 'reclaimed' but constructed as part of the social experience of language itself.

The success with which post-colonial societies have transformed the English language, through literature and other cultural production, is one of the most striking outcomes of the three centuries of British colonial adventurism. But the extent of that transformation is rarely sufficiently acknowledged because it disturbs the stereotypical binary relationship between colonizers and colonized. Caliban is imprisoned, in *The Tempest*, within Shakespeare's imagination, or, more specifically, within the inability of sixteenth-century English society to imagine a different role for the colonial subject. The monster is the example of the worst excesses of Nature (indeed he exceeds Nature itself) "on whom nurture can never stick" and can only profit from the elevating powers of Prospero's Art – the technology of civilization. But Caliban as exemplar of the colonial subject is still imprisoned in the European imagination. We must follow him beyond the play, beyond the Shakespearean imagination (and, indeed, beyond the imaginations of Caribbean writers such as Lamming or Retamar) to see what he actually does with Prospero's language.

Situating *Caliban's Voice*

The discussion revolving around this topic has been lively but not extensively focused on post-colonial writing. Many linguistic texts have treated the subject of world Englishes from a purely sociolinguistic and often technical perspective (e.g. Fishman *et al.* 1996; Watts and Trudgill 2002). The attack on world Englishes began in earnest with Phillipson (1992) whose title *Linguistic Imperialism* indicates the tenor of his argument. Moore (2001) explores regional varieties of English in relation to the lively debate about the increasing 'globalisation' of English. The study posits that linguistic varieties have their own cultural valency, somewhat like Kachru's (1990) theory of particular linguistic ecologies. Hence a new 'threat' to regional varieties of English in the spread of 'global English' by electronic communication which has the effect of washing out difference and reducing the cultural diversity of World Englishes. One of the strongest attacks on the spread of world English occurs in many of the essays contained in Mair (2003). The volume is wide-ranging and indicates the disciplinary differences in approaches to the question, from accusation of English as a "killer language" destroying the linguistic bio-diversity of the planet, to discussions of Sri Lankan English literary texts as active in cultural conservation. In his Introduction Mair indicates the principal disciplinary difference of these scholars in the treatment of colonial languages: the widespread acceptance by many post-colonial literary scholars of the link between language and culture, and their unreserved endorsement of the Sapir-Whorf hypothesis, is largely refused by linguists.

The specific relevance of language adaptation to post-colonial writing has been addressed by a relatively limited number of works. *The Empire Writes Back* first introduced the significance of language appropriation in 1989, and Chantal Zabus made a seminal exploration of African adaptations of English in *The African Palimpsest* (1993 repr. 2007). More recent works (Skinner 1998; Talib 2002; Pennycook 1994, 1998; Phillipson 1992; Mair 2003) tend to divide on strongly political lines: either seeing the language use as a rich source of literary production or a demonstration of colonial power and imperial domination. Skinner avoids the theoretical debate to provide a taxonomy of fictional practices. He argues against terms such as Commonwealth Literature, Post-colonial Literature, New Literatures in English or World Literature in English and argues in favour of the adoption of the term Anglophone Literature. Talib (2002) argues that the language of English Post-colonial Literatures differs from British English mostly in the lexis and doesn't take into consideration the syntactical transformations of these writers. Pennycook (1998) bases his study of the discourses of English on Foucault. He offers an energetic argument but clings to a view of language as discourse in the Foucaultian sense that is profoundly erroneous and leads to a position against which this project wishes to argue: that language *embodies* cultural meaning rather than represents it.

This book does not approach the question from the perspective of a technical linguistic discussion, but from a perception of language as a strategic tool used by writers in the business of colonial resistance and post-colonial transformation. It will canvass some fallacious assumptions about language to confirm the exciting capacity of post-colonial writers to use English as a cultural tool. The alert reader will see that many of the conclusions I make about language are commensurate with a poststructuralist analysis. The reason I do not invoke poststructuralism is that by and large it fails, as structuralism fails, to account adequately for the fact that language is a *practice*. Although 'language speaks' in the sense that speakers cannot say more than the law of language allow, the inventiveness of speakers at the limits of those laws is the characteristic of post-colonial writing.

Poststructuralism also fails to take into account the *affective* dimension that makes language such a contentious cultural phenomenon. Affect means that language is not only a way of being in the world, but a site at which one's feelings about the self and the world continue to interfere with one's thinking about language. This is what makes the use of English such a contentious issue in post-colonial studies.

Caliban's Voice is by no means a defence of English, but rather recognises the extraordinary power of literary writing to intervene in the political domination of colonized cultures by the use of a global language. It celebrates the inventiveness, strength and power of writing from post-colonized cultures. These cultures are very often victims of a form of neo-colonial marginalization that continues to keep them economically and politically repressed. More troubling to these societies however is the imminent smothering of their cultural difference within a situation of potential global homogenization. The strategic capacity to adopt and adapt a world language (one often seen as the agent of homogenization) for the purposes of self representation may well be, therefore, one of the most exciting features of cultural globalization.

1 Prospero's language, Caliban's voice

It is probably no surprise, given the cultural consequences of the history of slavery in the Atlantic, where slaves were isolated from their language groups and developed an extensive range of linguistic variations, that Caribbean novelists and poets have been among the most energetic transformers of colonial language. Already competent in moving through various registers of English, within what Bickerton calls the "creole continuum" (1973), their inventiveness with language is virtually unparalleled in the post-colonial world. The Caribbean has also been a productive site for the re-reading and re-writing of the canonical texts of English literature. Barbadian George Lamming, for instance, although not the first to recognize the colonial implications of Shakespeare's final play, *The Tempest*, is the writer who most influenced contemporary post-colonial readings.

When we examine canonical works they often show themselves to be consummate reconstructions of the dynamic of imperial power. Reading them we discover why they have been so attractive to re-writings. *The Tempest* has been read for nearly half a century as a powerful and remarkably comprehensive allegory of colonization. First used, somewhat eccentrically, by Octave Mannoni to demonstrate the 'dependency' complex of the colonized in 1950 (Mannoni 1950), *The Tempest* has become, since George Lamming's reading in *The Pleasures of Exile*, a major allegory of the colonial experience, written back to, re-written and alluded to by one post-colonial writer after another.[1] Lamming dismantles the view of Caliban as a creature outside civilization "on whose nature/Nurture can never stick" (IV.i.188–9), showing him to be a human being (specifically a West Indian), whose human status has been denied by the European claims to an exclusive human condition (see Brydon 1984; Zabus 1985, 2002). In the relationship

---

1 Interestingly, the possibilities for reading this play in terms of the political and cultural relationship between Caliban and Prospero date from the last century. J.S. Phillpot's introduction to the 1873 Rugby edition of Shakespeare notes that "The character may have had a special bearing on the great question of a time when we were discovering new countries, subjecting unknown savages, and founding fresh colonies. If Prospero might dispossess Caliban, England might dispossess the aborigines of the colonies" (Furness Variorum Edition: 383). This edition precedes the rise of classical imperialism that culminated in the 'scramble for Africa' in 1882. Curiously, the colonial importance of Prospero and Caliban was not revisited until 1950 when the major European empires were beginning to be dismantled.

between Prospero, Miranda, Ariel and Caliban we find demonstrated in dramatic form some of the most fundamental features of the colonial enterprise: the consummate binary set up between colonizer and colonized; the nature of the power relationship which this binary facilitates; the hegemony of imperial notions of order and good government; the profound link between such ideas and the technology of the colonizing power (which in Prospero is symbolized by his magic Art); the racial debasement and demonization of the colonized (articulated by Prospero's, and the play's, attitude to Caliban); and the belief that goals of 'improvement', of the civilizing mission, are a justification for subjugation.

Because such texts allegorize so well the dynamics of imperial power, they offer a rich site for the consideration of post-colonial issues, and one of these is the future of Caliban's language. While *The Tempest* has been a classic subject of re-readings and re-writings, it is in Caliban's encounter with Prospero's language that some of the most interesting issues in post-colonial transformation emerge. The play provides one of the most confronting demonstrations of the importance of language in the colonial encounter, but it does not share our interest in Caliban. He disappears almost without trace, contrite and repentant, leaving us ignorant of the possibilities of his use of Prospero's speech. *The Tempest* is fascinating because while it liberally displays the power of Prospero's language it offers no view of Caliban's response, other than his resonant "You taught me language, and my profit on't is I know how to curse". Famous though this response has become, it fails to conceive any possibility of Caliban's power to transform language. Caliban remains an evocative and controversial symbol of post-colonial resistance: while many would hold that colonial language has no other function than oppression, good for nothing but cursing, writers throughout the colonized world have continued to transform it, and turn it into a vehicle that works for them.

Caliban becomes, therefore, a peerless figure of colonial ambivalence and the main reason for the many counter-discursive renditions of the play. Caliban is important for our purposes because he has no future, that is, Shakespeare is incapable of conceiving any future for him. Thus to see Caliban's cursing as the only response the colonized subject might have to the colonial language, is to accept Caliban as the play presents him: a vanquished and marginalized miscegenator with no hope and no future. Once we locate the colonial significance of the play, some very different possibilities open up. Because Caliban is so manifestly the cannibal/primitive, the abject other of European civilization in the play, he has become a symbol for representations of subaltern exploitation and resistance. His disappearance from the action invites us to extend the allegory and consider the trajectory of his future, specifically the future of his speaking, his use of the colonial language.

Caliban's virtual relegation to the status of cursing savage is curiously echoed in the writings of Roberto Fernández Retamar whose Spanish essays on Caliban – "Caliban" (1971) and "Caliban Revisited" (1986), both translated in his *Caliban and Other Essays* (1989) and "Caliban Speaks Five Hundred Years Later" (1992 in McClintock *et al.* 1997) – raised the character to almost iconic status in Latin America. Retamar's essays are a trenchant attack on the huge and flimsy edifice of European imperialism. Yet in launching the attack they have as little to say about Caliban's future as *The Tempest*. Caliban appears to be unable to do anything but curse in the dominant language. This strangely futureless positioning of Caliban's voice reaches a peak in Retamar's final essay, "Caliban Speaks Five Hundred Years Later," a long diatribe against Europe and its historic imperialist evils, in which the author adopts Caliban's identity, to, in a sense, 'curse' the effects of five hundred years of domination. For all its justification and political energy it becomes an interesting demonstration of the inability of some resistance rhetoric to take into account the kinds of transformations that have actually occurred in colonized societies. The paradoxical effect of this is to lock Caliban into the position of anti-European 'natural man'.

Clearly, Shakespeare endorses Prospero's project to civilize the 'natural man'. Prospero is also a model for the playwright himself, a creative authority at the height of his powers who looks back in the play upon the capacity of creative art to change nature. But, perhaps for this reason, the contest between Nature and Art in the play is by no means a foregone conclusion: in a significant intervention into this argument the kindly Gonzalo proposes that in a Kingdom ruled by him "All things in common Nature should produce/Without sweat or endeavour" (II. i. 155–6). Furthermore, Caliban, so comprehensively demonized, is nevertheless given some of the most beautiful and powerful lines in the play. While the conflict between Prospero's Art and Caliban's Natural Man remains central, Caliban becomes, in a post-colonial reading, the lens through which the political issues of colonial subjection are focused. Caliban is the key to the transformation of this allegory in such a reading, for he is not only colonized by Prospero, but in a sense, also by the assumptions on which the play is based.

Caliban, as the marginalized indigene, is the antithesis of culture. He is ignorant of gentleness and humanity, he is a savage and capable of all ill; he is born to slavery, not to freedom, of a vile rather than a noble union and whose parents represent an evil natural magic which is the antithesis of Prospero's art. More importantly, his nature is one on which nurture, the benefits of imperial culture, "will not stick". So in every respect he is the antithesis of culture, and the terms by which he is described justify the colonizing process that subjugates him. Prospero's Art, on the other hand, is seen to represent civilized man's power over the world and over himself, a power over nature divorced from grace, of the mind over the senses.

The naming and depiction of Caliban (Carib – Canibal – Caliban) is a clear demonstration of the attempt by the text to refute the view of nature as that which man corrupts, and of Montaigne's view that the natural man enjoyed a naturally virtuous life uncorrupted by civilization (Florio 1603). Caliban's origins and character are 'natural' in the sense that they do not partake of grace, civility or art. Clearly Shakespeare's text resists the ambivalence that enters into the argument between Locke and Rousseau about the 'natural' state of the child. Caliban is ugly in body, associated with an evil 'natural' magic, and unqualified for rule or nurture. He is in every way offered as an example of the baseness of the life yet unordered by method, society, civilization or good government. The play contests categorically the assumptions of Montaigne or Rousseau that nature is that which human society corrupts (Rousseau 1755). Culture is that which necessarily turns the savage into a human being and it is the colonizing culture that provides the model *par excellence* of this process. But it is, above all, language that performs this civilizing and humanizing function.

Caliban is the prototype of the colonized subject, whose baseness, as constructed by the colonizer, is the justifying prerequisite of colonization. This is why Caliban has been so consistently fascinating to writers trying to understand their own colonial condition. Edouard Glissant says:

> This is the problem of Caliban, that island creature whom a prince from the continent wished to civilize. The theme of Caliban has touched Caribbean intellectuals in a surprising way: Fanon, Lamming, Césaire, Fernández Retamar. The fact is that Caliban, as the locus of encounters and conflicts, has become a symbol. Above and beyond Shakespeare's savage cannibal, a real dynamic is at play – not only in the Caribbean but in many places in the Third World – a dynamic constituted by encounters among these three necessities: the class struggle, the emergence or the construction of the nation, the quest for collective identity. The facts of social and cultural life are only rarely combined and reinforced in harmony. It is claimed in Panama that the negritude movement promoted by Panamanians of Caribbean origin is in opposition to the will to reinforce the Panamanian nation. It is asserted in Trinidad that the resolution of political or economic problems is achieved or not achieved (depending on the ideology of the speaker) by the aggressive affirmation of either Indian or African identity. It is argued in Cuba that the solution to problems of social inequality will mean the simultaneous removal of racism. All of that is the true Caribbean problematic. It is why Caliban deserves such a passionate scrutiny.
>
> (1989: 118–19)

It is not the simplicity of Caliban's rebellion and striving for identity that makes him so relevant to post-colonial experience, but its complexity. For every discourse of resistance there are several others vying for authority. The centre of this complexity, of the contending issues of class, race, nation, is the language he speaks. For in this language freedom resides, if only he can find the discourse that will liberate it.

Language, learning and colonial power

The domination of Prospero's Art over Nature is above all the domination of his language and books. Indeed it is, curiously, the reason for his overthrow and exile to the island.

> And Prospero the prime Duke being so reputed
> In dignity, and for the liberal Arts
> Without a parallel; those being all my study,

The government I cast upon my brother
And to my state grew stranger, being transported
And rapt in secret studies.

(I.ii.72–77)

Prospero is no cynical politician, indeed, by presenting him as deceived by his brother and naive about the politics of Milan, the play suggests that his Culture dwells in a rarefied dimension far beyond the hurly burly of ordinary political intrigue. Dedicated to "closeness and the bettering of my mind" (I.ii.90), he embodies the highest ideals of his culture which exist in the space of the 'timeless' and 'universal'. This, indeed, is precisely the way in which European culture maintains a hegemony of ideas and values that outlasts colonial domination itself.

There can be no doubt that the key to the moral superiority manifested in Prospero's art is the language with which he names and controls the island. His function as an educator nurtures the prototypical settler colonial – his daughter Miranda – but it has a very different effect on Caliban. In a scene between Prospero, Caliban and Miranda in Act I Scene ii (on which this chapter will principally focus) we discover how crucial language becomes in the process of colonial control.

Caliban: As wicked dew as e'er my mother brush'd
              With raven's feather from unwholesome fen
              Drop on you both! a south-west blow on ye
              And blister you all o'er!
Prospero: For this, be sure, tonight thou shalt have cramps,
              Side-stitches that shall pen thy breath up; urchins
              Shall, for that vast of night that they may work,
              All exercise on thee; thou shalt be pinch'd
              As thick as honeycomb, each pinch more stinging
              Than bees made 'em.
Caliban: I must eat my dinner.
              This island's mine, by Sycorax my mother,
              Which thou tak'st from me. When thou cam'st first,
              Thou strok'st me, and made much of me; wouldst give me
              Water with berries in't; and teach me how
              To name the bigger light, and how the less,
              That burn by day and night: and then I lov'd thee,
              And show'd thee all the qualities o' th' isle,
              The fresh springs, brine-pits, barren place and fertile:
              Curs'd be I that did so! All the charms
              Of Sycorax, toads, beetles, bats, light on you!
              For I am all the subjects that you have,
              Which first was mine own King: and here you sty me
              In this hard rock, whilst you do keep from me
              The rest o' the' island.

Prospero:	Thou most lying slave,
	Whom stripes may move, not kindness! I have us'd thee,
	Filth as thou art, with human care; and lodg'd thee
	In mine own cell, till thou didst seek to violate
	The honour of my child.
Caliban:	O ho, O ho! would't had been done!
	Thou didst prevent me; I had peopled else
	This isle with Calibans.
Miranda:	Abhorred slave,
	Which any print of goodness wilt not take,
	Being capable of all ill! I pitied thee,
	Took pains to make thee speak, taught thee each hour
	One thing or other: when thou didst not, savage,
	Know thine own meaning, but wouldst gabble like
	A thing most brutish, I endow'd thy purposes
	With words that made them known. But thy vile race,
	Though thou didst learn, had that in't which good natures
	Could not abide to be with; therefore wast thou
	Deservedly confin'd into this rock,
	Who hadst deserved more than a prison.
Caliban:	You taught me language; and my profit on't
	Is, I know how to curse. The red plague rid you
	For learning me your language.

(I.ii.332–67)

This scene plays out many of the major linguistic, racial and cultural issues emerging from the historical trauma of colonialism. Caliban's famous reply is a tortured and resonant confirmation of the various processes of colonial domination that have been articulated in the previous exchange. Language is not one aspect of a broad range of colonizing strategies. It is the very mode of cultural control, the vehicle in which those strategies are effected. But what are these processes of domination? When we examine the scene closely we will see that it rehearses several of the most profound and troubling aspects of linguistic colonization: the connection between language and race; the issue of place and the power of imperial technology; the power of naming; the relationship between language and power itself; and the constitutive and therefore putatively ontological power of a dominant language.

Language and race

Prospero's response to Caliban demonstrates his power to name and thus define his slave. The 'gift' of language with which Prospero 'educates' Caliban interpellates him as a linguistic subject of the master tongue. The question of Caliban's resistance therefore hinges at precisely this point, for the power of demonization lies in the capacity to make names stick, to make them the frame of one's self-representation. The colonized being whom Prospero at first stroked and 'made much of' is now constructed as a 'lying slave', 'filth', 'hag-seed', while to Miranda he is an 'abhorred slave', 'savage', 'brutish', of a 'vile race'. What motivates this change? Nothing less than the horror of miscegenation.

> Thou most lying slave,
> Whom stripes may move, not kindness! I have us'd thee,
> Filth as thou art, with human care; and lodg'd thee
> In mine own cell, till thou seek'st to violate
> The honour of my child.

To which Caliban replies:

> O ho, O ho! would't had been done!
> Thou didst prevent me; I had peopled else
> This isle with Calibans.

This passage radically skews the play against Caliban, undermining his protestations of hospitality to the father and daughter (I.ii.333–46). The effect of this charge is to show that he is incapable of recognizing proper civil boundaries, thus abrogating any rights to the island he occupies. This failure to recognize proper boundaries is a sign of primitiveness that predicts the discourse of race. The attempted rape threatens to introduce a race of hybrid post-colonial subjects, a threat of an almost dehumanizing racial pollution.

The link between language and race has existed since the emergence of racialist theory in writers such as Buffon, and becomes a key feature of imperial discourse as racial dominance is encouraged and ratified by the political, cultural and racial assertions of a dominant group. This link is foreshadowed in the exchange between Caliban and Prospero and Miranda, although not explicitly, for it is important to remember that the formal categorization of races had not yet occurred in European thinking when the play was written. The language which enabled Caliban to "name the bigger light and how the less" (I.ii.337) and which therefore becomes commensurate with reality itself, is a language in which the consequent assumption of authority cannot brook any thought of racial (nor linguistic) intermixing. In his play *Caliban*, Rénan has Ariel say "Prospero taught thee the Aryan language, and with that divine tongue the channel of reason has become inseparable from thee" (Rénan 1896: 18). There was a very deep investment in the link between language and culture in nineteenth-century thinking (when Rénan wrote his play); indeed it is the force of this link that carries over into assumptions about language today. Hybridity represents not merely a racial impurity, but more profoundly, threatens to disrupt the link between language and race so important to racialist thinking and hence, to the civilizing mission of imperialism. According to Rénan, if one is fortunate enough to speak "Indo-European" one benefits from all the qualities of that race (1896: 145).

Indeed, the myth of the authority of the dominant (Aryan) tongue as a discourse of knowledge rests upon its inviolability. As George Lamming asks:

> Could Prospero really have endured the presence and meaning of a brown skin grandchild? It would not be Miranda's own doing. It would not be the result of their enterprise. It would be Miranda's and Caliban's child. It would be *theirs*: the result and expression of some fusion both physical and other than physical.
>
> (1960: 102)

It is these "other than physical" possibilities that are the most far-reaching. For quite apart from issues of rape and miscegenation is the possibility of the emergence of a hybrid 'decolonizing' language which might completely transform the nature of the colonial relationship and consequently Caliban's power over discourse, and thus over the island itself.

The terms used to describe Caliban are so confused and contradictory that they give a clear insight into how the language of power operates. Caliban is such a 'monstrous absence' in contrast to the 'civilized presence' of Prospero, that it becomes impossible to visualize him by the descriptions the play gives of him. He is "a strange fish!" (II.ii.27); "Legg'd like a man! and his fins like arms!" (II.ii.34); "no fish" (II.ii.36); "some monster of the isle with four legs" (II.ii.66); "a plain fish" (V.i.266); and a "mis-shapen knave" (V.i.268). Morton Luce sums up this contradiction succinctly: "if all the suggestions as to Caliban's form and feature and endowments that are thrown out in the play are collected, it will be found that the one half renders the other half impossible" (Hulme 1986: 107).

The ambiguous representation of Caliban comes about because notions of race had not clearly coalesced when Shakespeare wrote, and were not to be so for a century and a half. The ambiguous directions, intimations and descriptions of Caliban in the play come about because, although the concept of the 'cannibal' had become entrenched in the European psyche as the absolute sign of the other, it had not yet been connected to the category of race. What we discover here is the origins of racism in a more radical distinction – that between humans and animals, and the subsequent connection between race and slavery. Miranda calls Caliban "slave" as well as "monster", and indeed he has been enslaved. But the concept of Caliban's animalistic, language-less identification with Nature rather than Culture, locates the origins of racism in what Peter Singer calls "speciesism".

"Speciesism"

In 1873, Daniel Wilson, attempting to argue that Shakespeare had predated nineteenth-century evolutionary theory by constructing Caliban as an example of the 'missing link', compared Caliban's relationship with Miranda to that of Ariel:

> Caliban is her fellow creature, in a way that Ariel could never be, and provokes comparison such as the other in no way suggests. For his is the palpable grossness of the lower nature, a creature of earth, not unredeemed by its own fitting attributes nor untrue to itself, but altogether below the level of humanity.
>
> (Vaughan and Vaughan 1991: 61)

Wilson's language, although aimed at a pseudo-scientific outcome, is a telling demonstration of the capacity of nineteenth-century eugenic discourse to relegate the racial other to a liminal space of abjection and sub-humanity. Although he wishes to make a distinction between Caliban and the human 'savage', the language he uses renders the boundary between the human and sub-human somewhat vague.

> After all that has been most strongly dwelt upon which seems to degrade the brutified Australian Bushman, Andaman Islander or other lowest type of human savage, he is still human. It can with no propriety be said of him that he has only doubtfully attained to the rank of manhood.
>
> (Vaughan and Vaughan 1991: 27–8)

A different way of understanding this discourse can be provided in the concept of what Peter Singer calls "speciesism" (Singer 2003). The indeterminacy of Caliban's representation in the play is an indeterminacy of species. It is his animal-like nature, confirmed in his lack of language, that constitutes him as both a lesser race, if human at all, and a slave. "The one special advantage we enjoy over animals," writes Cicero, "is our power to speak with one another, to express our thoughts in words" (Greenblatt 1990: 23). The 'civilizing' mission is based on the profoundly speciesist assumption that 'barbaric' languages have placed other men at the level of animals, placing them in need of cultural redemption. It remains a given that animals are irredeemable, they remain the ultimate binary – non-human. One of the most common attitudes of colonizers was the constitution of the indigenous inhabitants as a part of nature and therefore, by implication, not human, but merely one feature of an environment that needed to be tamed. Identifying humans with animals rests on the presumption that animals are beneath consideration.

Consequently speciesism and racism are not merely analogous, but one preceded and justified the other. We afflict other races because we first afflicted animals. As Carey Wolfe puts it:

> "Our humanist concept of subjectivity is inseparable from the discourse and institution of speciesism" since the "human" is *by definition* the *not* animal or "animalistic." This in turn makes possible a symbolic economy in which we can engage in "a non-criminal putting to death," as Derrida phrases it, not only of animals, but of other humans as well by marking them as animals.
>
> (Wolfe 2003: 40)

Caliban, in his contradictory and inexplicable monstrosity, demonstrates the European discourse of racial othering in the process of coming into being. He precedes the link between cannibal and race in the distinction between animals and humans.

This conflation of racial 'barbarism' with inhuman animalism appears from the beginning of racialist thinking (and the word 'barbarous' still has the synonym 'inhuman' in Roget's Thesaurus). When speaking of negroes Buffon never fails to mention "that their heads are covered with wool (like sheep) rather than hair, and he betrays no discomfiture in writing that 'Negroes and Negresses, when transported to the coldest climates always continue to produce animals of the same kind'" (Todorov 1993: 101). But eerily reminiscent of Prospero's view of Caliban (and indeed, of the way he is situated in the text), Buffon has a ready explanation for the African's animal nature: "It is not improbable that in warm climates apes have ravished girls" (101). This bizarre assertion has its antecedents in Edward Long's *History of Jamaica* (1774), which was quoted as late as 1857 by Armand de Quatrefages. Long presumed the existence of two kinds of sterile mulattos, of whom one lot were produced by the coupling of Blacks with Whites and the other of Blacks with Orang-Outangs, adding, "I do not think an Orang-Outang would be any dishonour to a Hottentot female" (Poliakov 1977: 178). We can see how clearly this version of polygenism demonstrates the importance attached to keeping the races separate. Given Rénan's commitment to the importance of the link between the Aryan language and racial improvement in his play *Caliban* it is not improbable that the idea came from Shakespeare, certainly from the same racial fear.

Visually, Caliban is a kind of absence in the play, represented only by Prospero's discourse. He takes shape completely within the language of the colonizer and by "learning to curse" through that language (I.ii.367) he fulfils the only expectations we may have of him. Linguistically, Caliban, the non-human monster, has been taught language itself, not just the invaders' language, so that he might "know his own meaning", a meaning provided, of course, by Prospero. If we ask the question, "How would Caliban seem if it weren't for the consequences of his bondage and imprisonment?", we find that we cannot answer it. In both his depiction as "hag seed", monster, lying slave, filth, and his imprisonment in the colonial language by which this construction is borne, Caliban fulfils all prophecies of his debasement.

Language and place

The threats exchanged between Caliban and Prospero in this key scene appear equally malicious. Yet there is a very subtle difference in their nature. Caliban calls upon a "wicked dew" from "unwholesome fen" (324) to drop on them both; that a "south west blow on ye and blister ye all over" (325–6). Caliban's resource is the place itself, the conditions of that island which he takes for granted as his home. Prospero's threats are more sinister and painful, for they emanate from his Art and are directed at Caliban's body. "Tonight thou shalt have cramps" he says, "Side stitches that shall pen thy breath up"; urchins and bees will do their work on Caliban's body at Prospero's behest.

Although Caliban belongs to the place and can call upon the natural resources of the island, Prospero's art intervenes in nature, for this intervention is the very function of culture and it becomes directly responsible for Caliban's physical pain. That separation between the base materiality of colonial subjection and the erudite power of imperial learning is completely dissolved the moment the colonized subject offers resistance. The link between Prospero's superior technology and the intention to torture Caliban's debased body is a profound metaphor of the actual material consequences of an eloquent and 'civilizing' imperial culture.

It is clear that there is a distinct difference in the play between the ways in which Prospero and Caliban relate to place. Prospero's primary modality is mastery, effected through his 'Art' and represented in his language. To Prospero, Caliban has no place – he is the place. He is the place in its most primitive and unimproved state. As an indigenous subject, he is outside the colonizing language and therefore beyond culture. He is part of the wilderness, to be tamed, subdued and civilized. His 'gabbling', which passes for language, predicates, in Prospero's mind, a lack of any civilized comprehension of his island as a location. By teaching Caliban to "name the bigger light and the less" Prospero not only provides Caliban with a medium of representation, but to his own eyes, provides Caliban with a world. Without that language Caliban is effectively 'erased' – part of the uninhabited, uncultured wasteland, the *Terra Nullius* whose unoccupied state invites colonial occupation.

Prospero, for all his geographical control of the island, cannot see it as home, and chooses a power over Caliban's body. The match is an unequal one for Prospero's force is consummate. But it suggests very different ways in which the combatants are located. Caliban is constructed by the play as part of Nature. His ability to experience the island 'instinctively', beyond the domination of Prospero's art or language, is elaborated later when Trinculo and Stephano hear Ariel's music.

> Be not afeard; the isle is full of noises,
> Sounds and sweet airs, that give delight, and hurt not.
> Sometimes a thousand twangling instruments
> Will hum about mine ears; and sometimes voices,
> That, if I then had wak'd after long sleep,
> Will make me sleep again; and then, in dreaming,
> The clouds methought would open, and show riches
> Ready to drop upon me; that, when I wak'd,
> I cried to dream again.

> (III.ii.132–41)

Whereas Prospero uses music to charm, punish and generally consolidate his power, music provokes in Caliban an enjoyment of the dream-like riches of the island. In one view this is a moment of excess that exists beyond the restricting language of the colonizer. "Caliban's production of the island as a pastoral space, separated from the world of power, takes *literally* what the discourse in the hands of a Prospero can only mean *metaphorically*" (Brown 1985, in Bloom 1988: 149). In this reading Caliban desires to escape reality and return to dream as the only way to evade the control of Prospero's language. Yet it is in this very language that Caliban reveals the delights of the island to the drunkards. Even in this eloquent description of the dream-like qualities of the island (or perhaps *particularly* in this description) Caliban engages the language that 'interpellates' him in a way that sets his experience of the island apart. The power of a dominant language to construct the physical environment is one with which the colonized must always contend. Whatever the sense of inherent or cultural 'belonging' to place which Caliban may have, it is clear that place may be 'controlled,' by being familiarized and domesticated through language.

Language and naming

The example of Prospero alerts us to the ways in which this apparently benign discourse of imperial naming may have actual, harmful effects on the lives and bodies of the colonized. In reply to Prospero's threat of torture, Caliban launches into a famous speech that confirms his own indigenous possession of the land, the power of Prospero's language and the ultimate hollowness of colonial control.

> This island's mine, by Sycorax my mother,
> Which thou tak'st from me. When thou cam'st first,
> Thou strok'st me, and made much of me; wouldst give me
> Water with berries in't; and teach me how
> To name the bigger light, and how the less,
> That burn by day and night: and then I lov'd thee,
> And show'd thee all the qualities o' th' isle,
> The fresh springs, brine-pits, barren place and fertile:
> Curs'd be I that did so!

Caliban's ownership of the island is based on prior occupation, which is the only practical measure of indigeneity, even though his mother Sycorax had migrated there. But the moral force of prior occupation pales into insignificance alongside the linguistic force of Prospero's power to name place, that is, establish *his* names as the authoritative ones. The power to name place, by locating the speaker within a world that is recognizable through a particular language, bestows the more far-reaching capacity to construct human identity. This is because those names represent not just a language but also an entire edifice of cultural assumptions: attitudes about time and space, about the relation between language and place and even about the operation of thought itself. In European colonization names become, in effect, metonymic of modernity, in terms of which the rights to dominance are assumed.

This assumption of dominance requires that the indigenous subjects be, in effect, dehumanized, their own capacity for naming erased. In Ernest Rénan's play *Caliban* the opening scene sees Caliban and Ariel discussing the issues that arise in Act I Scene ii of *The Tempest*. Here Ariel echoes the formative and strategic assertion of colonial occupation:

> Thou sayest without cessation that the island belonged to thee. In truth, it
> did belong to thee, just as the desert belongs to the gazelle, the jungle to the

tiger, and no more. Thou knewest the name of nothing there. Thou wast a stranger to reason and thy inarticulate language resembled the bellowing of an angry camel more than any human speech.

(Rénan 1896: 17)

The pronouncement of the inarticulacy of the indigenous occupants is an important erasure, a constitution of empty space on which 'place' can then be inscribed by the various processes of colonial discourse. One of these processes involves endowing or denying human identity to the indigenous inhabitants, a role in which Miranda functions by providing the terms by which Caliban may know himself. It was she who, teaching Caliban language, taught him to "know thine own meaning" (I.ii.358). The naming and re-naming of place is a potent demonstration of the ways in which the power of a discourse may operate. Re-naming operates as if it were the original and authoritative naming of the place, or any other concept, and it is this authority to describe the world that Prospero's language acquires. For to name reality is in some mysterious way to assume control of it, by fitting it into a scheme in which all things have their relation because they are related in language.

Language and identity

For George Lamming the language Prospero teaches Caliban is an unequivocal prison from which there is "no escape".

> Prospero has given Caliban Language; and with it an unstated history of consequences, an unknown history of future intentions. This gift of Language meant not English, in particular, but speech and concept as a way, a method, a necessary avenue towards areas of the self that could not be reached in any other way.
>
> (1960: 109)

Prospero's gift is the gift of method. To interpret the productive power of imperial representation as imprisonment is to ignore the transformative agency of those produced in this discourse. Does language provide an avenue towards areas of the self, unreachable in any other way, or does it provide the names by which those areas come into being? Prospero's names metonymise the power he has over Caliban's world, here and now, but not necessarily for all time. Caliban is not imprisoned in Prospero's language incontrovertibly because it is by *using* Prospero's language (or any other) that Caliban can actualize his own *possibility for being*. This power is the key to the transformative dynamic of post-colonial writing and cultural production. Such a dynamic emerges in Caliban's determination to answer back to one who has such manifest power over him.

All the charms
Of Sycorax, toads, beetles, bats, light on you!

> For I am all the subjects that you have,
> Which first was mine own King: and here you sty me
> In this hard rock, whilst you do keep from me
> The rest o' the' island.

This speech of Caliban's goes right to the heart of post-colonial subjectivity and specifically articulates the agency of the interpellated colonial subject to engage that power which produces him as subject. For, given the power of Prospero's language to interpellate Caliban, the discursive power that produces his subjectivity is neither absolute nor hierarchically fixed in those institutions – such as education, literature, and government – through which it is perpetuated. Clearly Prospero's power over Caliban is tangibly oppressive, he commands the means of physical torture and incarceration, not to mention the emotionally disabling impact of his personal treachery to one who loved him and showed him "all the qualities o' th' isle" (I.ii.339). But there is a place where the power of his language cannot reach. For Prospero's language can only have power over Caliban to the extent that it has power to cement his perception of himself, if Caliban comes to internalize the way in which he is situated in that language, accepting it as a true indication of his status and being.

Although such internalization may occur (and does occur often in the colonial experience) it is by no means inevitable or complete. Caliban's reaction demonstrates the limits of Prospero's power. For although his language assumes the status of an authoritative instrument for, in effect, bringing the world into being, it cannot obliterate Caliban's belief that he is the deposed king of the island and that Prospero's dominion is in essence pathetic, since Caliban is his one and only subject. Imperial power as *either* repressive force or productive energy is not absolute or static but transformable. Although it has the power to 'produce' Caliban, it cannot prevent him from 'entering' power and *reproducing* himself in the language.

Beyond cursing: Language and transformation

Miranda's response demonstrates the extent to which the filiative relationship with Empire constructs the discourse of settlement and to what extent she is placed in antagonism to Caliban through her ownership of language and her stewardship of education.

> Abhorred slave,
> Which any print of goodness wilt not take,
> Being capable of all ill! I pitied thee,
> Took pains to make thee speak, taught thee each hour
> One thing or other: when thou didst not, savage,
> Know thine own meaning, but wouldst gabble like
> A thing most brutish, I endow'd thy purposes
> With words that made them know. But thy vile race,
> Though thou didst learn, had that in't which good natures

Could not abide to be with; therefore wast thou
Deservedly confin'd into this rock,
Who hadst deserved more than a prison.

Miranda's language in this speech both embodies and describes the justification for the subjugation of the indigenous Caliban. Quite apart from his constitution as a rapist and miscegenator, he is an "abhorred slave", "savage", "brutish", "vile". What is being enacted here is the power of Miranda's language to construct Caliban racially, a power that is coterminous with Prospero's very tangible control of his body, his actions, his destiny. Caliban is the very nadir of the natural man – an 'animal' in fact – "which any print of goodness wilt not take". This is, of course, the inevitable retort of the civilizing mission to any rebuttals it might encounter from the colonized. The colonized subject cannot be endowed with the capacity for choice, can never be accorded the freedom to refuse incorporation. If he is recalcitrant he must be constituted as incapable of improvement: as Prospero says, he is "A devil, a born devil, on whose nature/ Nurture can never stick" (IV.i.188–9). The moral framework of the relationship is entirely constructed by the dominant party, the settler colonial Miranda, and it is a relationship dominated by a simple binary that remains central to imperial discourse.

By entering so effortlessly into the spirit of Prospero's language, Miranda reveals herself to be as formed by that language, by imperial discourse, as Caliban. Although she seems to further articulate the debasement of Caliban in which Prospero is engaged, her speech clarifies the link between the imperial and the patriarchal power. Miranda has clearly had a relationship as a child with Caliban and assumes the nurturing aspects of colonial control by being responsible for teaching him language by which he can "know himself". Caliban's response to Miranda's diatribe has become a resistance slogan:

You taught me language; and my profit on't
Is, I know how to curse. The red plague rid you
For learning me your language.

The play provides Caliban with no way in which he can make the language work for him. The curse is not Miranda's language but the way in which he has been situated in it. We have seen in this scene itself that Caliban does have the power of reply, he has the power of resistance, but his inability to appropriate the language of Prospero confines him as securely as does Prospero's Art. It is this acceptance of the link between Prospero's language and his Art, and hence the subtle acceptance of his domination, which traps Caliban.

What Caliban might do with this language constitutes one of the most pressing issues in post-colonial writing. For what he *might* have done has indeed been accomplished in post-colonial literatures. Until the middle of the twentieth century, says Vaughan, most critics implicitly sided with Prospero, blaming Caliban for his own linguistic limitations (1991: 166). But the relationship between Prospero and Caliban took a turn in George Lamming's essay

"A monster, a child, a slave" in 1960. When Lamming identified language as Prospero's "prison" he posited an ambiguous prison which maintained its power productively: its imprisonment was effected in the way it could "produce" Caliban.

No doubt Prospero remains convinced that his language is Caliban's prison, "the very prison in which Caliban's achievements will be realized and restricted" (110). This is a ubiquitous argument about the function of a colonizing language, although it is not always expressed so subtly: that for those for whom it is not a mother tongue the language is inevitably and essentially limiting. Language will not allow Caliban's expansion beyond a certain point, says Lamming. "This kind of realization, this kind of expansion, is possible only to those who reside in that state of being which is the very source and ultimate of the language which bears them always forward" (110). That is, expansion and true self-realization are only possible to those born into the language. But we must ask how that "state of being" becomes the inherent property of a mother tongue? Why is Prospero's language prevented from "bearing its speakers forward"? The history of post-colonial writing, including that of Lamming himself, would seem to suggest that language is a horizon into which all speakers may enter in different ways and along different trajectories.

Caliban "can never be regarded as an heir of that Language," adds Lamming, "since his use of Language is no more than his way of serving Prospero; and Prospero's instruction in this Language is only his way of measuring the distance which separates him from Caliban" (110). This embraces a *non sequitur* that denies Caliban any agency. Certainly it is undeniable that the colonizing language is taught and disseminated in a way that entrenches difference: the colonized speak dialect or marginal varieties, while the colonizer speaks, and has the status of, Standard English. But the idea that colonized peoples are unable to use the colonizer's language as anything more than a way of serving the colonizing power, is a myth about the function of language which falls into Prospero's trap.

But is it Prospero's trap? Is Prospero not as much a prisoner of language as Caliban? For, as Heidegger says: "Language speaks. Man only speaks in that he artfully complies with language" (1975: 32). That word 'artfully' opens up a marked and subtle ambivalence in Shakespeare's text. Why is it, for instance, that Caliban is given some of the most beautiful lines of the play? Could it be that the radical difference between Caliban and Prospero is seated in a kind of sameness, the similarity of their engagement with language? Both use threats of magic and curses and eloquent utterances of fearsome revenge. Both *use* language 'artfully'. To what extent is Caliban's agency embedded in his identification with Prospero? "I am all the subjects you have", he says at one stage to Prospero. Is Caliban's strategic intelligence, embedded so subtly in the present of the play, a premonition of his transformative agency in the future?

The answer to these questions may depend upon whether we see Caliban as a part of nature or a part of culture. Janheinz Jahn, building on Mannoni's and Lamming's interventions, offered a different prognosis for Caliban. Jahn suggests that Lamming is right, that "if Caliban is no more than a part of nature, he will never be able to break out of the prison of Prospero's language" (1968: 240). "But suppose Caliban is also part of a culture, a different culture unfamiliar to Prospero?" asks Jahn (240).

Suppose also, that Caliban carries out his revolt relying on his own resources rather than on the buffoons Stephano and Trinculo. In that event, the "thousand twangling instruments", the music of his island which he explains to them, might be considered the voices of his culture rather than the voices of nature. Or perhaps Caliban's culture is immersed in nature, in place, and therefore shows a different relationship possible between the two, a less hierarchic, un-European possibility. Caliban emerges from a culture very different from Prospero's book culture but able to utilize it.

> So he captures, in his own and Prospero's language, a culture Prospero did not create and cannot control, which he, Caliban, has recognized as his own. But in the process the language is transformed, acquiring different meanings that Prospero never expected. Caliban becomes a 'bilingual'. That language he shares with Prospero and the language he has minted from it are no longer identical. Caliban breaks out of the prison of Prospero's language.
>
> (Jahn 1968: 242)

Jahn explicitly dates Caliban's appropriation of Prospero's culture, the "successful revolt from the prison of Prospero's language" (242) from the rise of the Negritudinist literary movement between 1934 and 1948. According to Jahn, the escape was effected in three ways: in semantics, rhythm and subject matter. In particular, the use of French led writers such as Senghor, Damas and Césaire to construct a new literary culture which reconfigured Africa as "no longer exotic and 'primitive' but as a specific culture" (1968: 244). The limitations of the négritude movement have been widely discussed, but clearly the appropriation of French by these writers preceded a flourishing African literature in English in the post-independence 1950s. Caliban remained in Prospero's prison of language only as long as he could be deceived into believing it was a prison. The transformation of post-colonial literatures, which began in the negritudinist movement, was one that saw that language was not the repository of culture but its agent.

Prospero's books

From the position of inconsolable despair with which Caliban concludes his 'learning to curse' exchange with Prospero and Miranda, he is relegated to the role of comic foil for Stephano and Trinculo. But this comedy comes to revolve around an important accessory to Prospero's language – his books, which Caliban identifies as the source of his power, and which he entreats the two clowns to destroy. When plotting to overthrow Prospero, he advises Trinculo and Stephano:

> Remember
> First to possess his books; for without them
> He's but a sot as I am, nor hath not
> One spirit to command: they all do hate him
> As rootedly as I. Burn but his books.
>
> (III.ii.89–93)

The recognition of the power of books elaborates the very important link between language and writing in the colonial exchange. Shakespeare uses the term 'books' here, as he did in *The Merry Wives of Windsor* (IV.i.15) to refer to not only Prospero's physical collection of books, but also his book learning, his scholarship or study (OED). As Lord Macaulay put it in his infamous Minute to Parliament (see Chapter 2), knowing English gives anyone access to a "vast intellectual wealth", a literature that is intrinsically more valuable than any other, a corpus of arts and sciences that cannot be matched. The capacity to transfer this *belief* is the capacity to rule.

This ideological assumption of the power of print is replicated in *The Tempest* in the power that accrues to Prospero from his books. The play imprisons Caliban in a form of Orientalism: it describes Caliban's unquestioned acceptance of the fact that Prospero's power is located in a superior *culture* embodied in the written word, in his books; and it denies Caliban any opportunity to appropriate Prospero's technology. The play specifically denies him the opportunity to be nurtured by this Art, because, as an unreconstructed natural man, a "devil", he is one "on whose nature Nurture can never stick".

In his play *Caliban* Rénan elaborates the connection between Prospero's books and the power of his language, adding the extra dimension of those scientific instruments by which Prospero has developed his Art and representing what to Rénan is the ultimate secret of European supremacy.

> Those books of hell – ugh! how I hate them. They have been the instruments of my slavery. We must snatch and burn them instantly. No other method will serve but this. War to the books! They are our worst enemies, and those who possess them will have power over all their fellows. The man who knows Latin can control and command the people to his service. Down with Latin! Therefore, first of all seize his books, for there lies the secret of his power. It is by them that he reigns over the inferior spirits. Break, also, the glass retorts and all the materials of his laboratory.
>
> (Rénan 1896: 42)

There is both a class and a race dimension to Caliban in Rénan's play. The slave has been taken with Prospero back to Milan and his vengeful nature has become the instigator of rebellion amongst the disaffected classes in this 'civilized' duchy. Once Caliban has assumed power as the result of the revolution his rule also assumes the moderation of princes, but Prospero's counter-attack through Ariel is fruitless because, as Ariel suggests, the power of Prospero's art lies in its capacity to persuade people of its reality.

> Whence did it come that our magic prevailed so easily over our adversaries in the enchanted island? It lay in the fact that Alonzo and those minds that were so accessible to it perceived and believed in it …
>
> (Rénan 1896: 53)

Prospero's cultural power fails in Milan because he fails to convince the ruled that the power lies with him. More significantly, once Caliban assumes power, his fear of Prospero's books wanes.

The actual relationship with these books is a source of extreme ambivalence in the colonial relationship. Ideologically, they purport to give access to the "vast intellectual wealth" of the colonizer. But *strategically*, if Caliban were to acquire those books rather than burn them, would he not have access to an empowering counter-discourse? All Prospero's and Miranda's language can teach him is how to curse. But the example of post-colonial literatures reveals that Caliban can take hold of the language and make it work for him. And not only language, for this is but one feature, although a key one, of a set of relations of power that constitute imperial discourse. Rejecting the language will not alter the fundamentally productive power of the discourse itself. The future of Caliban's language is not cursing but transformation. By appropriating Prospero's language, his books, indeed the whole technological edifice of his 'Art', Caliban may determine not only his own future, but Prospero's as well.

This also raises to prominence the issue of the associated technologies of communication, particularly global electronic ones. Prospero's books stand for much more than books today just as they did in Shakespeare's time. But where they suggested scholarship, learning and erudition, today they suggest technology, the means of communication and information capital. Caliban's problem was not the language that represented him as a slave, but the fact that he was allowed only an incomplete access to Prospero's discourse (he is never allowed to touch the 'books'). Caliban's partial literacy renders him incapable of engaging his master in a war of words – and thus he is forced to adopt physical violence as an alternative – an alternative that we soon realize is inadequate given Prospero's frequent demonstrations of magical power. The significance of this for the theme of colonial resistance is poignant – particularly in the present world dominated by a hyperpower ever ready to invade weak nations in case they may be thinking about conflict. The option of violent political resistance to colonial control simply invites the exertion of even greater force. But the capture of the source of Prospero's power offers the true means of social and political transformation. In this one fact we discover the very centre of the post-colonial method of transformative resistance.

2 Language, learning and colonial power

When thou cam'st first,
Thou strok'st me, and made much of me; wouldst give me
Water with berries in't; and teach me how
To name the bigger light, and how the less,
That burn by day and night
  (*The Tempest* I.ii.333–8)

Prospero's language was a medium of slavery because it enabled him to give orders that could be understood and obeyed on pain of torture. But the language was hegemonic in a much more subtle way: it gave Caliban a world by constructing a particular kind of reality for him, showing him how to "name the bigger light and ... the less", naming his island with the names that signified Prospero's control. Prospero's language also provided Caliban with a hierarchy of values, a fabric of distinctions and associations predicated on a particular way of seeing the world and hence a clear understanding of his place in the colonial relationship.

The unreflective certainty of Prospero's authority is repeated many times in the history of European invasion and colonisation, but none is more striking than the example of the *Requerimiento* mentioned by Stephen Greenblatt, which was composed by the Spanish conquistadors to be read aloud to the inhabitants of the New World. The following demand for obedience is to be read to the Indians *in Spanish*. If obedience is not immediate:

> We shall take you and your wives and your children, and shall make slaves of them, and as such shall sell and dispose of them as their Highnesses may command; and we shall take away your goods, and shall do you all the mischief and damage that we can, as to vassals who do not obey, and refuse to receive their lord, and resist and contradict him; and we protest that the deaths and losses which shall accrue from this are your fault ... .
>
> (cited in Greenblatt 1990: 29)

Not satisfied with the absurdity of reading this directive to the inhabitants in a language they do not understand, the *Requerimiento* proceeds to validate its own authority by the power of writing.

And that we have said this to you and made this Requisition, we request the notary here present to give us his testimony in writing, and we ask the rest who are present that they should be witnesses of this Requisition.

(Greenblatt 1990: 29)

The legendary critic of the Spanish occupation Fr. Bartolomé de las Casas "didn't know whether to laugh or cry" at this absurdity, yet it is, in its own way, a sophisticated document. "A strange blend of ritual, cynicism, legal fiction, and perverse idealism," says Greenblatt, "the *Requerimiento* contains at its core the conviction that there is no serious language barrier between the Indians and the Europeans" (29). Linked to this power, of a language the victims cannot understand, is a perfect and unambiguous *inversion* of justice, based on nothing more than the authorisation of the written text. The astonishingly unreflective assertiveness of this injustice is not an isolated aberration, but can be seen to be emblematic of the assumption of the right of dominance, a view of a higher good which motivated the most unshakeable aspects of European hegemony.

For the British Empire, the sense contained in the posting of the *Requerimiento* – the refusal to accept any serious language barrier between the colonizers and their subjects – was subtly embedded in their decision to educate Indians in English. It is possible that situations as bizarre as this occurred in the British administration of its Empire. But the overriding assumption was that English was the peerless language, and if colonial peoples were to be educated it would have to be in this medium.

The ideological support for the spread of the English language through colonial control is both powerful and deeply rooted, the process having long been presented in philanthropic terms. It is possible that every linguistic group believes its language to be incomparable and beneficial, but political, economic and military power allow some groups, rather than others, to put this assumption into practice. It is interesting to see how far the idea of English as a global language extends back in history. In 1599 Samuel Daniel wrote in his poem *Musophilus*:

And who in time knows whither we may vent
The treasure of our tongue, to what strange shores
This gain of our best glory shall be sent,
To enrich unknowing nations without stores?
Which worlds in the yet unformed Occident
May come refined with the accents that are ours.

(Daniel 1599)

The assumption that the beauties and accomplishments of a particular language, like the benefits of 'civilized' culture, should be 'shared' with the world is, of course, at the very heart of the 'civilizing mission' of European imperialism, an undisputed belief in their own 'civilization' which provided much of the moral self-justification for the political and economic exploitation of colonization. In a lecture given to the Alliance for the Propagation of the French Language, Ernest

Rénan says: "The preservation and propagation of the French language are important for the general order of civilization" (Todorov 1993: 146). The assumption that the language, whether French or English, is so superior that the world would *want* it, remains unquestioned. It is in this *engagement* with imperial language conducted by the colonized that we find embedded many post-colonial issues of cultural contact and change.

The belief that English provided the most comprehensive strategic advantage to the Empire was expressed as early as 1801 when the British philologist William P. Russel proclaimed that:

> … the English language … is already the most general in America. Its progress in the East is considerable; and if many schools were established in different parts of Asia and Africa to instruct the natives, free of all expense, with various premiums of British manufacture to the most meritorious pupils, this would be the best preparatory step that Englishmen could adopt for the general admission of their commerce, their opinions, their religion. This would tend to conquer the heart and its affections; which is a far more effectual conquest than that obtained by swords and cannons: and a thousand pounds expended for tutors, books, and premiums, would do more to subdue a nation of savages than forty thousand expended for artillery-men, bullets, and gunpowder.
>
> (Russell 1801: 93–5)

This nicely apprehends how important the role of language actually became to the ideology of the civilizing mission. This mission was not only to civilize the world but also to spread the benefits of the British race. Writing in 1850 Martin Tupper wrote in the journal *The Anglo Saxon*:

> Stretch forth! stretch forth! from the south to the north,
> From the east to the west, – stretch forth! stretch forth!
> Strengthen thy stakes and lengthen thy cords, –
> The world is a tent for the world's true lords!
> Break forth and spread over every place
> The world is a world for the Saxon race![1]

Although imperial sentiments were not always expressed with such unabashed jingoism the assumption that the world was a world for the Saxon race was usually couched in philanthropic terms.

One exception to this philanthropic dressing up was the case of Celtic languages. In the middle of the nineteenth century Parliament appointed three English Anglicans – Lingen, Symons and Johnson – as commissioners to investigate the

---

1 Tupper recited this poem in the village of Wantage on Thursday 25 October 1850 at the celebration of the millennium of King Alfred's birth at which he proposed a toast to "the Anglo Saxon Race all over the world".

quality of education in Wales, and in particular whether the – largely monoglot, Welsh, and nonconformist – working class was being adequately trained in the use of English. The report of the Welsh Education Commission was bound in three blue-covered volumes, which are known unsurprisingly as the Blue Books, published in 1847. They concluded that the education system in Wales was inadequate – no doubt a reasonable conclusion, given the paucity of education spending in Wales. But their explanation of this was that the Welsh were indolent, filthy, superstitious, corrupt, intoxicated and that the principal reason for these personal inadequacies of the Welsh was the combination of Nonconformism and the Welsh language.

Needless to say this was an extremely contentious conclusion, coloured in part by the appointment of non-Welsh speaking English commissioners, and is seen by many to be the origin of both the modern self-concept of Wales as a nation, and the somewhat prickly relationships with England, with the established church, and with the English language. It is certainly the foundation of some of the class distinctions that were so important in the politics of Wales in the subsequent century. The popular reference to "Brad y Llyfrau Gleision" – the treason of the Blue Books – is contemporary with the publication of the report, and harks back to "Brad y Cyllyll Hirion" – the night of the long knives – when their Danish mercenaries slaughtered the British at the court of Gwrtheyrn (see Davies 1994).

As is so often the case, language was held by the Welsh to be a crucial, even incomparable, marker of identity, however much or little it was actually spoken. More than any other feature of life language seems to most clearly embody one's national or cultural identity. Language acts as a sign rather than a mode of referring: it is a sign of *us* and is therefore held to embody *our* meaning. The Welsh language is very much like a Welsh national flag. For the Welsh, an attack on the language was an attack on the culture as significant as war. Because the Celtic languages were much closer than overseas colonies they were treated less paternalistically and are therefore a very clear demonstration of the link between language and political power.

English and colonial education

The idea that colonial subjects *should* be educated at all was not a foregone conclusion in the nineteenth century. But the situation changed radically in the drama played out in the British parliament when Lord Macaulay rose in 1835 to deliver his Minute to Parliament, arguing the case for the teaching of English in India. This occasion, as Gauri Viswanathan explains (1987; 1989), signified the rise to prominence of the Anglicists over the Orientalists in the British administration of India. The Charter Act of 1813, devolving responsibility for Indian education on the colonial administration, led to a struggle between the two approaches, ultimately resolved by Macaulay's Minute, in which we find stated not just the assumptions of the Anglicists, but the profoundly universalist assumptions of English national culture itself. For Macaulay, the link between the majesty and achievement of Western culture and the English language is unarguable.

How, then, stands the case? We have to educate a people who cannot at present be educated by means of their mother tongue. We must teach them some foreign language. The claims of our own language it is hardly necessary to recapitulate. It stands pre-eminent even among the languages of the west. It abounds with works of imagination not inferior to the noblest which Greece has bequeathed to us … . Whoever knows that language has ready access to all the vast intellectual wealth, which all the wisest nations of the earth have created and hoarded in the course of ninety generations.

(1835 in Ashcroft *et al.* 2006: 374)

The astonishing cultural arrogance of this Minute is now widely recognised for the clarity with which it represents Eurocentric and imperial cultural pretensions. But the assumption that the colonized would appreciate the benefits of an imperial language had a long pre-history in English thought. Of the many aspects of the imperial mentality Macaulay's Minute displays, one seems most potent: the pre-eminence and power of the English language. But why is it so pre-eminent? In Macaulay we find a slippage that always occurs when language is being discussed, a slippage between the qualities of a language and the uses to which it is put, the texts in which it is found.

For Macaulay the pre-eminence of English arose from the wealth of expression in "works of imagination" and works of science and history. In other words, what English brings with it is not so much a peculiarly potent way of talking about the world, but an immense cultural gift, a history of aesthetic and scientific achievement, which becomes conflated with the language itself. This "vast wealth" of works of imagination, this history of western textuality, stands behind any utterance in the English language, and this historico-political inheritance, its eminent universality, lends the language its peculiarly hegemonic power. However it is precisely this conflation of the products of a linguistic culture with the inherent character of the language, its function as a way of engaging and constituting the world, which most confuses discussion of language use in the cross-cultural text.

English worked so well as a form of cultural indoctrination because "the strategy of locating authority in the texts of English literature all but effaced the sordid history of colonialist expropriation, material exploitation and class and race oppression behind British world dominance" (Viswanathan 1987: 22). English literature "functioned as a surrogate Englishman in his highest and most perfect state" (23). One could add that without the profoundly universalist assumptions of English literature and the dissemination of these through education, colonial administrations would not have been able to invoke such widespread complicity with imperial culture (see Said 1993).

Language education in Africa

Despite the professed determination, after Macaulay, to teach colonial students in English and to teach civilized values through English literature, the commitment of the Colonial Office to colonial education throughout the nineteenth century was erratic and desultory and nowhere more so than in Africa. The business of

education in general in the African colonies was left to missions for most of the
nineteenth century. The problem with this situation for the colonial administration
was that mission schools were firmly committed to vernacular teaching. The West
African Education Ordinance of 1882 marked the beginning of a defined relationship between the colonial government and the mission schools (Tiffen 1968:
70) creating a general Board of Education, local boards of education and the
appointment of Inspectors of Schools to ensure a strictly English-style curriculum.
But the missions and the Government clashed immediately over vernacular policy.
The first Inspector of Schools for the British West African territories, Mr Sunter,
declared in his 1884 report that "the natives must and will know English in spite
of all such well-meaning but diseased notions [of vernacular teaching]; it is the
language of commerce and the only education worth a moment's consideration or
attainable" (Hilliard 1957: 70). The Government, concerned about the missionary
schools' largely pro-vernacular policy, began to open Government schools in those
areas not served by mission schools, or in areas where vacuums had been created
by the deportation of the Bremen and Basel missionary societies (1957: 76).

The government's general neglect of language education in Africa continued up
to the 1920s. It wasn't until 1911 that British state involvement in colonial education began in earnest with the Imperial Education Conference. This conference
was less interested, however, in the issues of language education, than on purifying
and simplifying the English language so that it could be more easily disseminated.
However the 1911 conference marks the beginning of a systematic restructuring
of English to facilitate its spread throughout the world.

The second imperial conference of 1923 was more sensitive to language issues
and especially to the question of bilingualism, but unsurprisingly, the opening
address of the Duke of York left no doubt about the role of language in the civilizing mission. "Events conspire," he observed,

> ... to make us all Imperialists today, in no militant sense, but as upholders
> of the ideals which have already exercised a widespread influence on the
> progress of civilization, and which hold in no slight measure the future
> hope of humanity at large.

Language emerged quite clearly as a vehicle for the "ideals ... of civilization"
to be distributed to the world through British education. The Duke continued:

> It is well, therefore, that the children who are growing up in this and other
> Empires should realise the full meaning of the Imperial partnership, and
> should be reminded that they are destined to inherit a great trust, which it
> will be their duty to hand on to those who come after.
>   (Advisory Committee of the Imperial Education
>   Conference, Report 1923: 181)

It took until the 1920s for a commission of enquiry into African education to
be mounted by the Phelps–Stokes fund. The commission's 1923 report, *Education
in Africa* (Lewis 1962) set out principles that guided British educational policy in

West Africa for the four decades until independence. Curiously this report returned, probably subconsciously, to the general tenor of the Macaulay Minute by insisting on the need for a native elite who could learn standard English while the rest of the population could learn a more Africanised version. Despite the apparently liberal nature of the report in its recognition of the importance of vernacular languages, its language betrayed its sentiments:

> All peoples have an inherent right to their own language ... the vernacular is the means of giving expression to their own personality, *however primitive they may be.*
>
> (Lewis 1962: 63, my italics)

The vernaculars of these primitive personalities were to prepare the way for the civilizing influence of the colonial language:

> The more real the insight into Native life through the Native language, the more real and the more intelligent will be the demand for the European language to serve as the medium for the transfer of ... civilization to primitive Africa ... .
>
> (Lewis 1962: 66)

Thus, despite the fact that the Phelps–Stokes Report supported vernaculars as a medium of instruction and self sufficiency as an educational objective for native elites, its attitude was ambivalent because "multiplicity of Native dialects and languages" presented "one of the most perplexing problems confronting those interested in [African] education", so that "no phase of educational adaptation requires more careful consideration than the languages of instruction" (Jones 1922: 25). The emphasis on English as a medium of instruction, and as a political tool, becomes clearer in the case of the education of the native leadership. The first foreign language to be taught should be that of the European power in control, the report observed, since "[n]ative leadership must be able to confer freely with the government" (Lewis 1962: 153). In other words the native elite should learn the language to act as a conduit for colonial control.

The Phelps–Stokes report is a fascinating demonstration of the actual complexity of imperial rule. Here a report with a comparatively liberal approach to vernacular languages and a genuine concern for the linguistic autonomy of colonial peoples was caught up in the unquestioned acceptance of the superiority of the colonial ('civilized') languages, leading to the ambiguity of its summary:

1. Every people have an inherent right to their Native tongue;
2. The multiplicity of tongues shall not be such as to develop misunderstandings and distrust among people who should be friendly and cooperative;
3. Every group shall be able to communicate directly with those to whom the government is entrusted; and
4. An increasing number of Native people shall know at least one of the languages of the civilized nations.

(Advisory Committee Report: 80)

The linguistic policy in the Phelps–Stokes report resulted in a self-perpetuating system of English teaching in British West Africa. The 'civilizing mission' was thus transferred over to the native leadership, surrogates for European linguistic and cultural imperialism. The British government used this report as the foundational text for colonial language policy for the years that followed. Whether consciously or not, this ensured that the power invested in the language should be conducted *through* the native elites in belated continuation of Macaulay's principle that Englishness might be taught, and civilized values conveyed through language education.

Learning Englishness

The point was, of course, that 'Englishness' *could* be conveyed by the use of the language – not inherently, but in practice. Language used within certain forms of discourse may encapsulate all the problems of cultural hegemony. It also captures the source of the enduring debate about the cultural specificity of language. V.S. Naipaul demonstrates this in *The Middle Passage* (1962). Traveling back to the West Indies on a Spanish immigrant ship, the "Francisco Bobadilla", Naipaul encounters the West Indian disdain for the non-English-speaking waiter:

> 'But look at this, nuh,' Correia boomed. 'And I got to spend fo'teen days on this ship. Look here, man, look here. I want some tomatoes. You got that? Tomatoes. Having a lil trouble with the stomach,' he explained to us. 'Tomatoes. You got that? Me. Wantee. Tomatee. Me wantee tomatee. I don't know where they pick up these people who can't talk English.'
> The Spanish lady couldn't speak Spanish; Correia himself couldn't speak Portuguese. West Indians are English speaking, and when confronted with the foreigner display the language arrogance of all English speaking people.
> (Naipaul 1962: 16)

Naipaul's work speaks volumes about the historical importance of language in imperial power. Language means entry into the 'charmed circle' of empire (Narasimhaiah 1978: 2), an entry that Naipaul, of course, valued very greatly. To possess the language, suggests Narasimhaiah, is to have the imprimatur of the centre and a share in its pervasive cultural power.

Language has remained the key to colonial education policy, and the enforced spread of the colonial language has specific cultural effects. Ali Mazrui explains that in Africa many schools and governments opted for English because it was a "neutral" language, which would eliminate the problem of favouring one African tongue and its people over another. However English disseminated naturalized ideologies of British cultural and racial superiority, he claims, which legitimated British colonial power, while serving to subjugate Africans through an unconscious process of self-denigration (Mazrui 1975: 13).

The cultural effects of an education in English (and in most colonies an education meant learning English) were more numerous than those applying to colour terms. In his *History of the Voice*, Edward Kamau Brathwaite describes the effect of the educational system, which

> recognize[d] and maintain[ed] the language of the conquistador – the language of the planter, the language of the official, the language of the Anglican preacher. It insisted that not only would English be spoken in the Anglophone Caribbean, but that the educational system would carry the contours of an English heritage. In other words, we haven't got the syllables, the syllabic intelligence, to describe the hurricane, which is our own experience, whereas we can describe the imported alien experience of the snowfall. It is that kind of situation that we are in.
>
> (1984: 8)

Brathwaite explains how the language achieves its hegemony firstly by means of its cultural content. Not only is the literature written in the language of a distant land, but it comes to affect an individual's way of experiencing life in subtle ways:

> Paradoxically, in the Caribbean (as in many other 'cultural disaster' areas), the people educated in this system came to know more, even today, about English kings and queens than they do about our own national heroes, our own slave rebels – the people who helped to build and destroy our society … And in terms of what we write, our perceptual models, we are more conscious (in terms of sensibility) of the falling of the snow for instance – the models are all there for the falling of the snow – than the force of the hurricanes that take place every year.
>
> (1984: 263)

When Brathwaite claims that Jamaicans "haven't got the syllables, the syllabic intelligence" to describe the hurricane, he is giving a metaphoric twist to a situation of cultural dominance. What remains powerful in colonial dominance is the representation of imperial society as the model – implicitly and explicitly – for living. Thus the child, so used to images of an English winter writes "the snow was falling on the canefields" (1984: 264). "But," says Brathwaite, "that is creolization" (264). Out of the catachreses of an imported reality may emerge a new and vibrant 'nation' language. This could be a point at which we see the value of literary writing when looking at the effects of language education policies. Remarking on the attitudes of the English to colonial speakers of the language, Mazrui observes that "[w]e have had, then, the spread of English, capturing peoples and nations, and yet having those new 'converts' rejected as linguistic equals by the originators of that language in the British Isles" (1975: 78). But he assumes that post-colonial peoples universally *wanted* to be 'linguistic equals', that they wanted to speak the English of the British. 'Nation language' demonstrates that the colonial language could be the vehicle for a different kind of power, the creative power of literary language, the power of self-representation, operating in resistance to, and dialogue with imperial power.

The productive power of language

The proposition that power is mediated in language is by no means universally accepted although colonized intellectuals have predominantly held that view. But it is important to recognise that power does not operate in a simple top-down way, percolating down through a hierarchy of institutions exerting and distributing itself through strata of dominated subjects. "Power is everywhere," says Foucault, "not because it embraces everything but because it comes from everywhere … Power comes from below; that is, there is no binary and all-encompassing opposition between ruler and ruled at the root of power relations" (1980: 93). Imperial power, for instance, is *transcultural*, it circulates (through subjects as well as on them), and when it operates in language such transculturality is demonstrated by the capacity of speakers to transform the language by interpolating their own styles of usage into its wider circulation.

Foucault's radical re-evaluation of power is important for understanding how imperial power operates. Most contemporary analyses of power portray it as *only* negative and repressive. This is common in analyses of colonial power which tend to constitute it as hierarchical, teleological, invasive and repressive, which it undoubtedly is in terms of its historical and institutional perpetuation. But negativity and oppressive force do not explain what makes power so powerful, just as military force does not explain the power of cultural hegemony, the *desire* of the colonised to adopt the colonising culture. Power obtains its force from its power to produce. Foucault urges that "we must cease once and for all to describe the effects of power in negative terms: it 'excludes', it 'represses', it 'censors', it 'abstracts', it 'masks', it 'conceals'. In fact, power produces; it produces reality; it produces domains of objects and rituals of truth" (1980: 194).

The discursive power of language, that is, its function within the ensemble of relations which constitute the power of imperial discourse, is demonstrated precisely in Prospero teaching Caliban how to "name the bigger light and how the less". His language "produces" reality and in the colonial situation becomes a key agent in the 'production' of Caliban himself. The immediate power of Prospero's language lies in his role as 'teacher' that is enabled, in turn, by his physical enslavement of Caliban. This power is not contained as an inherent property of language (that is, language itself is not 'discourse' as Foucault uses the term, it does not itself embody the limits within which subjectivity is constructed); rather it is a social practice; it becomes intelligible in the techniques through which language is used (abuse, control, racialization, marginalization). The linguistic system (the *langue*) is not the source of (imperial) discourse but one instance of a set of *relations* of force that constitutes power.

> The colonizer's language and discourse are elevated to the status of arbiter of truth and reality, the world comes to be as the authoritative discourse says. For discursive practice does not simply represent colonialism after the fact but rather functions as a means to order colonial relations and to

establish meaning of those relations, in short, to define the world for the benefit of the colonizer.

(Arteaga 1994: 16)

This power is metonymic. For Prospero's capacity to teach Caliban how to "name the bigger light and how the less" signifies the discursive range of Prospero's power itself. The names he provides metonymise the power of imperial culture to determine the way the world is. It is the absolute character of Prospero's language, his books, his Art, in the face of all other possible discourses that characterises the colonial relationship. But this power is not irrefutable. It is not as if Caliban does not recognise the difference between the sun and moon, nor does it mean that he could not name them in another way. The question is, how different a person would he be if he did? The key to the engagement of postcolonial discourse with power is that language does not only repress Caliban, but *produces* him. It produces him in very material ways, for not only does it produce his self-representation but what he can say, where he can say it and when are all constrained by other dominant participants. In 'discourse analysis' (that is the analysis of language as a social practice) power is all about "powerful participants *controlling and constraining the contributions of non-powerful participants*" (Fairclough 1989: 46). How Caliban engages language will be vitally linked to how he engages powerful participants and will hence be a key to how he transforms power to work for him.

Standard English and power

Clearly, language accords power by its place in social discourse, by providing an entry into certain class and cultural situations, by being *used* in a particular way. This applies even to the central sign of power – Standard English – which itself could be regarded as one dialect among others. As Fairclough reminds us, "There is an element of schizophrenia about Standard English, in the sense that it aspires to be (and is certainly portrayed as) a *national* language belonging to all classes and sections of the society, and yet remains in many respects a *class dialect*" (1989: 57). The social practice of Standard English has nothing to do with the language but with the performance of a particular dialect. 'Dialect', is, of course, a pejorative term, which admits, by implication, to the existence of a 'monolect', a central and standard language. We do well to remember Max Müller's assertion that all languages are dialects. There is a saying that 'a language is a dialect with an army and navy'. What we call a 'language' is that dialect that has gained social and cultural power. It may assume the status of a Standard even when, as in the case of Standard English, very few people actually speak it.

Standards in language are a function of political power, being first *inscribed* and then *prescribed*. The 'standard' has little to do, in the long run, with the dynamic flux of ordinary speech. The 'standard code' has very little to do with the way language is learnt and how people use it to communicate, to identify themselves as individuals and members of a group, to express attitudes and experiences, to give shape and substance to their world or to share it with others. Ultimately the 'standard' code or 'correct' code is appropriated by people according to their perception of its use as a tool of power in certain circumstances. This code is inscribed and prescribed in grammar texts as the standard, because grammar texts are an artefact of education, and education is the prized domain of social power. But speakers may proceed without ever being able to describe what is standard, and the standard code will never be able to account for all occasions of language because the meaning and function of languages depend upon practice rather than its codification.

The tension between the 'standard' and the variant is a political tension, but it produces a great store of linguistic energy. In most colonial and post-colonial countries, education, as a mode of instruction, a body of texts and ideology, or a discourse of aspiration, has been overwhelmingly monolingual, with a complete disregard for the home spoken pidgin, creole, dialect, vernacular, regional variant or first language (including the home spoken accents), which are invariably constituted as 'vulgar' or 'crude'. The normative code thus installed as 'correct' or 'standard' has provided the framework (ironically) for a multiplicity of English variants given shape by the oppressive reality of a discourse of power. The metaphor of language as a tool is a useful one at this point. For the world that is sculpted by the tool is not the tool itself. Although speakers are *used* by the 'tool' of language to the extent that it provides a finite lexicon, they may also use a language by recreating and expanding it, as in fact happens in the registers of English spoken in the world today.

The power invested in language becomes very clear when pidgin and Creole forms are transcribed in the post-colonial text as a form of class distinction bearing the trace of the power relationship operating in colonial relations. Class in the post-colonial text is more than economic; it is racial and cultural as well. The pidgin forms inherited from British occupation serve ostensibly to perform the same function as they performed in colonial times: to provide a serviceable bridge between speakers of different languages in everyday life. But in the literature (written by English speakers who are *ipso facto* members of a higher class) pidgin and creole do not indicate the communication between people of different regions (because the varieties of standard English perform this function for members of the educated class) so much as a communication between classes. In this way the post-colonial text indicates the inheritance of the political as well as the linguistic reality of pidgin and creole as it functioned in colonial times. Pidgin was inevitably used in the context of master–servant relationships in European colonisation. So the social and economic hierarchies produced by colonialism have been retained in post-colonial society through the medium of language. Of course, pidgin remains a dominant mode of discourse among all non-English speakers in those countries where it exists, but its role in most literature, except that of the polydialectical communities of the Caribbean, is both to install class difference and to signify its presence.

Amamu sat in the living room, not exactly sober, and not exactly drunk. Yaro came in reeking of his own sweat and muddy. He had been arranging his flower pots. His master had called him thrice.

Yes sah, masa.

You no finish for outside?

No sah.

Finish quick and come clean for inside. We get party tonight. Big people dey come. Clean for all de glass, plate, fork, spoon, knife everything. You hear?

Yes sah. Yaro shuffled off on silent feet. Amamu stretched himself in the armchair, covering his face with yesterday's *Daily Graphic*.

(Awoonor 1971: 123)

The *Daily Graphic* with which Amamu covers his face is a clear sign of his mastery. The English language newspaper is the purveyor of those mysteries which will always be inaccessible to the 'uneducated', for education, class status and an ability to speak 'standard English' will usually be synonymous. Dialect is yet another demonstrations of the place and political function of the concept of 'correct' or 'standard' English in all English-speaking societies.

Standard English, because it is an example of discursive performance, rather than class dominance inherent in the language, demonstrates that the field of power introduced by language is a negotiable or contestable terrain. This is subtly demonstrated in the post-colonial text when a particular form of code-switching – from Creole to Standard – demonstrates the opportunity to appropriate power. In the story "Betel-nut is Bad Magic for Aeroplanes", by the Papua New Guinean writer John Kasaipwalova, code-switching is used not only to demonstrate the different registers of social and cultural power signified by the different codes, but also to demonstrate the way in which code-switching can operate overtly in a power struggle.

Straight away my face blooded because many black, white and yellow people, they was watching us too and this white papa dog, he was talking bad like that way to me. Plenty times I hear white people calling black men 'bois' so this time I hear it and my mind was already fire. I wanted to give him some. Maybe good English or maybe little Strine. So I says loudly to him, 'All right white man, on what moral grounds is it unlawful for me to chew betel-nut here? This is a free country of which we black people are citizens and unless you can show me the moral basis for your "so called laws" I cannot recognize and therefore comply to that law!'

(Kasaipwalova 1971: 71)

The passage shows the agency of speakers in appropriating the power represented by the code. Language variance can be a powerful form of resistance, but just as powerful is the capacity to assume power by *performing* the code in which discursive power is lodged. The adoption of the Standard code is a direct challenge to power, regardless of what is said, and it reconstitutes the linguistic terrain of colonialism as a contestable and transformable field.

A superb example of the importance of the capacity of colonized speakers to appropriate the power resident in the dominant code is provided by Selwyn Cudjoe's analysis of the politics of language in the speeches of Trinidadian states-man and writer Eric Williams. Cudjoe's discussion reveals the actual ambivalence of the hegemony of English in the colony. The enthusiasm of social elites such as Williams' father for obtaining, and encouraging their children to obtain, a profi-ciency in the English language is a familiar response throughout the colonial world. But Williams demonstrated how the power attached to or invoked by the language could be appropriated. On the occasion of his ejection from the Caribbean Commission, Williams gave a speech that demonstrated unequivocally the oppositional power available to the colonized subject proficient in the domi-nant tongue, and indeed, the dominant culture. As Cudjoe describes Williams' speech: *My Relations with the Caribbean Commission*: "he establishes his intellectual and moral superiority over his superiors and, in the process, describes how he ren-dered the former speechless; that is, for a moment, he had taken away his speech" (1993: 61).

This is perhaps the pivotal act of empowerment through the acquisition of the dominant tongue. To render the colonizer silent is to reverse the power inherent in the possession of the dominant language, to use the 'master's tools' to obtain mastery over the master:

> In fact, Mr X, his superior, had not only become speechless, he was at a loss even to construct meaning ... Williams had literally beaten his superior (both figuratively and literally) at his own game and rendered him mute, one of the major weapons that the colonizer always held over the heads of his subjects.
>
> (1993: 61)

At times, says Williams, his superior in the Commission "was quite incoherent, and I had to ask him at least twice to explain what he meant" (62). The silencing is achieved entirely on the terms of the dominant discourse. Williams displays a proficiency with language, a knowledge of history and a legal, moral and intel-lectual right for which his interlocutor had no answer.

Williams' famous speech *Massa Day Done* owes its power, according to Cudjoe, to his perception that language should be regarded not in terms of meanings but rather in terms of a constant battle for power between speakers (80). This characterises very well his confrontation with the Caribbean Commission, but his range widened to take in the *Trinidad Guardian* and others "who controlled the word and the way they represented the colonized people" (80). The power of language to literally silence one's opponents is well known and widely used. That it should be employed against the colonizer in the colonizer's own language is a particularly resonant example of the transformative power of language appropriation.

Literacy and power

The linguistic power appropriated by Eric Williams might best be described as 'rhetoric'. But the examples given from novels and other literary works are framed by another access to power in discourse – literacy itself. One of the criticisms of post-colonial writing is that it is accessible only to a small elite. Ngũgĩ wa Thiong'o famously contended that English is the province of an educated elite who perpetuate colonial class values and class structures. The effect of the colonial presence was to "create an élite who took on the tongue and adopted the style of the conquerors" (1981: 10).

But we might ask: Isn't every writer in every society a member of an elite? Does membership of an educated elite necessarily oblige one to reject one's roots? Does it obviate political activism? Aren't educated elites just as likely to be in the foreground of social reform in their societies as they are to perpetuate subservience to colonial values? Historically, the role of the intelligentsia has been crucial in all resistance movements. This, of course, is true of Ngũgĩ himself. The issue is rather one of a distinction between bourgeois intellectuals and what Gramsci calls 'organic' intellectuals. The former identify readily with the institutions of hegemonic power while the latter are those who often work outside those institutions. It may well be that many, even most of those intellectuals who become proficient in English in colonized societies may identify with colonial power, but it is not the English language which makes them do so, neither is it an inevitable process, for there are many intellectuals who resist that domination.

Achebe suggests that on the contrary, some contemporary writers "repudiate the crippling legacy of Europe-oriented protest", and see that "we were bound to violence long before you came to our shores" (1975: 51). "As if any intelligent writer of protest," he says, "had ever taken a starry eyed view of Africa or doubted the reality of evil in Africa" (51). For Achebe the intelligent writer of protest is a person whose existence and role are undisputed. The term "intelligent writer of protest" is an important one, for protest can be more enduring, wide-reaching and effective if put into print. Certainly it is a risky business, when writers deal with powerful institutions such as the publishing industry. But African writers have demonstrated the extent to which the consciousness of a world reading public can be affected. The larger issue here may be that in general post-colonized societies often have limited access to advanced literacy. However, rather than describe post-colonial literatures therefore as elitist, it is more useful to recognise that in any society, access to literacy means access to power and one prime access to post-colonial power has always been access to writing.

Literacy therefore operates as a powerful form of "cultural capital" (Bourdieu and Passeron 1977). We see numerous examples of this acquisition of imperial culture by colonial elites – study at Oxbridge, academic distinction, a knowledge of and familiarity with High culture, often including a propensity to quote Shakespeare – a capital which is then transmuted into anti-colonial struggles (most of the founding fathers of independent post-colonial states were educated at metropolitan centres). Significantly, this is an operation of sometimes quite selective consumption, in which the cultural product (such as various prominent authors in the canon of English literature) may become transformed in the process. But crucially, the cultural capital is not acquired formally, but is acquired during the socialization associated with, but not limited to, formal education. The attainment of cultural capital in the colonial situation is more than a function of class and the social *habitus* of students, because literacy functions as a rather special kind of capital. Literacy is not, ironically, limited to elites, unless we regard anyone who learns to read and write as elite, because the ideological function of colonial education meant that the teaching of literacy became relatively widespread.

Education and post-colonial power

We see from the evidence of the power acquired as cultural capital from the colonial education system that neither education in general nor literacy in particular worked quite the way they were intended by the colonial administrators. Lord Macaulay's Minute had most unexpected consequences. The discipline of English literature, more or less launched by Macaulay's intervention, a discipline that became, after the Newbolt Report in 1921, the very centre and lynchpin of British and Commonwealth education, was affected by two intellectual revolutions in the post-war period: the structuralist revolution and the rise of post-colonial writing. On the one hand the structuralist revolution, which introduced a notion of the text that still holds today, and initiated the rise to prominence of literary theory in general, was a revolution in the institutional character of English study that went hand in hand with the post-war growth of university education in the English speaking world. (Of course, literary theory was deeply and permanently affected by the feminist revolution of the 1960s and 1970s but this was not solely a feature of English.) On the other, the radical growth of writing by writers from formerly colonized societies, and from neo-colonized societies, changed the nature of the practice of literature, changed the nature of what we take to be English.

In this way, post-colonial writers who were taught in the colonial education system appropriated the cultural capital resident in literacy, interpolated the systems of publishing and distribution that kept the power of English in place, and acquired a power in a way that had not been foreseen. Literacy is the cultural capital of most interest to this book, but it was not the only way in which power was acquired from the education system. Norrel A. London, discussing English language education in Trinidad and Tobago shows how the power embedded in colonial education policy can be transformed in unexpected ways. The study focuses on a period late in the colonial administration but it demonstrates the way in which education could be used as a means of empowerment. There was no debate at all about the suitability of teaching English by this time, either amongst students, teachers or community.

> English by this time was 'right'; all other languages were 'wrong' as mediums of schooling and education, an ideology which spoke loudly and clearly to two issues on the colonial frontier: the inequitable distribution and unethical use of power on the one hand, and the extent to which consent for the dominance of English had been manufactured.
>
> (London 2003: 107)

English performed a gatekeeper function in that proficiency in English was essential for academic achievement. However London detected a development that complicates the issue of power in language education. For as proficiency in English increased so did Creole proliferate. Furthermore, the creole counterparts which "settled" during this period of entrenchment are not devious forms of or mistakes in the English language that was taught in the schools, but are rather "parts of a separate and genuine linguistic sub-system which approximates, but which is distinct from, the source language, English" (106–7).

London's discussion emphasizes the function of power in the colonial education system; a power that constituted different colonized groups as undifferentiated, uneducated and ripe for an education, a power that operated, as it had throughout imperial history, as a process of civilizing. However the unexpected consequence of education here – although somewhat distinct from the emphasis we are giving to language transformation – was to provide the capacity for developing a facility in non-English-based Creole, a Creole adapted from "the various languages occasioned through slavery, indenture, earlier colonization by Spain, and the prevalent use of French even during the early days of British occupation" (107).

We see from this that the post-colonial situation modifies Foucault's otherwise unremarkable contention that "any system of education is a political way of maintaining or modifying the appropriation of discourses, along with the knowledges and powers which they carry" (cited in Fairclough 1989: 65). Clearly the process of appropriation slips out of the control of the educating body as individual learners and writers utilize the power activated by the discourse. Among the most powerful technologies appropriated is literacy, but the power operating in the education situation flows, as Foucault suggested, in a capillary way, producing reality rather than repressing it.

Laughing at learning

The productive and transformative nature of this power is remarkable given the nature of the disciplinary technologies by which educational subjects are produced. Foucault says of the educational institution:

The activity which ensures apprenticeship and the acquisition of aptitudes or types of behaviour is developed there by means of a whole ensemble of regulated communications (lessons, questions and answers, orders, exhortations, coded signs of obedience, differentiation marks of 'value' of each person and of the levels of knowledge) and by means of a whole series of power processes (enclosure, surveillance, reward and punishment, the pyramidal hierarchy)

(Foucault 1982: 218–19)

Yet what we find in the disciplinary regime of the colonial educational institution, particularly when concerned with inculcating civilized values through English, is a disjunction that occurs at the very site of the language itself. This emerges, curiously, from the blindness of power, a display of arrogance not unrelated to that of the *Requerimiento* mentioned earlier. But rather than a refusal to countenance any lack of knowledge of the Spanish language, there is here a refusal to countenance any cultural situation for language outside England. Consequently the *Royal Reader Series* produced for colonial schools was distributed all over the world regardless of the conditions of life in that colony. The result of this was that by the 1950s, schoolchildren in places as diverse as Ireland, Australia, India and Jamaica would find themselves reading the inevitable fare of the English education system. Children who had never seen a daffodil would be required to read, and understand as 'great', Wordsworth's "Daffodils". This produced a situation of linguistic and cultural hegemony lamented by critics such as Brathwaite. But because of the disjunction, the language became a prime target for appropriation.

Given the undisputed power of Prospero's educational regime, was Caliban able to see the way that world interpellated him? Was he able to use the language without being *trapped in it*? We have seen how important language has been to imperial control. How successful that language has been in fulfilling the colonial project – trapping the colonial subject in a particular cultural discourse, a particular view of the world – is a question that continues to generate debate because that language has now been appropriated by post-colonial literatures and other forms of cultural production. By such means colonial peoples have transformed, for their own purposes, the discourses that have oppressed them. One of the most ironic aspects of that appropriation is the mockery of the institution of language learning itself.

The Calypso poet Slinger Francisco or 'The Mighty Sparrow' demonstrates the resistances to the pressure of imperial education upon the colonies through the strategy of parody. When he takes the nursery rhymes and nonsense poems of early education as representatives of the absurdity of English education the result is deeply satirical. In "Dan is the Man in the Van" the nonsense rhymes are taken to be the sign of the infantilization of the colonial population by colonial education. The education system operated on the binary of parent/child, teacher/pupil to the extent that the capacity of the colonial subject for independent thought, or the relevance of local culture, is completely excluded.

1
According to the education you get when you small
You'll grow up with true ambition and respect from one an all
But in my days in school they teach me like a fool
The things they teach me I should be a block-headed mule.
Pussy has finished his work long ago
And now he resting and thing
Solomon Agundy was born on a Monday[2]
The Ass in the Lion skin
Winkin Blinkin and Nod
Sail off in a wooden shoe
How the Agouti lose he tail and Alligator trying to get monkey liver soup[3]
II
The poems and the lessons they write and send from England
Impress me they were trying to cultivate comedians
Comic books made more sense
You know it was fictitious without pretence
J.O. Cutteridge[4] wanted to keep us in ignorance.

Humpty Dumpty sat on a wall
Humpty Dumpty did fall
Goosey Goosey Gander
Where shall I wander
Ding dong dell ... Pussy in the well
RIKKI ... TIKKI TAVI.
Rikki Tikki Tavi[5]

(Thieme 1996: 543)

The fantasy and fable that had provided stimulation to the imaginations of generations of English children is seen, in the colonial context, to be completely absurd. This poem inverts the absurdity detected by Brathwaite above at the sight of schoolchildren writing their essays about "snow on the canefields". Sparrow's final couplet – "They beat me like a dog to learn that in school / If me head was bright I woulda been a damn fool" – is a comical subversion of the whole process of imperial enculturation. The brightest achievers in the colonial system are at the same time the biggest fools for being duped by the process.

The example of the nursery rhymes in "Dan is the Man in the Van" is the tip of a very large iceberg in the business of enculturation. Because people in the

2 Solomon ... Monday: from a nursery-rhyme, like many of the references in this calypso, which was one of those for which Sparrow, the most famous of postwar calypsonians, won the 1963 Calypso Monarch crown in Trinidad.
3 A Trinidadian Anancy story. The agouti is a guinea-pig × 2 type rodent.
4 Cutteridge – an English Director of Education in Trinidad, who edited the six-volume *West Indian Readers* widely used in Caribbean schools in the late colonial period.
5 Mongoose hero in one of the stories in Rudyard Kipling's *Jungle Book*.

Caribbean are educated in this system, they are – as Brathwaite reminds us – still dominated by the literary models of Britain. But the value of Sparrow's poem, as it ridicules the colonial education system, is to remind us readers, both Caribbean and non-Caribbean, that the disciplinary regimes by which the colonial education system sought to inculcate civilized values were ultimately vulnerable to a resistance located at the centre of that system itself – the English language – through which power could be appropriated by a transformed English that might operate as a cultural vehicle, a vehicle of re-directed and re-disseminated power.

3 Language and race

But thy vile race,
Though thou didst learn, had that in't which good natures
Could not abide to be with.

(I.ii.359–62)

The basic assumption of the civilizing mission – that the imperial nations had a duty to impart the benefits of modernity to subject peoples – went hand in hand with the assumption that such benefits were accessible through the imperial language. But this raises several questions, not the least of which is: What made imperial nations think that 'subject' peoples might want their language? Clearly this question never entered their heads. Macaulay's Minute gives a good demonstration of the arrogance with which the colonizers took their cultural power for granted. This attitude was justified, for them, not only because they maintained power over these subject peoples, but because their attitudes were embedded in a long-standing discourse of discrimination. In short, 'subject peoples', were subject *races*. This justified the exertion of power over them, but it raises another fundamental question: How are language and race interconnected? It becomes clear that the connection between race and language, evident in the attitudes of imperial powers, became formalized in the nineteenth century because of a quite extraordinary development of race-based philology.

There is a case to be made for the assertion that the idea of race exists almost entirely in language. As Prospero's terms of address to Caliban: "hag-seed", "lying slave", "vile race", "freckled whelp", "tortoise", indicate, the language of authority and discrimination, which underlies the language of race, need bear no empirical relation to its subject. Indeed the terms deployed during the flourishing of race thinking in the nineteenth century very often bore only the most fanciful relation to the appearance of actual human beings. "Who has seen a black or red person, a white, a yellow, or brown?" asks Henry Louis Gates (1986: 6).

Nevertheless, no two words have had the momentous and catastrophic consequences, in human history, of the words 'white' and 'black': no two words so completely encompass the binarism of Western culture, no two words have such profound cultural ramifications. As Ali Mazrui explains, this binary was the source of deep self-denigration amongst Africans.

> The English language, because of its origins as a language of white-skinned people, has accumulated a heritage of imagery which invested the word 'black' with negative connotations. The 'black market' was a market of illicit merchandise; 'blackmail' was an exercise in the exploitation of fear ... Of course, users of [such] phrases ... are not always conscious of the neo-racialist implications of their usage. But it is arguable that unconscious self-denigration is even more alarming than purposeful self-devaluation.
>
> (Mazrui 1975: 13)

Yet these two words, which have bound us firmly into a race discourse based on the binary of light and its absence, were not inevitable signifiers of human difference. Other words, even colour terms, might have been employed to describe the gradation of physical types conceived by Francois Bernier. But white, black, red, yellow, came to be the markers of racial difference. Would not some other, more specific, less arbitrary words have served better? Or was the distinction between light and darkness, purity and corruption, good and evil an already overdetermined binary into which racial classification slipped effortlessly?

Light has had an importance in Western culture since the Greeks, and the concomitant link between seeing and knowing, the link between light and spiritual illumination have had a profound effect on Western thinking. But why didn't blue, the colour of the sky, or yellow, the colour of the sun, and brown, the colour of the earth, emerge as the dominant binary? Why this ultimate polarity of white and black? The reason seems to lie in the fascination light had for the western imagination, both in religious and philosophical terms. The ultimate binary – white and black – embodied the distinction between light and its absence.

These two words have so completely captured racial discourse that there appears no escape: a 'white' person (who, unless an albino, is never white) cannot claim to be a 'black' person (who is very seldom black). The secret of this stunningly economical binary is the very secret of race, the secret of the persistence of this quite spurious category of human identification. But the question remains: what do these terms signify? Does racial classification offer the ultimate deconstruction of language itself? It is in these words, black and white, that we see the true complexity of 'racial' difference and at the same time the deferral of signification. Needless to say, black and white have no substantive meaning as racial classifiers outside the context of their use.

The English philosopher, David Hume, who at one time served in the British Colonial Office, wrote:

> I am apt to suspect the Negroes to be naturally inferior to whites. There scarcely was ever a civilised nation of that complexion, not even any individual eminent in action of speculation. No ingenious manufacturers amongst them, no arts, no sciences. On the other hand, the most rude and barbarous of the whites, such as the ancient GERMANS, the present TARTARS, have still something eminent about them.
>
> (*An Essay on the Nature and Immutability of Truth in Opposition to Sophistry and Skepticism* cited in Eze 1997: 7)

Here the difference between whites and "Negroes" (*negre*, black) is a constant, original distinction established in nature. The black race is cast as existing outside 'proper', i.e. white, humanity. "And," says Eze, "for the Enlightenment philosophers, European humanity was not only universal, but the embodiment of, and coincident with, humanity *as such*, the framing of the African as being of a different, subhuman species therefore philosophically and anthropologically sanctioned the exploitations of Africans in barbaric ways that were not allowed for Europeans" (1997: 7).

It is significant that in Enlightenment thinking the colour hierarchy of the races was cast in terms of the *primary* colours, for the primary colours represented a taxonomy that had a purchase in Nature. Thus the 'natural' gradation of colours could be adapted to a gradation of race, the only connection being the colour word. The step from the physical taxonomy to the assumption of inherent qualities was apparently very simple. Kant presented this hierarchy thus:

STEM GENUS: *white brunette*
First race, very blonde (Northern Europe)
Second race, Copper-Red (American)
Third race, Black (Senegambia)
Fourth race, Olive-Yellow (Indians)

Kant's statement: "This man was black from head to toe, a *clear proof* that what he said was stupid" (cited in Eze 1997: 7) indicates the core feature of Enlightenment race thinking, that colour was the *self-evident* sign of inherent rational and moral capacities, diminishing as they deviated from the white.

The biological, phrenological, craniological and philological studies that defined, categorized and described racial types in the nineteenth century appear now to be elaborate fictions, invested with an absurd amount of intellectual energy. But the experience of race, the "fact of blackness" as Frantz Fanon put it, is no less real for its empirical fictionality. Language has always 'inscribed' rather than 'described' human difference through such chromatic signifiers. Those signifiers have had an indispensable function in colonial relations and have been notoriously difficult to dislodge. But the paradox of race is that the reality of racial experience centres, not in physical typology, or 'community of blood', or genetic variation, but in language. This occurs in two ways: the development of the concept of linguistic races which saw language and race as inseparable, and the figurative power of language in which chromatic signifiers performed the cultural work of racial 'othering'.

The very term 'black' achieved its connotation in Plato as a sign of lack, of absence. Black came to evoke evil very early in European history, and was allied to concepts of sin, treachery, ugliness, filth and degradation, night and mourning, while 'white' came to be associated with cleanliness, purity, beauty, virginity and peace (Bolt 1971: 131). These terms re-emerged ambivalently in abolitionist literature such as Blake's "Little Black Boy".

> My mother bore me in the southern wild
> And I am black, but O! my soul is white;
> White as an angel is the English child:
> But I am black as if bereaved of light.

The development of the language had its broadest and most influential significance in the emergence of the myth of the 'Dark Continent' shaped by the political and economic pressures of the Victorian period (Brantlinger 1988: 173–97). The strength of such representation in colonialism arises from the arbitrary adaptability of these signifiers which circulate within the very clear boundaries of imperial binarism, binaries such as: colonizer/colonized; white/non-white;civilized/primitive. Whatever cultural, biological or pseudo-scientific terms have been invoked to describe 'racial' variation, the distinction comes down finally to that existing between the imperial powers and their others. Consider the assertion by William Lawrence in 1822:

> the mind of the Negro and the Hottentot, of the Calmuck and the Carib, is inferior to that of the European and also their organization is less perfect … In all particulars … the Negro structure approximates unequivocally to that of the monkey. It not only differs from their Caucasian model; but is distinguished from it in two respects; the intellectual characters are reduced, the animal features enlarged and exaggerated.
>
> (Stepan 1982: 15)

Here, Lawrence conflates several kinds of non-European together in his racial classification, supported by assertions which, though absurd, had become commonplace because they attempted to explain the biological continuity from ape to *homo sapiens*. The significant feature of this statement is not the issue of evolution but the attitude to animals themselves. The treatment of animals was justified because they do not have language, and by extension, such treatment could be meted out to 'barbarous' races, who appeared to have no civilized language either. But the mechanism by which this distinction was kept in place was chromatic.

This fundamental distinction between white and non-white holds today, as does the unstable and arbitrary nature of racial signifiers. This racial Manichaeism, arising to appease the hegemonic pretensions of imperial powers, was greatly advanced by the invention of the concept of the Aryan race, which itself was the product of the new science of philology. Despite the heavy investment in biological taxonomy in nineteenth-century anthropology, it was the link between race and language that most firmly embedded the concept of race in western thought. Curiously, the vagueness and imprecision of racial terms, far from diminishing this fixation, merely served to exacerbate it, by fostering a language that was protean in its application. As Henry Gates points out, race "is the ultimate trope of difference because it is so very arbitrary in its application" (1986: 5). "The biological differences used to determine 'difference' in sex simply do not hold when applied to 'race'. Yet we carelessly use language in such a way as to *will* this sense of *natural* difference into our formulations" (5). For these reasons race has become "a trope of ultimate, irreducible difference between cultures, linguistic groups, or adherents of specific belief systems". Paradoxically, in the wake of colonial occupation, with its strongly developed practical racism, race remains the most unstable and misleading, yet strategic focus of representation in post-colonial societies.

Our interest in race in this chapter comes firstly from the ways it reveals the function of language in constructing the most profound and pervasive category of human difference. Second, the language of race has become particularly instrumental in post-colonial writing, in the process of Caliban articulating the nature of his displacement of, as well as his cursing of, Prospero's domination. Third, the language of race unveils the difficulties which exist in other categories of human discrimination and identification, categories such as 'culture' upon which we might rely while rejecting the arbitrary classifications of racialist terminology.

'Race' was first used in the English language in 1508 in a poem by William Dunbar, and through the seventeenth and eighteenth centuries it remained essentially a literary word denoting a class of persons or things. It was only in the late eighteenth century that the term came to mean a distinct category of human beings with physical characteristics transmitted by descent. Humans had been categorized in terms of their biological difference from the late 1600s when Francois Bernier postulated a number of distinctive categories, based largely on facial character and skin colour. Soon a hierarchy of groups (not yet termed races) came to be accepted, with white Europeans at the top. The Negro or black African, or later the Australian Aborigine, was usually relegated to the bottom, in part because of black Africans' colour and allegedly 'primitive' culture, but primarily because they were best known to Europeans as slaves.

Immanuel Kant's use of the German phrase for 'races of mankind' in his *Observations on the Feeling of the Beautiful and Sublime* in 1764 was probably the first explicit use of the term in the sense of biologically or physically distinctive categories of human beings. Kant here elaborates on Hume's 1748 essay, "Of National Characteristics", which makes the familiar claim that there "never was a civilized nation of any other complexion than white". Hume averred that "such a uniform and constant difference" could not happen if it was not a fundamental fact of nature. Clearly then, Kant's use of the term 'race' was based on a deep and pervasive chromatism, a sense that a group's unchangeable physical characteristics – its colour – could be linked in a direct, causal way to psychological nature or intellectual abilities. Kant claims that "so fundamental is the difference between the races of man ... it appears to be as great in mental capacities as in colour" (1764: ix). The term 'race' was therefore inserted by Kant into a vocabulary of discrimination, already present in taxonomies such as Bernier's, which were firmly based on colour difference. By the nineteenth century colour had become the unquestioned sign of the relation between external characteristics and inner capacities, despite its complete metaphoricity, arbitrariness and unreliability in describing those external features.

Widespread interest in the link between language and race really began in the late eighteenth century with the discovery of the Indo-European family of languages. The link between language and race tightened as the science of philology grew, but the races with which philology was concerned were almost exclusively those of the Semitic and Indo-European, or 'Aryan' language groups.

Consequently, the English historian Edward Freeman could say with confidence in 1879 that the "doctrine of race, in its popular form, is the direct offspring of the study of scientific philology" (Freeman 1879: 31). Although "language is no certain test of race, the men who speak the same tongue are not therefore necessarily men of the same blood", nevertheless, "the natural instinct of mankind connects race and language" (32). Freeman, writing around the height of Britain's own imperial expansion, sums up a century of thinking on the difficult links between language and identity:

> If races and nations, though largely formed by the workings of an artificial law, are still real and living things, groups in which the idea of kindred is the idea around which everything has grown, how are we to define our races and nations? How are we to mark them off from one another? ... I say unhesitatingly that for practical purposes there is one test, and one only, and that that test is language.
>
> (33)

Freeman is splendidly vague about how that test may be applied, how language and race are linked, or even how the communal metaphors of nation and race may be distinguished. His confidence rested on a century of philological study, but neither the difficult distinction between nation and race, nor the precise way in which languages could be said to characterize groups of people had been resolved. Clearly the establishment of an empire extends the qualities of the (English) nation into the qualities of the (Anglo-Saxon) race. Although as J.A. Hobson pointed out at the turn of the century, imperialism is "the expansion of nationality", it was overwhelmingly conceived in terms of the expansion of the British, or Anglo-Saxon, race.

Language was only one feature of a broad array of concepts invoked to elaborate the idea of racial grouping and inheritance. Freeman demonstrates something of the mental gymnastics employed by those determined to propound the link:

> Community of language does not imply community of blood; it might be added that diversity of language does not imply diversity of blood. But community of language is, in the absence of any evidence to the contrary, a presumption of community of blood, and is proof of something which for practical purposes is the same as community of blood.
>
> (1879: 34)

There is no link between community of language and community of blood yet "for practical purposes" we can pretend they are the same thing. The almost meaninglessly figurative, and much used term – "community of blood" – becomes a tautology for 'race' which language is supposed to define. In this circumlocution we find the beginnings of the paradox with which race is to gain its grip on contemporary thought. Though a widely disputed category of biological variation, the assumption of its presence in language, including the protean nature of racial metaphors, means that linguistically it becomes ineradicable.

Ernest Rénan and the racial origin of language

The assumption that language is so integral to human life that it determines the way one sees the world, or conversely, that the character of one's social and cultural being determines the language one speaks, has been a persistent feature of discourse on language. The emergence of racialist theory in the nineteenth century found many of its principal exponents in those French thinkers most deeply influenced by the emerging Orientalism of Napoleonic France. People such as Buffon and Gobineau are well-known for their development of race thinking and for ideas that, from the perspective of the late twentieth century, seem absurdly ethnocentric. But the philologist-historian who had the most to say about the link between race and language was Ernest Rénan. Rénan was a voluminously productive Orientalist whose career spanned three quarters of the nineteenth century. Much of his writing is perhaps less interesting for its originality of thought than for the extent to which it reflected the European intellectual milieu of the time. In this respect he is most interesting in his discourse on language for the ways in which he conflated 'race' and 'culture'.

In many ways a contradictory figure, Rénan's life work was a monumental description of the Semitic language, religion and history, yet his fundamental belief was that this "race of religions" was destined to give way to the "Indo-Germanic" race whose inheritance of science and rationality gave them the final responsibility for the philosophical search after truth. The opposition between the Semitic and the Aryan, was, for Rénan, incontrovertibly in favour of the latter, being an "opposition between reason and faith, between truth and revelation, between philosophy (or science) and religion", between Semitic unity and Aryan multiplicity (Todorov 1993: 146).

Rénan rejected the notion of biological races, proffering instead the theory of 'linguistic races', which demonstrate a cultural determinism every bit as rigid as the biological determinism of people such as Gobineau. For him there were no pure races, indeed "the noblest countries, England, France, Italy are those in which the blood is most mixed" (Todorov 1993: 140). Rénan is adamant that 'race' itself refers to two things: a physical race and a cultural race, and that one must be careful not to confuse the two. Language is the key for Rénan, because language plays a dominant role in the formation of a culture. "Language is thus almost completely substituted for race in the division of humanity into groups, or rather the word 'race' changes meaning. Language, religion, laws, mores brought the race into being much more than blood did" (*Histoire du peuple Israël* 1887: 32). The Semitic race and the Aryan race, which focus most of Rénan's attention, are not physical races but linguistic races. "As the individuality of the Semitic race has been revealed only by the analysis of language, an analysis particularly well corroborated … as this race has been created by philology, there is just one criterion for recognizing Semites, and that is language" (*Histoire générale* 1855: 80).

However Rénan avoids a simple correspondence between language and race. There are five 'documents' which determine a race within the human species: a separate language, a literature with identifiable characteristics, a religion, a history, and a civilization. Clearly, what he is talking about, without being explicit, is 'culture'. But Rénan encounters two problems here: first, the concept of a linguistic race is haunted by the presence of biological race. As Todorov observes,

> when he [Rénan] writes in *De l'Origine du langage*, 'The race that speaks Sanscrit [is] an aristocratic and conquering race, distinguished by its white colour from the darker shades of the former inhabitants [of India]' (*Oevres complétes*: 109–10), we can attribute the aristocratic and conquering spirit to culture; but can we do the same for light and dark skin?
>
> (1993: 143)

Is the reference to skin colour meant to be seen as arbitrary, or does the colour of the skin provide the biological frame for cultural dominance? The concept of linguistic race does not seem to be able to extricate itself from the racialist priority of colour, because linguistic races are, like biological races, situated on a hierarchy of value (indeed the hierarchy of languages is a key feature of Rénan's theory).

Second, when positing the deterministic link between language and culture, Rénan encounters the problem of priority: which comes first, language or culture? "The spirit of each people and its language are very closely connected: the spirit creates the language, and the language in turn serves as formula and limit for the spirit" (Todorov 1993: 96). On the face of it, this seems to describe the complex interactive relationship between language and culture, but it represents precisely the dilemma we encounter when we attempt to posit, in a deterministic way, that a culture somehow precedes language. As Todorov asks pertinently, "can the spirit, as a product of the language, really create the language?" (1993: 143). Or, does the phrase "formula and limit of the spirit" let Rénan off the hook, by suggesting that the spirit of a people somehow creates its own formula and limit? Either way Rénan is caught in a circularity that becomes completely tautologous when he says, "It is in fact in the diversity of races that we must seek the most effective cause of the diversity of idioms". Either 'race' means a linguistic race in which case the "diversity of idioms" explains the "diversity of idioms", or else race retains its "biological" meaning, in which case physical difference somehow causes linguistic difference.

But this contradiction – that the language to which a culture gives birth becomes its restraint and limit – is often repeated by Rénan. "As language is, for a race, the very form of its thought, the use of a common language over the centuries becomes, for the family encompassed by it, a mold, a corset, as it were" (*Histoire du peuple Israël* 1887: 32). At what point, we might ask, did the energy and creativity of that 'race' which formed the language dissipate into a passivity unable to escape from its limits? This dilemma can be found at the very beginning of Rénan's career when he makes an explicit link between race and grammar: "All the grammatical processes proceed directly from the manner in which each race treated ideas" (*Future of Science* 1891: 253). If language is the very form of the race's thought, how does its treatment of ideas *precede* the language in which they are conceived?

We may examine this problem where Rénan becomes more specific about language and race. For at one point he sheets the entire supposed superiority of the Aryan race to its ability to conjugate verbs:

> The Aryan language was highly superior, especially as regards verb conjugations. This marvelous instrument, created by the instinct of primitive men, contained the seeds of all the metaphysics that would be developed later on by the genius of the Hindus, the Greeks or the Germans. The Semitic language, on the contrary, got off to the wrong start where verbs are concerned. The greatest mistake this race ever made (because the most irreparable) was to adopt such a niggardly mechanism for treating verbs that the expression of tenses and moods has always been imperfect and awkward in its language. Even today, the Arabs are still struggling against the linguistic error committed by their ancestors ten or fifteen thousand years ago.
>
> (*Histoire du peuple d'Israël* 1887: 35)

This is a racial dichotomy quite breathtaking in its scope and we could hardly imagine a more explicit example of cultural determinism. Ten or fifteen thousand years ago the Semitic forefathers omitted to conjugate verbs properly and because this "marvelous instrument" contained "the seeds of all the metaphysics" of the Aryan race (ranging from the Hindus to the Germans!), the Semitic speakers have been stuck with an inferior culture ever since. "If today's Arabs are wretched while Germans are prosperous, the fault lies with their ancestors, who created [?] their languages" (Todorov 1993: 147).

Putting to one side the ethnocentric assumption that the Semitic cultures are inferior to the Aryan (and the many other questions we might ask, such as: Exactly how are the seeds of the metaphysics of Aryan races 'contained' in the instrument of verb conjugation? How does an 'imperfect' expression of tense and mood affect the philosophical and metaphysical ideas of a culture? How many 'cultures' are represented by a 'linguistic race'?) we find here in explicit form the logical problems of a deterministic view of the relationship between language and culture. For how does the 'instinct' of one people create an instrument that contains the seeds of its metaphysics, while the instinct of another becomes circumscribed by its inferior language? If the seeds of a culture's metaphysics are contained in its conjugation of verbs, do those seeds exist before the evolution of verb conjugation or after? If creating the language creates the seeds of its metaphysics, why does that instrument proscribe the 'genius' of the race? At what point does the creative instinct of a people become bound and limited by the genius of the language it has created?

In *The Future of Science* Rénan, while not directly addressing this problem, suggests that the answer lies in the region of the sublime. We can never really know how language emerges at the dawn of time. How could our refined sensibilities ever grasp "the antique harmony then existing between the thought and the sensation, between man and nature? Looking back to that horizon where heaven and earth become confounded with one another, man was god and the god was man"

(1891: 156). The device of an unapproachable 'primitive man', however lame it may be, is the only way of escaping the paradox of a people becoming confined within its own creative genius.

> We must assume primeval man to have possessed an infinitely delicate tact which enabled him to grasp, with a *finesse* of which we can no longer form an idea, the qualities 'to be felt' which were to be the basic of the nomenclature of things.
>
> (156)

However this cannot release Rénan from the logical absurdity of a language being simultaneously both a peoples' creation and prison. Unless we suppose that the creative energy of language invention withers:

> If man were to lose language, he would once more create it. But he finds it ready made, hence his productive force, in default of an object, withers away like every faculty not exercised. The infant still possesses it before it is able to speak, but loses it as soon as science from without renders the creation from within useless.
>
> (1891: 159)

So, in a conveniently neat, though unconvincing supposition, the 'genius' of a people creates a language, after which the creative faculty withers away, and the society becomes molded and constricted by the language.

In *Islamism and Science* Rénan says, "All the grammatical processes proceed directly from the manner in which each race treated ideas" (1888: 104). Yet the way a race treats ideas is determined by the grammar of its language. Clearly, the complexity of the relationship between language and culture requires some other explanation. Either the linguistic identity of a culture lies in the ways it uses the language available to it, or the culture can never change, and can never appropriate that which lies outside it. Since the latter is disproved by history, we must conclude that the culture of a people does not lie within language as an inherent property, but in the complex ways in which that people creates, uses, develops, deploys, and engages language. These ways will interact with the historical, geographical, climatic, religious and material experiences of its speakers and the discourses within which those experiences emerge.

The significance of Rénan's thought lies in the connection he makes between race and culture. For what we find is that many of the assertions which seem so absurd when referring to a race appear less absurd when referring to the more complicated and unspecific concept of culture. We might also contend that the pervasive assumption of the cultural properties of language is itself a consequence of imperialism. When Rénan writes "The great Indo-European race [is] obviously destined to incorporate all the others" (*Histoire générale* 1855: 587) and when he predicts that "after thousands of years of efforts, the Aryan race will have become master of the planet it inhabits", he is basing his assertion on the link between language and culture. The claim by Ariel in Réna's play *Caliban* (1896) that with the divine Aryan tongue the channel of reason has become inseparable from Caliban, he is formulating a myth which generations of decolonizing writers have accepted in its obverse form: the colonial language embodies a culture which cannot be escaped.

Clearly centuries of use create cultural habits and tendencies which come to be identified with the culture. But these uses are epistemological and relational, not onto-logical. The simple principle of language *use* rather than grammar itself may resolve the question of which comes first, language or culture, and explain the paradox of a language being created and yet apparently having the power to *direct* a social group's forms of thought and ways of seeing. The key is the power of individual speakers to change and develop the language. For the language may better be seen to be the elastic and transformative mode of a people's becoming rather than the 'corset' and 'mould' of its being. The assumption that language is deterministically connected to a culture's way of seeing the world privileges the static and rigid over the changing and developmental. A member of a race, according to Rénan, can never escape its denomination; education does not make much difference. "All the progress of mod-ern science leads us, on the contrary, to envision each race as confined to a charac-teristic type that it may or may not achieve but from which it cannot escape" (1891: 145). However, if creative adaptation of the language were so thoroughly circum-scribed how could poetry and literature exist? Rather than a static limit, how much more useful it is to see that the language provides a range of possibilities from which further cultural change develops. If this were not so, how could any culture, any race, adapt to global cultural changes? Conversely, as Todorov asks, how could a particular culture produce something so apparently universal, such as science?

Indeed, at base Rénan's work is fundamentally about race, with all the assump-tions of hierarchy that this involves. This becomes most obvious when he takes his connection between language and race to its logical extreme. But it is then that we see most clearly the absurdity of an ethnocentric view of language. For Rénan, the French language:

> will say quite diverse things, but always liberal things … It will never be a reactionary language, either … This language improves [those who learn it]; it is a school; it has naturalness, good-naturedness, it can laugh, it conveys an agreeable skepticism mingled with goodness … Fanaticism is impossible in French … A Mussulman who knows French will never be a dangerous Mussulman.
>
> (1891: 145–6)

No matter how indulgently we concede the metaphoric tone of this assertion, the absurdity of such polemic is patent and stems from a very simple inability to con-cede the validity of individual agency, of the capacity of individual speakers and writers to use the language.

By the turn of the century the link between language and race, advanced by Rénan and others, had undergone some modification. In 1902, Baldwin's *Dictionary of Philosophy and Psychology* defines philology as "a department of study which seeks to restore a vital sympathy with a past form of civilized life, chiefly through the medium of its language". Although cautious about including the concept of race, we find in Baldwin's definition a consolidation of the persistent myth that a community's language somehow embodies its identity:

> The relics or monuments of such a life surviving in the form of language, whether as literature, inscriptions, glosses, or other record, constitute, *in connection with the language itself as an embodiment of the folk-spirit and an index of the national consciousness*, are the central objects of attention … .
>
> (emphasis added)

The conflation of race, culture and language continued to haunt race theorists. When C.G. Seligman published his classic but controversial *Races of Africa*, the first problem he had to confront was the problem of race. He admitted that language itself was not an adequate guide to race:

> Yet the study of the races of Africa has been so largely determined by the interest in speech, and it is so much easier to acquire a working knowledge of a language than of another part of a man's cultural make-up, that names based upon linguistic criteria are constantly applied to large groups of mankind, and indeed, if intelligently used, often fit quite well. Hence, in describing the great racial groups of Africa, terms such as Bantu, which strictly speaking have no more than a linguistic significance, are habitually employed.
>
> (Seligman 1957: 1–2)

Seligman used a mother tongue to define a language, but as Mazrui and Mazrui point out, while the Baganda may be those to whom Luganda is the first language, "imagine applying the same criterion to the English language. The English are those to whom English is the first language? What would the Scots have to say about this? Imagine the response of the Jamaicans and Trinidadians" (Mazrui and Mazrui 1998: 18).

Mazrui and Mazrui attempt to solve this problem by positing the existence of 'communal' and 'ecumenical' languages.

> Communalist languages are those, like Luganda and Luo, which can be used to define a race or tribe. Communalist languages are 'race-bound' or 'tribe-bound', and define as communities those who speak them as mother tongues. Ecumenical languages are in fact extra-communalist. They transcend the boundaries of racial or ethnic classification.
>
> (1998: 18)

Philology and race

How then did this stubborn belief in the link between race and language come about? The answer to this is to be located in the rise of philology – comparative or historical linguistics – which developed in the eighteenth century out of an interest in the link between language and the essential identity of communities, and of which Ernest Rénan was a principal exponent. While the concept of 'race' might exist entirely in language, a convenient and protean trope of otherness, philology became the major impetus in the myth of the link between language and race as the diversity of languages was used to explain the diversity of races.

The interest in the link between race and language arose largely as a result of the discovery of the Indo-European family of languages and particularly the emergence of the theory that all European languages developed from Sanskrit. The championing of Sanskrit as the source tongue for Indo-European is a fascinating chapter in the rise of Orientalism. British Orientalist and jurist, William Jones, gave a presidential address to the Bengal Asiatic Society in 1786 which is generally regarded as the first clear statement of the existence of the Indo-European family of languages.

> The Sanskrit language, whatever its antiquity, is of a wonderful structure, more perfect than the Greek, more copious than the Latin, and more exquisitely refined than either, yet bearing to both of them a stronger affinity, both in the roots of verbs, and in the forms of grammar, than could possibly have been produced by accident; so strong, indeed, that no philologer could examine them all three, without believing them to have sprung from some common source, which, perhaps, no longer exists.
>
> (Asiatic Researches 1788, cited in Poliakov 1977: 190)

Jones' statement was revolutionary because existing conceptions of linguistic history supposed that language development had taken place within six thousand years since creation, with Hebrew as the source language and other languages emerging by a process of degeneration. Jones' declaration ushered in a new conception of linguistic history, elaborated in 1819 by Jacob Grimm's *Deutsch Grammatik* which put forward the law of the permutation of consonants within the Indo-Germanic group of languages, and placed on a firm scientific basis by Franz Bopp's *Comparative Grammar*, 1833–5. However, it was Friedrich Schlegel who gave Jones' statement an anthropological twist by deducing from the relationship of language a relationship of race (Poliakov 1977: 191). In his enthusiastic prospectus for a science of comparative philology Schlegel announced that:

> the decisive factor which will clear up everything is the inner structure of languages, or comparative grammar, which will give us altogether new insights into the genealogy of languages, in a manner similar to that in which comparative anatomy has shed light on higher natural history.
>
> (Stocking 1996: 23)

Schlegel's lasting legacy was to galvanize German youth with the myth of an Aryan race. "This linguistic research," says Poliakov, "produced fateful results in a field where everything depends on words". Henceforth, "the authentic and useful science of linguistics became absorbed in the crazy doctrine of 'racial anthropology'" (1977: 193).

Jones' pronouncement initiated what George Stocking calls "a kind of 'Indomania' as the spiritual coherence of the Middle Ages was rediscovered in a primitivist Indian Golden Age" (1996: 23). What remained in the aftermath of Indomania was Orientalism and philology. The latter tended to be assimilated to the natural sciences "because it revealed a natural human capacity expressing itself in a deterministic manner, beyond the control of individual human will, but susceptible to a rigorous systematic study that demonstrated underlying laws" (24). Consequently it provided the basis for the study called 'ethnology' or 'the science of human races'. Philology lent its methodological, rigour to "trace the affinities of all the various 'races' of man, and if possible to reduce their present diversity to a primitive unity analogous to that of the Indo-European language family" (24).

The persistent confusion between language and race (underpinned no doubt by the need of imperial powers to find some basis for defining their dominance over their colonial populations) was compounded by the developing belief that languages were species with lives of their own. In 1863 August Schleicher in his *Die Darwinische Theorie und die Sprachwissenschaft* contended that languages possess "that succession of phenomena to which one ordinarily applies the term 'life'", from which he concluded that "linguistic science is therefore a natural science" (Brew 1968: 176). The very concept of an Indo-European 'family' of languages and the development of a linguistic family tree inevitably encouraged the perception that language evolution replicated biological and cultural phylogeny. Although the organic analogy had many detractors it maintained a hold on popular thinking in a way that inevitably cemented the link between the racial characteristics of speakers and the languages they spoke. Furthermore, a family tree diagram posits a hierarchy of branchings over time which rests on a view of history as a movement from primitive to ever more highly developed languages and peoples. This, of course, as Schleicher's book demonstrates, links the development of languages to Darwin's theory of species evolution and its associated doctrine of the survival of the fittest. Influential British anthropologist, Edward Tylor, held that although words such as 'savage' and 'barbarous' had come to mean "such behaviour as is most wild, rough and cruel", "savage and barbarous tribes often more or less fairly represent stages of culture through which our own ancestors passed long ago ..." (Bolt 1971: 25).

The increasing attempt to provide comparative linguistics with a firmly scientific base parallels the late nineteenth-century attempts to provide a scientific basis for the analysis of race. Both rested on rigid hypotheses that ignored exceptions and bore little relationship to empirical evidence. An example of this was the 'neogrammarian' hypothesis, which provides a telling example of the strong appeal of scientific laws to linguistics analysis. The hypothesis that *the laws of phonetic change admit of no exceptions* was first stated by August Leskien in 1876, and again by Herman Paul in 1879: "*Every phonetic law operates with absolute necessity; it as little admits of an exception as a chemical or physical law*". This is an example of a tendency towards the rigid structuration of language which has dogged linguistics. "On the face of it," says Brew, "the neogrammarian hypothesis appeared to ignore, and to be flatly contradicted by, the known exceptions to every one of the major regularities of phonetic correspondence between related languages" (1968: 177). We will see this disturbance of linguistic theory time and again as post-colonial societies appropriate language for their purposes, demonstrating the extreme elasticity of languages.

The rise in philology and the rise in the interest in races which it fostered occurred in a political environment highly charged with the competing imperial pretensions of European states, dominated by the industrial strength and consequent rising imperial supremacy of Britain. The beginning of serious opposition to the slave traffic near the end of the eighteenth century made the question of the status of, and relationship between, the different races more urgent. The major question about race had long focused on the issue of their origin and was characterized by conflict between the monogenesists, who believed that all races descended from Adam, and polygenesists, who believed in multiple origins. Language appeared to support the theory of human descent from a plurality of races, but in some respects both of these theories could be marshaled in support of imperialism. The triumph of polygenesis, however, with the publication of Darwin's *Origin of Species*, laid the foundation for the racial interpretations of history on which imperialism depended.

British historians such as William Stubbs, writing at the height of British imperial power, tended to link linguistic heritage to a Teutonic racial inheritance.

> The blood that is in our veins comes from German ancestors. Our language, diversified as it is, is at the bottom a German language; our institutions have grown into what they are from the common basis of the ancient institutions of Germany. The Jutes, Angles, and Saxons were but different tribes of the great Teutonic household.
>
> (1900: 3)

The concept of monogenism is expressed in statements such as that of Mallebranch that "all trees exist in miniature within the germ of their seed" to which Vallisneri added that "the whole human race which is and shall be till the end of the world was thus created in Adam" (Poliakov 1977: 159). This produced modifications such as the belief that the language groups descended from the sons of Noah – Shem, Ham and Japheth – giving rise to the Semitic, Hamitic and Japhetic languages, the last being the term for Indo-European proposed without much success by Leibnitz.

It is into this debate between monogenism and polygenism (single and multiple origins) that philology and its concern with different racial groups emerges. Indeed the emergence of philology itself, the coining of the term 'race' as a description of biological variation and the increasing need of an expanding Europe to justify its increasing dominance over subject peoples, all appear to overdetermine the dominance of polygenism in the nineteenth century. Ironically the great achievements of the abolitionists, which gradually abolished slavery, were overtaken by nationalism and imperialism, which sought the deepest racial basis for the concepts of national and imperial dominance. More and more scientists were drawn to the view that "the human races were separated from each other by such profound mental, moral and physical differences as to constitute separate biological species of mankind" (Stepan 1982: 2). Polygenism, to people such as Voltaire, amounted to a strident rejection of the monogenism of the church. Whatever might be said by "a man dressed in a long black cassock", declares Voltaire in his *Traité de méta-physique* (1734), "bearded whites, fuzzy negroes, the long-maned yellow races and beardless men are not descended from the same man" (Poliakov 1977: 175).

Max Müller felt very keenly the resistance to the discovery of a common root to languages.

> "Nations and Languages against Dynasties and Treaties", this is what has remodeled, and will remodel still more, the map of Europe, and in America comparative philologists have been encouraged to prove the impossibility of a common origin of languages and races in order to justify, by scientific arguments, the unhallowed theory of slavery.
>
> (1882: 13)

Müller has been proven right with regard to Europe. The link between race thinking and slavery, if not a hindrance to the ending of slavery, certainly remained a hidden dimension in the concept of race, which increasingly came to stand, in the common imagination, for colour difference, particularly black and white.

Ideas about the purity of language draw their energy directly from the impor-tance of maintaining the purity and separation of the (white) races. But notions about the link between language and race are undergirded by an unshakeable though unexamined assumption of the link between the moral and the material:

> Let us note here a striking feature of Buffon's scientific discourse: before *telling* us that there is a continuity between the physical and moral realms, Buffon *suggests* this indirectly. The major figure of this monist determinism, as practiced by Buffon, is precisely this type of *coordination*: on the strength of a comma, a conjunction or an enumeration, the author insinuates with-out asserting; the reader absorbs what is 'presupposed' much less skeptically than what is 'posited'. By setting out to deal with both physical *and* cultural differences in a single passage, Buffon behaves as if the correlation between the two were already established: when he reaches the point of stating this correlation in the form of a thesis.
>
> (Todorov 1993: 102)

A classic example of this is the sentence: "The natives of this country are very black, savage, and brutal." "Who would notice," asks Todorov, "that the main assertion here is conveyed by a comma?" (102). In this sentence we find the essence of Eurocentric (and imperialistic) racism, along with its major discursive feature – conflation. In the phrase "black, savage, and brutal" we find embedded the entire doctrine of racialist thinking: the existence of races is self-evident, the physical and moral realms are interdependent, the characteristics of the individual are determined by the group, the races exist in a hierarchy of values, and political and practical consequences, such as slavery, colonization, and subjugation stem from these assumptions.

Sartre, Fanon and the decolonization of race

The foundational place of race in the emergence of post-colonial theory in Frantz Fanon can therefore be seen to have quite a long prehistory. The energetic intervention of Fanon and Sartre into the issue of race and colonial power builds upon a foundation of race thinking in Europe as seen in Rénan and the entire history of philology. There is, in particular, a strong tradition in French writers for describing the way in which the French language both dominated and inhibited the expression of 'black' reality.

In *Black Orpheus* Jean-Paul Sartre claims that black poetry is essentially a fierce response to the inadequacy of language: "this feeling of failure before language ... is the source of all poetic expression" (1972: xix). Language, for the black writer was not a neutral, transparent instrument, but the determining medium of thought itself. In his pursuit of self-definition, the black artist saw the inherited colonial language as a pernicious symbolic system used by the European colonizer in order to gain total and systematic control of the mind and reality of the colonized world. In the face of Prospero's hubris, his signifying authority (*langue*), the African or Caribbean Caliban deployed his own militant idiom (*langage*).

The first chapter of *Black Skins White Masks* is called "The Negro and Language" and like *Black Orpheus* conflates blackness with culture. For Fanon, to speak means "above all to assume a culture, to support the weight of a civilization" (1952: 17–18). This is a belief that will reappear many times in this book. But is it the language or the act of using the language, the linguistic tool itself or the fact of one's proficiency in it, which does this cultural work? "The Negro of the Antilles," claims Fanon, "will be proportionately whiter – that is, he will come closer to being a real human being – in direct ratio to his mastery of the French language" (18). As we have seen in the discussion of language and power, what Fanon means here is that proficiency in language *represents* civilization. When Fanon says, "A man who has a language consequently possesses the world expressed and implied by that language" (1952: 18), he is articulating one of the central problems of the question of post-colonial language use. For such a person "possesses" the language, not as a receptacle of culture, thus making him (or her) white, but as a *signifier* of culture, which, like whiteness, signifies social and cultural dominance. This seems a moot point but it is in fact crucial to the whole debate over language. The use of language is a signifier of culture, language does not contain that culture: "The colonized is elevated above his jungle status in proportion to his adoption of the mother country's cultural standards. He becomes whiter as he renounces his blackness, his jungle" (Fanon 1952: 18). This sentence is irrefutable ... metaphorically. The problem is that discussion of language such as Fanon's constantly slips between metaphor and literalism. This sentence is preceded by such a conflation, when he says that every colonized people "finds itself face to face with the language of the civilizing nation; that is, with the culture of the mother country". How effortless it is to slip between metaphor and metonymy, between the figurative and literal.

We can compare this assumption of status through the use of language with the ways in which language operates as a class marker. Speaking in a refined way acts as a class marker, a sign of elevation, and indeed the speaker may be taking great pains to change into someone of a different class. But the language will only ever be a signifier of that change. There is no secret formula that causes a language *in and of itself* to effect an inner transformation. However, in Fanon's view, the change in behaviour is often so marked that the changed language and the changed person are the same thing: "The black man who has lived in France for a length of time returns radically changed. To express it in genetic terms, his phenotype undergoes a definitive, an absolute mutation" (1952: 19). But what he means by this is explained in a footnote: "By that I mean that Negroes who return to their original environments convey the impression that they have completed a cycle, that they have added to themselves something that was lacking. They return literally full of themselves" (19). What Fanon is saying here is an important indication of the social function of language performativity.

However, the problem of a slippage between metaphor and metonymy comes about because of the extreme Manichaeism of race. Fanon, discussing Mayotte's *Je suis Martiniquaise* says that it would seem "that for her white and black represent the two poles of a world, two poles in perpetual conflict: a genuinely Manichaean concept of the world" (1952: 44–5).

> I am white: that is to say that I possess beauty and virtue, which have never been black. I am the colour of the daylight … .
> I am black: I am the incarnation of a complete fusion with the world, an inuitive understanding of the earth, an abandonment of my ego in the heart of the cosmos, and no white man, no matter how intelligent he may be, can ever understand Louis Armstrong and the music of the Congo.
>
> (45)

Consequently, for Fanon: "The Negro enslaved by his inferiority, the white man enslaved by his superiority alike behave in accordance with a neurotic orientation" (60).

Race and writing

Fanon gives voice, perhaps ironically, to the assumption that had driven the imperial use of language as a medium of power. The question that becomes pertinent to post-colonial writing is: How can black writers intervene in and 're-write' this structure of unequal relations? Writing on the connection between 'race' and 'writing', Henry Louis Gates voices a widespread disillusionment with the political possibilities of 'black' writing.

Can writing, with the difference it makes and marks, mask the blackness of the black face that addresses the text of Western letters, in a voice that speaks English through an idiom which contains the irreducible element of cultural difference that will always separate the white voice from the black? Black people, we know, have not been liberated from racism by our writings. We accepted a false premise by assuming that racism would be destroyed once white racists became convinced that we were human, too. Writing stood as a complex "certificate of humanity", as Paulin Hountondji put it. Black writing, and especially the literature of the slave, served not to obliterate the difference of race; rather the inscription of the black voice in Western literatures has pre-served those very cultural differences to be repeated, imitated and revised in a separate Western literary tradition, a tradition of black difference.

(1986: 12)

When we remember the history of these race terms 'black' and 'white' we see how much our problems of race are problems of language. This metaphoric term coined with so little regard for the complexity and diversity of ethnic groups, is now deployed as a universal political identifier. But Gates identifies the true func-tion of post-colonial and 'black' writing – the insertion of difference.

'Black' and 'white' simply *reverse* the hierarchy of binary terms rather than *erase* the binary. The broad sweep of post-colonizing literatures brings together a much more diverse constituency. But the very use of the terms 'black' and 'white' show that we cannot escape history, nor escape that discourse which constantly attempts to construct us. For many people the question of identity is, as a consequence of that history, overwhelmingly a question of colour, no matter how metaphoric those colour terms may be. And the dominance discourse will continue to construct its others. For both 'black writing' and 'post-colonial writing' (which are not the same thing) the alternative to taking Prospero's voice and speaking back is Caliban's – silence or cursing. Despite this pessimism it is evident that Gates is talking about a revolution in literary expression that aims at a true appropriation rather than a literature that becomes absorbed by the canon.

The linguistic character of 'black writing' will be very much like that of post-colonial writing in general. Edward Kamau Brathwaite refers to Caribbean writ-ing in English as implicating an African presence, which involves the use of "African rhythms" (1984: 8). It is true that writing in West Africa, particularly from Igbo-speaking regions, adapts a specifically rhythmic and proverbial style to written English and this rhythmic, oral and performative language use can be detected in Caribbean writing. But this is not so much a function of 'race' as a function of the originating culture, particularly the rhythms of the culture's lan-guage. In the regions of the creole continuum in the Caribbean the fluidity and malleability of language has a marked effect on the writing. Such writing is not 'black' but transformative in the way of much post-colonial writing in English.

When Henry Louis Gates turns to criticism his alternatives are much more cannily expressed. Speaking of Jacques Derrida's challenge "to speak the other's language without renouncing [our] own" Gates observes that he once thought that the task of the black critic was to *master* the Western critical canon and *apply* it but "now I believe that we must turn to the black tradition itself to develop theories of criticism indigenous to our literatures" (13). This is indeed the discovery of post-colonial criticism: theory does not exist in a vacuum; it has a history and a culture. Theory that takes no account of the local becomes imperial by default. But whether theory also has a *colour* is less evident. Indeed it is difficult to see how the concept of 'black' literature and theory, a "black tradition", can avoid the imperial dynamic it aims to combat.

Nevertheless, race continues to form a nexus for the transformations of post-colonial writing. In an article called "The African Presence in Caribbean Literature", Edward Kamau Brathwaite identifies four kinds of written African literature in the Caribbean: the rhetorical (whereby the writer "uses Africa as a mask"); the literature of African survival, which deals with African survivals in Caribbean society; the literature of African expression, rooted in folk material; and the literature of reconnection, written by writers "who are consciously reaching out to rebridge the gap with the spiritual heartland" (1974: 80–1). Each of these forms of African presence in Caribbean writing comes about as a combination of style and linguistic adaptation. This writing Brathwaite talks about is writing in English, and the capacity of Caribbean writers to appropriate the colonial language in such a way as to infuse it with what he calls a "sense of race" contests the deep link between language and race made by nineteenth century philologists. 'Race' now becomes a feature, and according to Brathwaite, an organic feature of literary representation. How it might do that is the focus of discussion in Chapter 9.

4   Language, place and nature

This island's mine, by Sycorax my mother,
Which thou tak'st from me.

(I.ii.332–3)

… then I lov'd thee,
And show'd thee all the qualities o' th' isle,
The fresh springs, brine-pits, barren place and fertile.

(I.ii.338–10)

A key to the invasion of Caliban's place by Prospero's language was the assumption that Caliban, a creature so racially inferior that he less than human, did not *have* a place but was a part of, a *feature* of, the place. This attitude is played out time and again as colonizers invade and occupy indigenous lands. Although an integral part of the land, the inhabitants are not regarded as *owning* the land because they do not farm it. The struggle over place that ensues from this is also a struggle in language even though it is a war in which the coloniser appears unassailable. The physical invasion and occupation of colonial space is a small part of the contest, for this struggle issues from a profoundly different conception of space, grounded in a profoundly different conception of language.

Language is a key to the colonizing of place in at least three ways: erasing, naming, and narrating, and it is in the linguistic engagement with these discourses that 'post-colonized' place comes into being. The link between language and space can be described in Saussurian terms. "Language, like topographic space," says Kirby, "can be described as a loose unrealized network (*langue*) organized by relative distances, proximities, connections and chasms between terms. Its potentials are activated and actualized only in moments of utterance, just as physical terrain is only realized in traversal" (Kirby 1993: 179). Place is the equivalent of *parole* – utterance itself rather than the potentiality of utterance that is space. Place, we might say, is uttered into being and maintained by narrative.

Most people see 'place' as a concrete physical setting, but this distinction between space as unbounded extension and place as a location is peculiar to the English language and doesn't exist, for instance, in other languages such as German. The German *raum* encapsulates both space and place in a way that provides an extremely dynamic sense of spatiality (Olwig 2002). This is a critical starting point for considering the link between language and place: the distinction between space and place in English is important for the particular nature of the occupation of space by British imperialism.

Olwig argues that the distinction between space and place has become blurred in English-language geographical thinking because it has been influenced by the dual nature of German *raum* through the avenue of influential Swedish geography which uses the cognate *rum*. "My thesis," says Olwig, "is that the apparently anomalous tendency for English language geographers to confound the meaning of space may be traced back to a long-standing German fixation on '*Raum*'" (2002: 1). This has far-reaching consequences in German nationalism through the dominance of terms such as *lebensraum*.

Historically, we may say that the distinction between space, which can be 'emptied' by means of the mathematical coordinates of the world map, and 'place', which can be appropriated, and effectively 'owned', by situating names on that map (and subsequently fencing off portions of it), has been extremely important to the progress of British imperialism. The understanding of a place as a site has been essential to Empire's need to establish colonial sites of its dominance, *at the same time* as the coordinates of the world map have allowed European modernity to empty out the human dimensions of space. The link between the control of space through cartography and the location of authority in monuments and buildings is a peculiarity of the British (and French) forms of imperialism.

While the duality of space and place is important to imperialism the ambivalent tension between these concepts, the ambiguity between Modernity's empty space and the controlled, named, fenced and commodified colonial place, is a balancing act that remains central to imperialism's linguistic strategy of control. The problem is that the balance between empty space and *colonial* location keeps overstepping its bounds. There is a constant slippage between space and place that stems from the capacity of place to signify difference and construct identity. The space/place distinction thus keeps slipping into something like German *raum*. Colonial displacement renders the environment so distinct that in Australia, for instance, the very limitlessness of space characterizes the Australian sense of place. It is out of this disruption of the space/place binary that the continuing and sometimes obsessive struggle over settler colony identity emerges. My 'place' becomes an extensive tract of space I will never visit because it operates mythically in my sense of being.

Place is a text, this is an important feature of its cultural density. On one hand place can be constructed by the interactive operation of various texts – not only written media such as documents, books, and brochures, but also spoken, visual and non-verbal media including photographs, architecture, advertisements, performance media, and the artifacts of material culture (national parks and forests might be seen as one example of a social text). But place is also a 'text' itself, a network of meaning, a production of discourse that may be 'read'. The sense of place an individual might develop is never entirely separate from the text created by cultural discourse, the "social place" known and understood by the society, formalized in social behaviour. The text of place becomes embedded through a continual process of narration, the reality of the world itself "sustained through conversation with significant others" (Berger and Kellner 1964: 1). Subjects actively create meaningful places through conversation and interaction with others.

Systems of speaking and writing invent, rather than reflect, the reality of place, and spatial discourse enables observers to imagine their worlds (including its significant places) as stable, reliable, and certain. The task of making place is a political and moral act because representation itself is a process of giving concrete form to ideological concepts. Place is never neutral but corresponds to a normative landscape – ideas about what is right and appropriate (Cresswell 1996: 9) as well as ideas about how the world is structured. Thus texts function symbolically to either unite or distance groups or individuals from one another. In the post-colonial setting the texts of place are a locus of continual political and linguistic struggle. Places are always in the process of being created, always provisional and uncertain, and always capable of being discursively manipulated towards particular ends. This is strikingly demonstrated in the processes by which colonizers construct colonial space. Value and meaning do not somehow inhere in any space or place but must be created, reproduced, and defended – whether by indigenous or colonial discourse. Post-colonized place is therefore a site of struggle on which the values and beliefs of indigenous and colonizer contend for possession. Ultimately this possession occurs in language.

Just as place may be 'created, reproduced and defended' by the colonizer, it may also be produced and reproduced by the colonized. The success of colonized people, such as the Australian Aborigines, in *reinstating* an ancestral concept of place forces us to rethink the language by which we have come to understand place. The idea of place as a text can be both illuminating and misleading. For instance, the metaphor of the palimpsest has been extraordinarily successful in elaborating the textuality of place – a text on which previous inscriptions have been erased but remain as traces in the present. But the palimpsest suggests that place can be brought into the world *only* by erasure. It visualizes the text as a flat plane, a misleading view of the temporal continuity of the struggle out of which an experience of place emerges. The insistence on place as a rhizomic rather than palimpsestic text reveals that representations of place are always a potential product of the dis-articulated resistances and transformations of the inhabitants, the province of the hybrid, the mundane, the quotidian. While the image of the palimpsest might be the Egyptian papyrus scroll from which the word comes, the image of the rhizomic *text* would be the hypertext – an image that doesn't come immediately to mind when we are considering topography.

The acts of erasure, naming and narration, although they might invoke the metaphor of the text as a flat plane, occur vertically through time as well as laterally in space. They are always provisional, always contested. This introduces an ongoing problem in understanding the linguistic function of colonialism. Colonial power treats place as a physical text – erased, re-inscribed, identified, named, fenced and owned. But place is actually more like a disjointed, decentred, erratic hypertext. If the palimpsest describes the process of colonization, the rhizome describes the process of post-colonial transformation. The implication of stratification in the metaphor of the palimpsest invokes a linearity that is unable to deal with the complexities of spatial history. This is particularly revealed by recent events in Australia.

The most significant of these was the Mabo case, which reversed two hundred years of Crown sovereignty and in effect reversed the doctrine of *Terra Nullius*.[1] In terms of the palimpsest we could say that this judgment has uncovered the original 'parchment' first erased by colonial settlement. How does one conceptualize the process of scraping away the accreted palimpsest of two hundred years to 'uncover' what was original written on the *tabula rasa*? We can't wipe away two hundred years of history, nor can we guarantee the legal implications of this judgment for other Aboriginal people, so how can we conceptualize such an important excavation? This question doesn't simply refer to indigenous claims over land; it is fundamental to our conception of place itself. Clearly the idea of this 'text' issuing from innumerable centres augments the palimpsest metaphor with a concept of the living, uncentred network of social formations apparently repressed by the imperial 'inscription'. Place is 'written' at the various sites of this continual but erratic contestation.

Erasure

Considering the provisional nature of the idea of place as a text, the first act of place making – erasure – is decidedly metaphoric. The colonial story is a story of the (re)creation of place in language and this invariably requires a radical erasure of the existing place and its constitution as empty space. But we keep in mind that contesting acts of naming and narrating continue in the network of place despite the acts of *linguistic* violence by which place comes into being. Erasure takes place in various stages. The moment of contact is the first erasure because the place is regarded as empty, unoccupied and 'virgin' land. From Columbus onward, the erasure took the form of a sacred rebirth. The newly discovered country was "recreated" by the cross, as though it had no prior existence other than unredeemed wilderness (Eliade 1959: 32). Colonized space becomes described in many reports in the language of Revelation – a new heaven and a new earth.

The redemptive quality of the civilizing mission provides the sense of innocence that allows the colonizing powers to justify their subsequent depredations. The myth of a new earth begins with the impossibility of imagining the place before the colonizer arrives. As Paul Carter says:

> Before the name: what was the place like before it was named? How did Cook see it? Barring catatonic seizure his landing was assured: but where to land, where to look, how to proceed? Where was the place as yet?
>
> (Carter 1987: i)

---

1 On 3 June 1992 the justices of the High Court handed down a judgment in favour of Eddie Mabo against the Queensland government, confirming that the Meriam people were entitled 'as against the whole world' to the possession, occupation, use and enjoyment of the Murray islands in the Torres Strait.

Our first response is to characterise the place before Cook as "non-place". The erasure of indigenous place occurs in language and the linguistic erasure of pre-colonial space continues up to the present.

Terra Nullius

We may ask, as Carter does, "What was the place like before it was named?" But the invaders never ask this question. They do not notice that the place they encounter is already a richly inscribed text, dense with indigenous cultural meaning, a text intricately inscribed with centuries of interaction, mythology, travel and contestation. The act of negation, the perception of a *tabula rasa*, is the first act of erasure, and inscribed in British Law as *Terra Nullius*. The expression *terra nullius*, literally 'land belonging to nobody' comes from the Latin *terra* for earth or land, and *nullius* being no one or nobody. However, the expression is used in two ways: (1) A land where there is no sovereign (law, social order); and (2) A land where there is no recognizable tenure in land. Although the legal doctrine of *Terra Nullius* did not make its appearance until long after early settlement, around the beginning of the twentieth century, it defines very well the underlying assumptions of early contact.

The habit of the first European observers to categorize aboriginal people as 'part of nature' represented, in its more benign form, a continuation of Rousseauean ideas of the noble savage and primitive innocence. But the attendant identification of the inhabitants with animals was ultimately designed to render the place unpopulated. Yet the Aboriginal people lived in a remarkably humanized world. Nature was not polarized from its human inhabitants, but, as the Dreaming reveals, was itself appropriated into the narrative and substance of human cultural life. Rather than 'children of Nature', they were people who made Nature an aspect of culture.

> Almost any ethnographic report of a nonliterate people includes accounts of their legends, myths, and rituals, and of the natural objects they identify and classify for a variety of reasons and purposes. These are treated, usually in separate sections, as custom, social institution, and knowledge (or ethnoscience). Rarely are they taken to be, as a geographer would, verbal and gestural efforts to construct and maintain place – to create a world that resonated to human needs and desires out of neutral environment. Ethnographic reports of Australian Aborigines are an exception, for they almost always tell of how important places have come into being during ... the Dreamtime.
>
> (Tuan 1991: 687)

The first construction is that a land could be seen to be *terra nullius* where there was no established political system or no existing code of law. Claiming sovereignty over such a territory brought the indigenous people under the civilizing 'protection' of the British Crown. The second definition is open to conflicting interpretation, because it depends on the meaning of words like 'tenure' and 'ownership' and 'possession'. This interpretation has generated argument for two centuries.

Why the indigenous peoples' claim to a densely humanized space could be so summarily dismissed has several answers. Quite apart from the radical othering of a nomadic society that in and of itself justified invasion, the absence of agriculture meant that European consciousness was unable to comprehend the owner's relationship with the land. Right of occupation seemed to be established by Biblical authority. In *Two Treatises of Government* published in 1690, John Locke states that:

> 26. God, who hath given the World to Men in common, hath also given them reason to make use of it to the best advantage of Life, and convenience. The Earth, and all that is therein, is given to Men for the Support and Comfort of their being ...
> 27. ... Whatsoever, then, he removes out of the state that nature hath provided and left it in, he hath mixed his Labour with, and joined to it something that is his own, and thereby makes it his Property.
>
> (Locke 1690: 328–9)

In Book 11 Chapter 5 of the *Second Treatise of Government* Locke outlines the principle of enclosure (Locke 1690: 330). It is man's labour which removes the products from nature and makes them his. "*As much Land* as a Man Tills, Plants, Improves, Cultivates and can use the Product of, so much is his *Property*. He by his Labour does, as it were, inclose it from the Common" (1690: 332). For God "gave it to the use of the Industrious and Rational (and *Labour* was to be *his Title* to it)" (333). From the eighteenth century the words 'place' and 'property' became subtly but inextricably tangled.

Where there had been no improvement on nature, 'man' had not acted according to the Genesis directive and subdued the earth, creating 'property' in the process. Where the evidence of 'use' such as agriculture, buildings, monuments and temples was missing, it was assumed that the peoples did not have a concept of landed property, and therefore could not be seen as possessors. The Blackburn judgment of 1972 against the Yirrkala land claim determined that there was no such thing as community title in Australian law. But the aboriginal relationship with the land continued in different forms alongside the European (rather than 'beneath' as the palimpsest metaphor might imply), until the Mabo decision revealed (contrary to Blackburn) that this aboriginal relationship with the land had been sustained over centuries.

The establishment of settler colonies is the most obvious example of this process of erasure because it demonstrates an agrarian culture assuming its dominance and stealing the land belonging to hunter-gatherers. But a similar process occurs in grazing lands such as the African savanna, which were seen as "lost Edens in need of protection and preservation" (Neumann 1996: 80), specifically from the indigenous human occupants. In 1909, a French colonial botanist, Auguste Chevalier, reached the conclusion that the people in the savanna boundary in Guinea were clearing the forest at an alarming rate and the mosaic landscape was a consequence of this intervention. More recent investigation has shown that in fact the forested areas around the villages were a result of careful husbandry. Where the colonists saw a mirror of their own destruction of the ecology, the locals saw it very differently: not a forest landscape progressively losing its trees, but a savanna landscape filling with forest. The effects of colonial erasure are mourned by Hone Tuwhare in the first book of poems in English by a Maori writer, *No Ordinary Sun* (1964):

> O voiceless land, let me echo your desolation.
> The mana of my house has fled
> The marae is but a paddock of thistle,
> I come to you with a bitterness
> That only your dull folds can sooth.
>
> (1993: 25)

The erasure is one that occurs in language as it occurs in the materiality of place, and significantly the land *loses its voice*.

Because the process of erasure is continually resisted it must be continually re-asserted in language. Jay Arthur, for instance, analyzing various documents including government and private geographic, economic and demographic reports, finds a dizzying array of terms used right up to the present, to nullify pre-colonized space including: "unawakened, uncleared, undescribed, undiscovered, unexplored, unfamiliar, ungrazed, uninhabited, unknown, unnamed, unoccupied, unpeopled, unproductive, unsettled, untamed" (Arthur 1999: 66). The pre-colonized space continues to be erased and constituted by its 'un-ness' or 'not-ness'. The land is characterized by lack, absence, and nullity. Colonization does not necessarily fill this emptiness. Whereas pre-colonial space is 'timeless and age-less' post-colonial space is 'endless and featureless'. Place is now revealed to be "unawakened, uncleared, undescribed, undiscovered, unexplored, unfamiliar, ungrazed, uninhabited, unknown, unnamed, unoccupied, unpeopled, unproductive, unsettled, untamed" (Arthur 1999: 66). By means of such negation, language has cleared the ground, and continues to clear the ground, quite literally, for a disastrous influx of foreign plants and animals. Because agriculture was held to be the only medium of development, the 'unawakened' bush was cleared to expose fragile soils.

Naming

When Captain Cook, disobeying his orders to "Take Convenient situations of the Country" with the *consent* of the natives, or "if *uninhabited* take possession in the name of his Majesty", took possession of the whole of Australia for England by raising the Union Jack on "Possession Island", he gave it a name that both enacts and embodies the power of naming in creating place. Naming is, of course, an act of such enormous importance in the power struggle over place, that it always involves the violent act of erasure. "Possession Island" on which Cook formally took possession of the whole country, not only locates the moment but enacts the function of language in the process of possessing.

Names *of* places are names *in* language and are the most powerful means of cultural incorporation. Names invoke ownership, they invoke a cultural reality and a narrative of the future. Place names denote places and connote a certain ideology about the use of these names and the nature of these places. The name begins to insert the place in a narration. For instance to call a rise in the ground a 'mount' is not only to give it a certain character but also to locate it within a discourse. To call it Mount Misery is to locate within a narrative of arrival, exploration, alienation and domination. This name must be enhanced by further narration, but the name itself signifies the linguistic possession by the namer. It *inscribes* a certain experience of the place, rather than *describes* the place. This is perhaps more obvious with a name like Mount Misery but it is true of all names. The scientific naming of a region's climatic, geological, topographical and geographical features insert it into the more consuming global narrative of modernity itself.

The power of language is something with which colonized people must always contend, often, as we have seen in the history of colonial language education, with unexpected results. In particular, the power of language to construct the physical environment is ever present. Whatever the sense of inherent or cultural 'belonging' to place which the indigenous occupants may have, it is clear that place may be 'controlled', by being familiarized and domesticated through language. This assumption of dominance requires that the indigenous subjects be, in effect, dehumanized, their own processes of naming erased. A key feature of Caliban's education was being taught to "name the bigger light and the less". We saw this link between naming and civilizing in Chapter 1, in Ariel's speech to Caliban in Rénan's play *Caliban* when he says, "Thou knewest the name of nothing there. Thou wast a stranger to reason and thy inarticulate language resembled the bellowing of an angry camel more than any human speech" (Rénan 1896: 17).The presumption of the inarticulacy of the indigenous occupants is an important erasure, a constitution of empty space on which place can then be constructed by the various processes of colonial discourse.

In David Malouf's *An Imaginary Life*, the exiled Ovid, located at the margins of language, wonders how he can give the reader any notion of the place to which he has been exiled:

> you who know only landscapes that have been shaped for centuries to the idea we all carry in our souls of that ideal scene against which our lives should be played out – of what earth was in its original bleakness, before we brought to it the order of industry, the terraces, fields, orchards, pastures, the irrigated gardens of the world we are making in our own image.
>
> (28)

While we may think of Italy or any place as a land given by the gods, "It is a created place" created in our image, which is created in the image of, created by, our language. When Ovid discovers a poppy, the simple beauty and colour of which remind him of a whole way of life, he keeps saying the word over and over to himself, "scarlet, as if the word, like the color, had escaped me till now, and just saying it would keep the little windblown flower in sight" (31). So language creates being through its creation of experience. The poet's head fills with flowers, he has only to name them and "they burst into bud" (32). This process by which the landscape is given life is precisely the process by which we come into being. "So it is that the beings we are in process of becoming will be drawn out of us" (32). It would not be too much to say that the perception of the power of naming here is a perception of the post-colonial writer, his subject located at the distant edges of empire, where the transported names are the only link to a known world.

Renaming Palestine

A chilling demonstration of the power of naming and the political importance of names is the erasure of Arabic toponomy in Palestine and its reinscription with Hebrew names (Azaryhu and Golan 2001). The Hebraicization of the map began in 1949 with the establishment of Israel itself, a virtual erasure of Palestine and the inscription of the state of Israel. This erasure had been long preceded in Zionist propaganda by the slogan "A land without people (Palestine) for a people without land (Jews)". The erasure of the land, reducing it to *Terra Nullius*, was the necessary preliminary to the inscription of the Israeli State, an inscription that was conducted with a concerted state-funded programme of renaming.

The ideological basis of the process was indicated by Ben-Gurion who claimed that the lack of Hebrew place names meant that the land *could not be known* by the Jewish inhabitants. The Government Names Commission began by replacing Arab locations with Biblical names, but since only 174 Hebrew names are mentioned in the Bible, the process continued by erasing Arabic names and inscribing new Hebrew names that had no historical provenance. The British Mandatory Survey of 1940 recorded some 3700 Arabic names designating local topography, with little more than 200 Hebrew names designating Jewish settlements (Azaryhu and Golan 2001: 183). By 1960, virtually all these names had been replaced. Unsurprisingly, the Israeli army was ordered to publicize the new names, which were institutionalized in road signs and maps. "As long as the names did not appear in maps, they can not take possession in life", reported the Commission. The war against the Palestinians can be said to have begun in earnest with the erasure of Arabic names and the inscription of the Ismeli map.

For both sides the renaming of Palestine, the battle of toponomies, was an occasion of enormous cultural and historical significance, perhaps the most significant episode in the destruction of Palestine and the disenfranchisement of the Palestinian people. For the Jews the re-writing of the national map in Hebrew was inextricable from nationhood itself. For the Palestinians the erasure of names was metonymic of the erasure of their own nationhood. However, like the Aboriginal narrative of place, the Arab map is still there and has not been replaced by the Hebrew map of Jewish Israel in the minds of the people living there. Arabic toponomy further persists in the form of Arab folk geography and in Arab-Palestinian maps that assert the validity of Arabic place-names. Consequently, Hebrew and Arabic toponomies persist as two versions of a shared and contested national homeland (Azaryhu and Golan 2001: 193).

However, while the duality of the place persists, the rhetorical strategy of erasure demonstrates the connection between political and linguistic power in the representation of the place – in the eyes of the world the map of Israel is as fixed as if it had always been there. Ghada Karmi provides a wrenching account of the dilemma faced by Palestinian refugees driven out of their country in 1948 and living in London. Commenting on her father's obsession with knowing every inch of Palestinian geography, she says:

> For years, I thought this obsession with places and family names and 'who was related to whom' was just a quirk of my parents. My sister and I used to imitate them in our bedroom after a particularly grueling interrogation with some hapless Palestinian visitor, and laugh and shake our heads. It took me years to realize that after 1948, establishing a person's origin became for Palestinians a sort of mapping – a surrogate repopulation of Palestine in negation of the *nakbah* [the catastrophe]. It was their way of recreating the lost homeland, as if the families and the villages and the relations they had once known were all still there, waiting to be reclaimed. And indeed, for Palestinians in the immediate aftermath of the 1948 exodus, the prospect of a return to Palestine was very real.
>
> (Karmi 2004: 186)

This is a moving demonstration of the importance of place to identity, particularly the importance of the memory of place to the diasporic population. But it also shows the way place may operate as a hypertext rather than a palimpsest. The place remains a constant dynamic relation between memory, ancestry and location. But while the map is maintained by such means, the power of erasure is demonstrated even in the minds and memories of the former inhabitants themselves. Palestine became a faded dream for her since it disappeared so quickly from British memories.

> By 1953, when people asked me where I came from and I answered, "Palestine", they would respond with "did you say Pakistan?" The country, whose turbulent history had so frustrated Britain's government but five years before, simply vanished from people's consciousness. Instead, the talk was of Israel, "the new young plucky state which was making such rapid advances".
>
> (Karmi 2004: 210)

The fading of memory, the gradual disassociation of the second generation from the memory of the parents – suggests the success of erasure in the representation of the region. But by the 1980s the map of Palestine, the memory of Palestine, had become reestablished.

The power of language to construct the physical environment is one with which the colonized must always contend. Whatever the sense of inherent or cultural 'belonging' to place which the indigenous occupants may have, it is clear that place may be 'controlled', by being familiarized and domesticated through language. The process of naming is fundamentally an act of power and the most important power is the power over representation, the power to present a toponomy as the only representation of a real world.

Post-colonial naming and re-naming

However that power is never absolute, as post-colonial writing and the reemergence of Palestine demonstrates. The Palestinian poet Mahmoud Darwish says that "to resist means ... to be confident of your incurable malady / The malady of hope" (*State of Siege* 2002). The same determination to cling on to place 'No matter what some name it", is affirmed in a poem by Maureen Watson:

> Aboriginaland, yes, our birthright,
> No matter what some name it;
> So dig your fingers deep in the soil,
> And feel it, and hold it, and claim it.
> Your people fought and died for this,
> Tho' history books distort it all,
> But in your veins runs that same Aboriginal blood,
> So walk tall, my child, walk tall ...

(Watson 1982b)

Such a 'malady' of hope also describes Edward Kamau Brathwaite's poem "Naming", where we see the subtle way in which the rhythms of the natural world, rhythms that poetry apprehends, can overcome the strictures of naming.

> *Naming*
>
> 1
> How then shall we
> succeed?
> The eye must heed
> the meaning
> the eye must be free
> seeing.
>
> 2
> What is a word
> to the eye?
> Meaning.
> Seeing the pot-
> boil of leaves in the wind

it is a tree
watching the pale hoist
of shining
it is the moon
climbing.

3
The tree must be named.
This gives it fruit
issues its juices.
The moon must be named.
This renders love
madness.
There is a gladness
in the leaves
when the rain stops
before the rains stop.
This is the drought.
It is a fine haze.
On clear days
lifting from Africa
it is the desert's gift
of Christmas. By
April, deciduous trees
have lost their green
diligence. A broom
is sweeping the sky
of its leaves.

4
So the eye waits,
the sun's gold weight
lightens
rain remakes trees
leaves brighten the colour
the drying fish flies
in the pool.

(Brathwaite 1969: 60–1)

To the eye the word is "meaning". But the poem reveals that a meaning arises beyond the eye. Language is necessary to name the world, but there is a meaning beyond the name. There is deep irony in the lines, "The tree must be named./ This gives it fruit/issues its juices", as though the name supplied the fruit. Brathwaite acknowledges the extent to which language proffers and shapes experience by naming it. But the rhythms of the year – beginning with the drought that, lifting from Africa, is the desert's gift of Christmas – overwhelm language. The fact that the drought haze lifts from Africa is an indication of the roots that will allow the Caribbean poet to plug into a source of cultural and racial energy that cannot be contained by the language. The rain will remake the trees and the cycle of the natural world, the rhythms of a relationship with place that runs deeper than naming will continue in a ceaseless recurrence. Either indigenous or appropriated language has the capacity to reach beyond the name. But for the Caribbean poet there is no indigenous language, rather there is a continuum that offers, like the poem, the opportunity for continual, regenerative and creative engagement with the world. This is the point at which the name becomes subject to the narrative of place.

This is why Derek Walcott chooses to see himself in *Another Life* in the role of a symbolic Adam "exiled/ to our new Eden" (1986: 300).

> We were blest with a virginal, unpainted world
> With Adam's task of giving things their names
>
> (1986: 294)

The post-colonial writer can oppose the colonizer's naming of the world by taking over the role of name-giver and this is a specific function of the agency of literature. It is not limited to the post-colonial writer but in such a writer's hands it becomes powerfully political – "this process of renaming, of finding new metaphors, is the same process that the poet faces every morning of his working day, making his own tools like Crusoe, assembling nouns from necessity" (1996: 70). The irony of the comparison with Crusoe is patent. The writer can *choose* to be Crusoe rather than Caliban as he renames the world through his poetry, performing his own process of erasure and renaming, in a performance of the deepest functions of the creative act in post-colonial space.

In "The Muse of History" Walcott quotes Pablo Neruda:

> My land without a name, without America
> Equinoctal stamen, lance-like purple
> Your aroma rose through my roots
> Into the cup I drained, into the most tenuous
> Word not yet born in my mouth

It is this awe of the numinous, this elemental privilege of naming the new world which annihilates history in our great poets, an elation common to all of them, whether they are aligned by heritage to Crusoe and Prospero or to Friday and Caliban. They reject ethnic ancestry for faith in elemental man. The vision, the "democratic vista", is not metaphorical, it is a social necessity. A political philosophy rooted in elation would have to accept belief in a second Adam, the recreation of the entire order, from religion to the simplest domestic rituals.

(1974, cited in Ashcroft, Griffiths and Tiffin 2006: 330–1)

For Walcott the apples of the second Eden "have the tartness of experience" and the privilege or power of renaming comes with "a bitter memory and it is bitterness that dries last on the tongue" (331). But his philosophy is, ultimately, "rooted in elation".

The Caribbean experiences a new birth, as in Grace Nichols' poem "In My Name" in which a Caribbean girl gives birth to a child in a banana plantation.

> It is my tainted
> perfect child
> my bastard fruit
> my seedling
> my sea grape
> my strange mulatto
> For with my blood
> I've cleansed you
> And with my tears
> I've pooled the river Niger
> Now my sweet one it is for you to swim
>
> (1983: 56–7)

The river Niger has been "pooled" here in the Caribbean. The child is like the poem itself, given birth in the name of a new and hybrid, a renamed and renaming place, and thus becoming a result and an agent of that renaming process.

Narrating

The most important process in the struggle over place, the one that attenuates inscription, is the narration by which place develops its particular identity. It is the narrations and contesting narrations by which place comes into being – even names maintain power by being located in narratives. The sense of place an individual might develop is never entirely separate from the text created by cultural discourse, the "social place" known and understood by the society, formalized in social behavior. The text of place becomes embedded through a continual process of narration, in which subjects actively create meaningful places through conversation and interaction with others (Berger and Kellner 1964: 1). This contributes to the reality of the physical world itself.

Topographical features (such as Mount Misery) are already located in a discourse *before* they are encountered, inscribed and 'owned' and before they become the site of a continuing narration of occupation. This is because the names given to such space invoke the connotations of the culture from which they emerged. But it is narration that then confirms the place as place. Places "do not exist until they are verbalized, first in thought and memory and then through the spoken or written word" (Ryden 1993: 241). By narration, space is located in time. By narration the displacement characteristic of post-colonial discourse, the gap between language and place, becomes filled, and by narration culture constructs the text of place.

Johnstone, in her study of place making through story telling found that:

> Just as narrative structures our sense of self and our interactions with others, our sense of place and community is rooted in narration. A person is

at home in a place when the place evokes stories, and conversely, stories can serve to create places.

(1990: 5)

Stories represent, pattern, and express the meanings of place across society, and therefore the study of post-colonial literary and cultural narrative is a particularly strategic entry into the dynamic space of post-colonial place.

Narration is not only verbal. An important feature of the narrating process is that it includes forms of representation such as painting. Visual representation is an aspect of the narrative process because paintings occur within a particular discourse. The visual representation of Australia in colonial times fell into two broad discourses that had existed even before the arrival of European settlers. Visual representation narrated one of two stories: either the colony was Arcadian – nature as a place of freedom and possibility, a land where a new 'race' might develop – or it was Dystopian – a wasteland and prison at the edge of the known world to which people were relegated as punishment. One aspect of the Arcadian discourse was the element of sublime representation imported from German Romanticism. The ambivalent dialogue of these two discourses has dominated the representation of Australian place ever since.

The tension between a land as exile and Paradise has defined the ambivalence of Australian settlement and often in the literature the ambivalence is captured in the metaphor of distance and the settler's struggle to control it. This is the myth constantly recreated in the literature. As Patrick White says of Stan Parker in *The Tree of Man*;

> His Gold Coast still glittered in a haze of promise as he grubbed the weeds out of his land, as he felled trees and tautened the wire fences he had put round what was his. It was, by this time, almost enclosed. But what else was his he could not say. Would his life of longing be lived behind wire fences? His eyes were assuming a distance from looking into distances. So he did begin then with impatience, even passion, to hew the logs that still lay, and to throw aside his axe at the end, with disgust, apparently, for something wood will not disclose.

(38)

The narration of place here is one that hovers continually on the unspoken reality of erasure, a narrative of settlement built out of uncertainty and *unheimlichkeit*. Names are not given to place but the unconvincing fences perform the function of names – "what was his … almost enclosed" – and White captures beautifully here the continual horizon of something not yet realized, a discovery of sacred possibility, that characterizes Stan's life, and, by extension the life of white Australia.

One extremely subtle way of maintaining the integrity of settled land, despite the historical ambivalence that surrounds it, is by reformulating the concept of 'wilderness' as that which putatively lies outside civilized space. This is a paradoxical and perhaps unfortunate consequence of the genuine attempt to protect the natural environment. The conception of 'wilderness' was principally forged in the United States. Roderick Nash suggests that "a society must become technological, urban and crowded before a need for wild nature makes economic and intellectual sense" (1982: 343). Ruggedness, self-sufficiency and hardihood were to found in the wilderness rather than the effete lifestyles of the city, according to groups like the Boone and Crockett Club of 1887.

The original meaning of 'wilderness' was a wild place lacking human amenity or civilization: beyond settlement, of wild animals and wild people, unused and unusable (Schama 1995). Over this Lockean view was overlaid the Rousseauean sense of wilderness as a precious, unsullied, natural wonderland, a place of natural balance and wild order, providing a backdrop for human action and a moral baseline for destructive human engagements with nature (Cronon 1995). Wilderness implies a metaphoric boundary that ensures Nature is kept separate from Culture. The civilizing mission can always manage to keep these totally opposed ideas in balance, particularly as the Romantic view of wilderness begins to grow once the damage caused by agricultural development has begun to be felt. But with the boundary between wilderness and human space defined, the wilderness can be reinstated as the *tabula rasa* on which is inscribed the society's sense of ecological heroism. The establishment of 'wilderness' is a very good thing that has very ambiguous consequences, because outside the wilderness, the unawakened, undeveloped, unimproved, undiscovered, unutilized land can be drafted into the service of international capital.

The bounded wilderness is an oxymoron that absorbs the slippage between space and place: on the one hand it is boundless, in the sense of untamed extension, but on the other hand it is a place controlled by the processes of inscription: naming, mapping, boundary marking bring the wilderness within the spatial economy of colonized place. Wilderness is important to the imperial adventure narrative because it provides a place of primal innocence even though that native, child-like innocence hovers in an uncomfortable relation to the adult responsibilities of imperial development. In short, 'wilderness' is cultural because it produces another narrative alongside the narrative of uncivilized place as wasteland.

Re-narration: Writing post-colonial place

The various forms of 'colonial' narration serve to create a place that is both historically and culturally dense enough to occlude marginal stories. This is particularly true of place because its physical nature belies its existence as a function of representation. And yet, place is always *what it has become* rather than what it simply *is* because of the narratives in which it is represented. Post-colonial re-writing of place is therefore a central function of the appropriation of English. Writers such as Edward Kamau Brathwaite insist on the capacity of language to communicate a sense of place. The Caribbean hurricane, he says resonantly, "does not roar in pentameters. There is something in the style of language that invokes the hurricane but also invokes the heat, the drift, the serenity of tropical life" (1984: 13). There are many ways in which we might impute place as a feature of language. However, the post-colonial writing of place is more often a feature of narration and because it narrates a place in dialogue with the great weight of colonial representations, it is often a 're-narration'. Olmsted has used Brathwaite's description to illuminate the location of the central character, Merle Kinbona, in Paule Marshall's *The Chosen Place, The Timeless People* (1969). In particular Merle, who is identified with the place, uses a language that seems to evoke the *feel* of the place.

> When Merle speaks, her voice seems to be in a "downhill race with itself" (11); thus, her pace matches the pace of the island's "wrecked hills that appeared to be racing en masse toward the sea" (99). Sometimes her pace is so rapid that her sense is unintelligible. At other times her voice adopts the "exaggerated island accent she purposely affected" (71). Her voice ranges from shrill to unintelligible – when she is pleased, she "crow[s] her approval" (127). It is no coincidence that her voice can be "pitched to the highdrumming of heat" or the "unremitting whirr of heat rising", for Merle is as much a part of the island as the island is herself; her face is "despoiled . . . in much the same way as the worn hills ... their substance taken" (5). Saul notes on two occasions that, in order to get to know the island, he must know Merle first.
>
> (Olmsted 1997: 256)

Language in the novel – and its capacity to communicate what Brathwaite calls "African rhythms", as well as its ability to communicate place – becomes a combination of narrative pace, sentence structures and linguistic changes. This occurs also in the way Marshall identifies the immediacy of Merle's bodily experience. In this way, this novel is an example of the capacity of language to communicate place in the substance of language as well as the narrative structure. This substance is the substance of post-colonial transformation, in which language operates as a metonym of culture, and in Brathwaite's formulation, operates as a metonym for race as well. Very often the two are conflated. Brathwaite's contention is that Standard English creates a disjunction between language and experience in the Caribbean. The writer intervenes to produce a transformed English, moulded and shaped by the effects of the creole continuum.

The writers struggling for a language in which to narrate place come from various backgrounds. One of the classic struggles in nineteenth-century Australian writers was the struggle out of the straitjacket of an inherited language that did not have the vocabulary to deal with this new and threatening place. The word 'creek' rather than 'stream' or 'brook' in Henry Kendall's "Bell Birds" identifies a precise moment in the nineteenth century when a local idiom takes over from the inherited language. But a similar struggle has occurred in white writers in post-apartheid South Africa. As Michael Chapman remarks, 'the burden has been to write themselves out of a dead, white, racist and patriarchal past, and to reinscribe themselves in a society that does not yet exist" (1996: 415). Jeremy Cronin suggests how in "To Learn How to Speak":

> With the voices of the land,
> To parse the speech in its rivers
> To catch, in the inarticulate grunt,
> Stammer, call, cry, babble, tongue's knot
> A sense of the stoneness of these stones
> From which all words are cut
>
> (Hirson 1996: 169)

Aboriginal narrations of place in literature contest the inscriptions of an imperial Modernity with such "voices of the land", the rhizome of place continuing to accommodate an Aboriginal reality as it weaves itself into the institutions of contemporary Australia. Although contemporary Aboriginal writers might also have to learn (or re-learn) these voices we can describe the situation, metaphorically, as the 'uninscribed earth' irrupting into the inscribed world. Aboriginal writing, we find, interpolates the dominant discourse, disturbing the learned representations of Australian reality. The Australian Aboriginal writer Alexis Wright's monumental novel *Carpentaria*, is a novel that 'writes back' to previous novels of Northern Australia such as Xavier Herbert's classics *Capricornia* and *Poor Fellow My Country*. Herbert's novels were sympathetic to Aboriginal culture and often scathing about the white society of the North. But Wright's project is clearly one of reclamation: of reclaiming the North to the Aboriginal voice, and also to an Aboriginal cosmology. *Carpentaria* weaves a story of Northern Australia that at times is so fantastic it has been referred to as 'magic realism'. But this term, common though it has become, fails to capture the particular transformative strategies of the novel, especially in its perpetuation, in the demotic literary text. Take this description in the opening pages:

> Picture the creative serpent, scoring deep into – scouring down through – the slippery underground of the mudflats, leaving in its wake the thunder of tunnels collapsing to form deep sunken valleys. The sea water following in the serpent's wake, swarming in a frenzy of tidal waves, soon changed colour from ocean blue to the yellow of mud. The water filled the swirling tracks to form the mighty bending rivers spread across the vast plains of the Gulf country. The serpent traveled over the marine plains, over the salt flats, through the salt dunes, past the mangrove forests and crawled inland. Then it went back to the sea. And it came out at another spot along the coastline … When it finished creating the many rivers in its wake, it created one last river, no larger or smaller than the others, a river which offers no apologies for its discontent with people who do not know it. This is where the giant serpent continues to live deep down under the ground in a vast network of limestone aquifers. They say its being is porous; it permeates everything. It is all around in the atmosphere and is attached to the lives of the river people like skin.
>
> (2006: 1)

A number of strategies are being adopted here. First, what we have termed the 'rhizome of place' sees the Aboriginal sense of cosmology reasserting itself by irrupting through the surface of the contemporary spatial narrative. We saw the rhizomic character of place in the Mabo judgment in which Aboriginal communal title was recognized after presumably having *not* existed for two hundred years. But here the text narrates place in a way that reasserts Aboriginal cosmology as a conceivable feature of the present. This reassertion occurs with no linguistic markers apart from its verbal energy that might mark it off as 'myth'. The question here is: what is the status of the voice narrating? Is it ironic? Is it simply animistic and mythological? Or is it re-narrating the nature of place in a way that situates the metaphoric and metonymic reality of the Aboriginal Dreaming in the demotic English text? Though poetic and oracular, the lines also seem to be pushing the boundaries of realism. The last sentence states: "It *is* all around in the atmosphere and is attached to the lives of the river people like skin." In that sentence, in the *presence* of the Aboriginal reality, the boundary between reality and myth is crossed and the re-narration, re-creation of place begins to occur.

Second, the description includes no concessions to the contemporary reader. This is a refusal to 'translate' that we will look at more closely in Chapter 9. But by simply inserting the perception of place into the text a gap is established, what we will call a 'metonymic gap' that establishes the cultural difference without which a true dialogue between Aboriginal and non-Aboriginal Australia cannot begin. The assertion of Aboriginal reality occurs in the contemporary English text. The author has chosen her audience and the audience must enter into dialogue with the continuing reality of the Aboriginal Dreaming.

Here we see how powerfully the post-colonial English text can re-assert the experience of place that had been erased by two hundred years of colonial inscription. Just as the Aboriginal names of places had not been erased, so the Aboriginal experience of place, an experience quite contrary to the ocularcentric, commodifying and rationalist construction of White Australia. The passage continues:

> This tidal river snake of flowing mud takes in breaths of a size that is difficult to comprehend. Imagine the serpent's breathing rhythms as the tide flows inland, edging towards the spring waters nestled deeply in the gorges of an ancient limestone plateau covered with rattling grasses dried yellow from the prevailing winds. Then with the outward breath, the tide turns and the serpent flows back to its own circulating mass of shallow waters in the giant water basin in a crook of the mainland whose sides separate it from the open sea.
>
> (2006: 2)

The narrator addresses the reader – "picture" and "imagine" – words that belong to the ocular dimensions of the English text and to the modern reader. As with all literature, the reader "imagines", constructs the reality of, the novel and it becomes real. Oracular though the language is, it invites the reader to enter a dialogue with difference. This is partially because the text utilizes the nature of writing itself: for this moment at least, the Aboriginal experience of place exists. But it is also because place as *place* does not exist outside representation. There might be many pre-linguistic experiences of place yet these may only be situated, may only become actual, by being located in a coherent narrative of place. Post-colonial place is therefore a contest of representations, a dialogue in which different narratives break into the text to reveal the *heteroglossic* nature of place.

5 Language and identity

I pitied thee,
Took pains to make thee speak, taught thee each hour
One thing or other: when thou didst not, savage,
Know thine own meaning

(I.ii.356–9)

We may regard ourselves as belonging to a certain category of race, or being at home in a certain place, but for some mysterious reason we don't simply *have* a language. We tend to believe that our language *is* us – that it inhabits us and we inhabit it. This is why Miranda's claim that by teaching Caliban language he might "know his own meaning", is so significant. Language introduces us to an identifiable world, initiates us into a family, providing those most basic concepts – 'me', 'us', 'them'. Language itself identifies us, announces us, even, it seems, defines us, defines the space of being itself. Our language "is not just *a* language," says Edgar Thompson, "it is *our* language, the language of human beings".

> The language of those outside, or what they call a language, is the language of people who babble and answer to silly names; they are barbarians even when they use much the same vocabulary. But in our language we know ourselves as brothers and sisters or as comrades or as fellow countrymen. In it we make love and say our prayers, and in it, too, is written our poetry, our oratory, and our history.
>
> (Thompson and Hughes 1965: 237)

Languages may be held to represent various cultural traits, but *our* language is different, our language is transcendent, it is the language of God Himself. Language is an instrument of communication, but in our heart of hearts, we know God speaks only our language to us, because *our* language is *us*.

The attachment to one's language and the fear of its suppression or domination has been true of all languages and all societies. But in post-colonial societies the question of language has been both an historical and a very material question of struggle. Central to this struggle is the place of language within one's construction of identity. Language is associated with identity, indeed, can be said, metaphorically, to *construct* one's identity, in many ways: physical, psychological, geographical, social and ethnic. It constructs these principally, though not solely, through names which act as markers, signs of a particular identifying discourse. It constructs identity simply by being 'ours,' by constructing a sense of 'us' from the earliest interactions between parents and children. In this way a language is something like a national flag in that it signifies an imagined community of speakers. But unlike the flag it is something we also possess as an intimate part of our being. The anxious and febrile connection between language and *cultural* identity, the extension of the familial 'we', motivates many of the most heated debates about language and its negotiation with imperial and neo-colonial power. For if a language seems to represent 'us' because it is 'ours', what of a colonial language? It is not exactly 'ours' but it is not exclusively 'theirs' either. It is 'ours' because we make it ours, and when we do so we choose to identify ourselves in a particularly contested, a particularly ambivalent space. It is then no longer fully 'theirs' because in making it 'ours' we change its form. Quite simply, the post-colonial use of English problematizes all those questions of identity that linger round our possession of a mother tongue. Who owns the language? Does a completely bilingual child even *have* a mother tongue? The Indian poet Kamala Das offers a pragmatic view in her poem, "An Introduction":

> I am Indian, very brown, born in
> Malabar, I speak three languages, write in
> Two, dream in one. Don't write in English, they said
> English is not your mother tongue
> …
> The language I speak
> Becomes mine, its distortions, its queerness
> All mine, mine alone. It is half English, half
> Indian, funny perhaps, but it is honest
> It is human as I am human
>
> (1986: 7)

It was another South Asian who coined the term 'chutnification' in *Midnight's Children* as a response to linguistic and cultural essentialisms. A question that follows from 'Who owns the language?' is 'How culturally valid is post-colonial writing in English?' The assertion of this chapter, and this book, is that such writing has an almost unparalleled political agency. But the discovery we make is that language, far from being a mode of being locked up in a particular culture, is already an ambivalent 'third space' between people, a transcultural space that defies the essential location of subjects.

More than any other aspect of our social life, language, in its various modes, participates in the constant struggle to define some version of our 'self' over and against some 'other'. It is in the language learned and shared in the family that we discover that 'we' are different from 'them'. But we do not passively inhabit our language; it is the primary tool we use to fashion ourselves as subjects, in thought, poem, and song, in formal or casual speech. This active engagement with language, this constant performative use, is a key to the role of language in constructing a private, religious, national or cultural identity. The language we speak is very often crucial in establishing who we are. But it need not define the limits to what we can be. In fact, the idea of the *horizon* of language blurs those limits, because it reveals, yet again, that the limits of speech, what Wittgenstein calls the limits of my world, are a matter for speakers rather than languages.

The case of the complex position of Chicanos in America demonstrates how important language becomes in our political formation. Alfred Arteaga says:

> I define myself as a Chicano. I was born in California and am a citizen of the United States, but my relation to that nation is problematic. US Anglo-American nationalists define their nation to the exclusion of my people … that I am rendered alien by US jingoism remains a quotidian fact. My nation is not Mexico, yet I am ethnically Mexican and racially mestizo. But my people exist in the borderlands that traverse the national frontiers of the United States and Mexico. It is obvious for us here that the language we speak both reflects and determines our position in relation to the two nations.
> (1994: 3–4)

In the creased and untidy fabric of post-colonial language use the link between language and nation has been radically loosened by a great number of social and cultural groups. This chauvinistically established link between language and the nation state reflects the way in which nationalist resistance to imperial language policies has often historically replaced those policies with a restrictive concept of a national language. The case of the Chicano uncovers an example of the felt experience of *natio* existing outside, or beneath the racial and historical narrative of the nation state. In this cultural sense of nation, this existence in the border-lands of the state, the use of language is not only a central fact but also an empowering 'technology' for self-fashioning. The example of the borderland culture is important because it reveals a truth about all language: that while identity is usually held to reside in language, identity is actually performed in the range of different ways the language is used.

Is English egocentric?

The moment we begin to try to make specific connections between language and cultural identity, things become very blurry. Eugene C. Eoyang offers a curious discussion of the link between the capitalization of the 'I' in the English language and the Western obsession with self (Arteaga 1994: 93–112). "The concept of the individual self," says Eoyang, "as a separate, privileged entity set apart from the community, is a fairly recent development, even in the West" (98). But, the argument goes, the self is predominant in the West, and in English in particular because of the capital 'I' used to describe the self. Such an analysis of the properties of language is highly suspect. The first and obvious point to make is that England is not the West, and a 'European' obsession with 'Self' is also maintained in languages which do not capitalize the first person singular, probably because it is not a single letter. Indeed 'me' in English is not capitalized either, suggesting that there is a practical reason, and probably an historical etymological reason, for this convention. This is the kind of error Lacan addressed when he argues that the position of the 'I' within language, the subject, does not simply represent the presence of a subject that pre-exists it, but rather *produces* it. The 'I' is the 'subject' because it is the subject of the sentence.

But the more germane issue concerns the assumption that capital 'I' may *generate* a concern with 'self' in English speakers. There is no doubt that this concern exists in western society, but is it stimulated by the language? Does it exist in all speakers of the language? Is it limited to the language that capitalizes the first person singular? Is it really limited to western societies? The linking of an obsession with self in the identities of people who speak English is a good example of the conflation that often occurs between language and identity. But if we follow Lacan we see that it is the sentence, not the capital 'I', that counts. As the hybridization of languages, and the strategies by which English is transformed demonstrate, identities are much more fluid and adaptable than it might seem.

The employment of a second, dominant tongue, forces us to inspect some fondly held myths about the ways in which identity emerges in language use. What we find in this struggle, and what we will investigate further in later chapters, is that the politics of language is the politics of identity. Claims are made about the 'essential' character of a language that stem from the politics of its speakers, and indeed this myth of the inherent qualities of language becomes extremely important in nationalism. The issue is not the signifying qualities of a language but the negotiation of power and authority. Such a negotiation becomes a feature of daily discourse for the Chicano speaker.

> In poem and daily speech, English and Spanish bestow different levels of authority on text and speaker. The relative imbalance in authority grows daily in the present era of increasing legislative suppression of languages other than English. English carries with it the status of authorization by the hegemony. It is the language of Anglo America and Anglo Americans, whether or not they be ethnic Anglos. Further, it is the language of the greatest military and economic power in the world. Spanish is a language of Latin Americans, south of the border and north. Across the border, Spanish is a third world language; here it is the language of the poor.
>
> (Arteaga 1994: 12)

Language as a discourse of identity is primarily about power, about what the language as such signifies about the authority and status of its speakers. This is, and has always been, true for a colonial language, a characteristic Bakhtin calls 'monoglossic'. However the very ambivalent location of Chicano speakers and writers is indicative of the ways in which the political power and social implications of a language such as English can be subverted in its actual use. For the Chicano speaker is (often literally) a speaker in the borderlands, social, political and linguistic and it is out of the appropriation and hybridization of the dominant language, the "language of the greatest military and economic power in the world", that the unique nature of Chicano identity has been fashioned by writers, ethnic politicians and ordinary speakers. For Chicano discourse is archetypally heteroglossic. "To speak, or even attempt to learn to speak," says Arteaga, "sparks a display of power from the dominant group. It is within this system of unequal discursive relationships that Chicano speak and write" (12). However it is not the fact of linguistic suppression that is significant here, but of the capacity and success of Chicano speakers to use the turbulent, overlapping space of a multilingual environment to undermine the political power of the dominant language in the process of fashioning a Chicano identity. The idea that culture is somehow embedded in a particular language is disproved by the heteroglossic ferment of Chicano linguistic politics.

Clearly, the question of language use cannot be separated from the question of social identity. But how has this identity itself been subtly changed by the very experience of colonization? Octave Mannoni, whose study of the psychology of colonization (1950) first reawakened the symbolic importance of Caliban and Prospero in the fifties, contended that studies of traditional African societies and cultures had to make the colonial experience central, not discreetly tuck it away in a chapter on 'social change'. The cultural critique of anthropology that we find in such books as Talal Assad's collection (1973) demonstrate a growing awareness of the fact that one cannot locate some discrete 'traditional' or 'primitive' cultural reality that is somehow immune to the history of its colonization. If this is true then we are forced to question the idea that a culture's identity is somehow preserved intact in its language.

Many of us have encountered that sense of exclusion that comes when we cannot speak a foreign language. But even more than this, a language inherited from some other place (which is the common experience of post-colonial societies) seems to us to define and describe some different kind of reality. Few have been as forthright about the imprisoning effects of a colonial language as Gandhi, who said in 1908:

> To give millions a knowledge of English is to enslave them … Is it not a painful thing that, if I want to go to a court of justice, I must employ the English language as a medium; that, when I became a Barrister, I may not speak my mother tongue, and that someone else should have to translate to me from my own language? Is not this absolutely absurd? Is not this a sign of slavery?
>
> (Gandhi 1910)

Yet again the language is confused with its function as a political weapon. This was decades before his campaign against the British, in which he deployed the language to good effect, an effect that was far from 'enslavement'. However, the power divide that opens up between colonizing and colonized cultures seems to embed itself in the colonial language. In an essay written in the 1970s, "Language as a Boundary", Wole Soyinka stated that:

> of all the forms of boundaries known to man, encountered by him as an act of Nature, created by him for reasons or unreasons of his own, or imposed upon him through the innate conditions of his own struggle for

development or fulfilment, language as a boundary is one of the most persistent, insidious and tragic.

(1988: 82)

Yet ironically, these boundaries have always seemed the most potent expressions of self-determination against the homogenizing power of a colonial language. In 1959, at the Second Congress of Negro Writers, in Rome, the following resolution was passed:

(i)   that free and liberated black Africa should not adopt any European or other language as a national tongue
(ii) that one African language should be chosen ... that all Africans would learn this national language besides their own regional language
(iii) that a team of linguists be instructed to enrich this language as rapidly as possible, with the terminology for expression of modern philosophy, science and technology.

(Soyinka 1988: 89)

In 1974, Jomo Kenyatta, the president of Kenya, and instrumental in its colonial liberation, said that "the basis of any independent government is a national language, and we can no longer continue aping our former colonizers" (Crystal 1997: 114). Yet the need for a pan-African language and the undesirability of the intense exclusivism of regional languages has not yet been strong enough to lead to a solution. With monotonous regularity, linguistic groups continue to be expelled from African states. "At the very least," says Soyinka, "language is *one* of the key factors in embedding that separatist definition in social consciousness. The result, whenever the excuse is afforded from whatever direction, is the breakdown of the tenuous links of daily cohabitation, and the sudden resurrection of boundaries between linguistic groups" (Soyinka 1988: 84–5). Paradoxically, the boundaries may also be erected between linguistic groups oriented to one or another of the colonial languages. Soyinka relates a vigorous struggle in the UN between French-speaking and English-speaking Africans. Different colonial languages have themselves had an important role in reconstructing the boundaries of African identity.

Programs aimed at 'decolonizing' literature have been promoted in Africa since the 1960s, whilst in India the solution to these perceived failings has been subsumed in the general urge to writers to discard English altogether. In the Pacific, with an illiteracy rate of 75 per cent, English hardly reaches a local audience at all. In some respects the feeling about English in this region is more personal and impassioned and many of the battles resolved elsewhere are still being fought out. In the Caribbean, with no mother tongue to which to revert, the struggle with language is a struggle to create out of English a genuine 'nation language' – an appropriated mother tongue.

Writing 'identity'

Since so many formerly colonized people write in the colonizer's language we are bound to ask the question: 'What happens to one's identity when another language is spoken? How do we manage to maintain our identity while writing in a colonial tongue?' As Salman Rushdie puts it:

> To be an Indian writer in this society is to face, everyday, problems of definition. What does it mean to be 'Indian' outside India? How can culture be preserved without becoming ossified? How should we discuss the need for change within our community and ourselves without seeming to play into the hands of our racial enemies? What are the consequences, both spiritual and practical, of refusing to make any concessions to Western ideas and practices? What are the consequences of embracing those ideas and practices and turning away from the ones that came here with us? These questions are all a single existential question: How are we to live in the world?
>
> (1991: 17–18)

These questions apply to all post-colonial peoples: those whose national, racial, cultural and religious identities have been affected by the historical experience of colonization. 'How are we to live in the world?' is the question that must be asked by all those who dwell in the space between tongues, those whose use of a colonizing language demystifies language itself, revealing its pre-eminent function as a tool of self-fashioning. It is this experience and the thick palimpsest of cultural attitudes and influences it entails that distinguishes these users of English from those who simply learn it as a global communicative tool. For post-colonial peoples the language is deeply inflected with the troubling questions littering that liminal space where identity and culture mingle and scrape against one another.

The promotion, by many, of indigenous languages as the only proper medium for decolonizing literature, seemed to go along with a full-scale attack on the social provenance, stylistic choices and subject matter of writing in English. With the rise to global prominence of the United States, English, as a social institution, has become a pre-eminent language of authority. Consequently, writers who write in English have been accused of being elitist, urbanized, stylistically difficult and catering mainly for overseas audiences. The question many post-colonial writers have asked is: 'Since the historical phenomenon of English as an instrument of control has been so powerful and effective, what is to stop us taking it over for our own purposes?' What stops many is the thought that the essence of 'our' culture, and therefore of our identity, resides in 'our' language. The assumption is that to write in a colonial language is to be "marginal, anomalous, illegitimate, suffering, schizophrenic, treacherous, alienated, hybrid, separated from the Mother …" (McGuire 1992: 107). But Bengali poet and critic Sanjukta Dasgupta suggests that a consequence of linguistic confusion can be creative profusion:

> My mind was in a whirl
> First language – English, the Other tongue
> Second language – Bengali, the mother tongue
> Third language – Hindi, *filmi*, *oops*, the national tongue
>
> Which is which
> Bangla/English
> A twin togetherness

No comparatives or superlatives
My first language in school
My first language at home
A tangled tapestry of same and different words
Acquired skills both, after all
Obeying teachers, compulsory
Obeying parents, optional
So school skills prevailed on homely ones.

She recalls how there came a time when ...

I became not just bi-lingual
But bifocal too
Always sensitive to the local/global slash
Till there came a time
When a fountain of words
Began pouring out of me
I did not notice
Whether they were Romanic, Devnagiri or Kutil
As they were born in black scrawls on diary pages
But when I shared them with others
The skeptics boomed
Is it possible to create in the Other tongue
Can it be like the arrival of leaves to trees.

I felt confused, shy, shunned
But Other words flowed out of me
Like a river or a mountain stream
Romanic words grew on the page
Like a bed of green grass
Though the Other tongue
Was not my mother tongue
By years of nurturing this foster mother
And the one I ripped open to be here
Like Krishna's two loving mothers
Joyously merged and mingled
The language English
The text my own
Bengali? Indian? Anglo? Cosmo?
Four-in-one?
(You decide!)

(Dasgupta 2004: 8–9)

The bilingual writer discovers that complexity and (occasionally) confusion can be the rich ground of a transcultural creative process in which a "fountain" of words can never quite reach the limit of its possibilities.

In his defense of *The Satanic Verses* Salman Rushdie says:

> Throughout human history, the apostles of purity, those who have claimed to possess a total explanation, have wrought havoc among mere mixed-up human beings. Like many millions of people, I am a bastard child of history. Perhaps we are all, black and white, leaking into one another, as a character of mine once said, *like flavours when you cook.*
>
> (Rushdie 1991: 394)

The question Rushdie's metaphor addresses is: 'Is it impossible for signs of cultural difference to be communicated in a different language?' If those signs communicate difference rather than essence, the answer must obviously be – no! In fact the very existence of post-colonial literatures in English refutes this. If cultural difference can be communicated in a second language then these literatures also lead us to the conclusion that our identity, our subjectivity, is *performed by*, rather than *embodied in* language.

Ngũgĩ and Achebe

This argument about language and cultural identity has been remarkably intractable and widespread throughout the post-colonial world, but, as Kenyatta and Soyinka demonstrate above, Africa seems to have provided some of the most vigorous debates. Two African novelists, the Kenyan Ngũgĩ wa Thiongo and the Nigerian Chinua Achebe, have engaged these issues longer, more often and more resolutely than other post-colonial writers, so it is useful to see them as representatives of this longstanding, world-wide argument. Ngũgĩ, whose original *nom de plume* was James Ngũgĩ, came to reject his Christian name and the imperial language and decided to write his novels only in Gikuyu. Chinua Achebe whose novel *Things Fall Apart* is probably the most widely known, and some say the first, African novel in English, has consistently announced his view that English is a linguistic tool which can be creatively used. These are sides of a dialogue that continues throughout the world, but the African debate dates at least from the writers' conference in Makere, Uganda in 1962 (although as Wole Soyinka reveals, the conference of 'Negro' writers in Rome 1959 foreshadowed many of these issues).

　In essence, the conflict is simple: do writers who continue to write in a colonial language 'remain colonized' – by retaining a colonized identity – or can they appropriate the language as a tool for their own purposes? Does literature in a language such as English privilege western cultural values, and with them the whole history of colonial oppression and control, or does such a literature use English as a tool to reveal the non-western world and even record resistance to that colonial world view? The argument sometimes seems so old and battered that it is best avoided. But it needs to be addressed because it reveals some crucial issues in the transformation of language by post-colonial writers.

Ngũgĩ's position is stated early in his essay "Towards a National Culture"[1]:

> We have seen what the colonial system does: impose its tongue on the
> subject races, and then downgrade the vernacular tongues of the people.
> By so doing they make the acquisition of their tongue a status symbol; any-
> one who learns it begins to despise the peasant majority and their barbaric
> tongues. By acquiring the thought processes and values of his mother
> tongue, he becomes alienated from the values of his mother tongue, or
> from the language of the masses. Language after all is a carrier of values
> fashioned by a people over a period of time ... . We need to develop a
> national language, but not at the expense of regional languages. In a social-
> ist economic and political context, the development of ethnic languages
> would not be inimical to national unity and consciousness.
>
> (1981: 16)

This statement expresses the general objections to which Ngũgĩ and many others
after him have returned time and again: (1) the colonial tongue becomes a province
of the elite and thus the language itself reproduces colonial class distinctions; (2) language embodies the "thought processes and values" of its culture; (3) learning a
colonial tongue alienates a speaker from the "values" of the local language and
from the values of the masses (which to Ngũgĩ are the same thing); (4) national language should not exist at the expense of regional languages which can enhance
national unity "in a socialist economic and political context".

Ngũgĩ is right to suggest that colonialism has had a profound and often destructive
effect on local cultures, disrupting social structures and initiating changes in cultural values. The issue, however, with those writers, such as Achebe, who choose to write in
English, is whether a cultural identity can be communicated in a different language,
and whether that language can be a vibrant and creative medium for the expression of
such identity. "Those of us who have inherited the English language," says Achebe,

> may not be in a position to appreciate the value of the inheritance. Or we
> may go on resenting it because it came as part of a package deal which
> included many other items of doubtful value and the positive atrocity of
> racial arrogance and prejudice which may yet set the world on fire. But let
> us not in rejecting the evil throw out the good with it.
>
> (1975: 58)

The position of most African writers in English is as pragmatic as Achebe's.
The legacies of colonialism constantly need to be addressed, but, paradoxically,
they may best be addressed by some of the tools taken from the colonizers. We
have considered the question of literacy as the province of an elite, but what of
Ngũgĩ's three other assertions?

---

1 This was written in 1972 and is the essay to which Achebe responds in 1975 in *Morning Yet on
Creation Day*.

"Language embodies the thought processes and values of a culture"

'Is culture embodied in a language?' is the most crucial question in the link between language and identity. In *Decolonizing the Mind* Ngũgĩ states that, "Language, any language, has a dual character: it is both a means of communication and a carrier of culture". Where English is concerned, "It is widely used as a means of communication across many nationalities. But it is not the carrier of a culture and history of many of those nationalities" (13). The key question here is 'How does a language "carry" a culture?' 'Is it impossible for a language to "carry" a different culture?' Obviously what we mean by the term 'carry' will be critical in deciding this. Chinua Achebe says:

> I feel that the English language will be able to carry the weight of my African experience. But it will have to be a new English, still in full communion with its ancestral home but altered to suit new African surroundings.
>
> (1975: 62)

Clearly, what Ngũgĩ and Achebe mean by the term 'carry' are quite different things, and this points out some of the difficulty of the debate, because many people believe that to 'carry' does not mean simply to 'bear', but to 'embody'.

Underlying the language debate has been the assertion that English, whether transported into a foreign language or settler culture, is profoundly 'inauthentic' in its new place. If we are to regard an 'authentic' language as one that somehow embodies cultural uniqueness in a way no other language could, then English becomes linguistically inappropriate to the development of a non-British culture. But a truly 'authentic' discourse, one true to the actual life of a culture, must be one that is itself syncretic, dynamic, and constantly changing. European genres might equally be held to be inauthentic. For instance, the appearance of novels and plays in languages like Wolof, Yoruba, Gikuyu in Africa, and Bengali, Kannada and Malayalam in India, has in each case required the invention of an audience, the creation of audiences of readers to 'consume' literary works of a kind that had not previously existed in those languages.

Correspondingly, Ngũgĩ has no objection to Western political economy because he seeks to create a revolutionary culture in Kenya and instill a "new strength and new dynamic" (1981: 19) on Marxist principles. But could this new strength and new dynamic not be considered a different and subtler form of colonization? Is the social change brought about by the intervention of such alien philosophies necessarily bad? Clearly, for Ngũgĩ some "alien thought processes and values" are better than others, but who makes the decision that socialist principles are more in tune with indigenous values if the end of the exercise is to dispense with tribal groups in favour of a global community?

Ngũgĩ goes on to say that "we" can then "utilize all the resources at our disposal – radio, television, film, schools, universities, youth movements, farmers' co-operatives – to create such a society" (1981: 20). Clearly there are institutions that can be utilized, however deeply embedded they are in western cultural history and values, to the benefit of local societies, but this doesn't include language. Language is special because it 'embodies' these thought processes, values and cultural history in some more mysterious and organic way than any other colonial institution or discourse.

Achebe responds that it is the way the language is *used* which counts.

> Allow me to quote a small example, from *Arrow of God*, which may give some idea of how I approach the use of English. The Chief Priest in the story is telling one of his sons why it is necessary to send him to church:
>
>> I want one of my sons to join these people and be my eyes there. If there is nothing in it you will come back. But if there is something there you will bring home my share. The world is like a Mask, dancing. If you want to see it well you do not stand in one place. My spirit tells me that those who do not befriend the white man today will be saying *had we known* tomorrow.
>
> Now supposing I had put it another way. Like this for instance:
>
>> I am sending you as my representative among these people – just to be on the safe side in case the new religion develops. One has to move with the times or else one is left behind. I have a hunch that those who fail to come to terms with the white man may well regret their lack of foresight.
>
> The material is the same. But the form of one is *in character* and the other is not.
>
> (Achebe 1975: 61–2)

This demonstrates, yet again, that what we often take to be a *property* of language is in fact a *function of its use*. The Africanness of the first passage is a function of the way in which the English language is used. It is no more an embodiment of Africanness than the English language – more specifically, the range of Englishes used around the world, including the United Kingdom – is an embodiment of Englishness.

Ngũgĩ provides us with a very evocative account of his childhood, an account in which the language connotes for him the range of experiences, the gradual emergence of his identity as he listened to, and used the language. "We spoke Gikuyu as we worked in the fields," he says. "We spoke Gikuyu in and outside the home. I can vividly recall those evenings of story telling around the fireside" (1981: 10). He goes on to describe the kinds of stories, particularly stories about animals with whom the listeners identified, in their struggle against hostile nature and their struggles amongst themselves. There were also stories about humans in which many of the cultural values of his society were transmitted. This, indeed, indicates the function of myth in society, for myths are stories that embody constitutive cultural meanings. This is an incontrovertible way in which language 'carries' cultural meanings. But to what extent do these uses of the language enter into the language itself? When Ngũgĩ attempts to describe how this happens, things get very blurry:

> We therefore learnt to value words for their meanings and nuances. Language was not a mere string of words. It had a suggestive power well beyond the immediate and lexical meaning.
>
> (1981: 11)

But this is something that happens in all cultures, for this is the way language means. It is not a specific cultural property but a process that occurs in all language learning since all language has a "suggestive … power".

> Our appreciation of the suggestive magical power of language was reinforced by the games we played with words through riddles, proverbs, transpositions of syllables, or through nonsensical but musically arranged words. So we learnt the music of our language on top of content. The language, through images and symbols, gave us a view of the world, but it had a beauty of its own.
>
> (11)

Again the values of the language are carried in the way it is used, the kinds of games played to emphasize its evocativeness. The key statement in this passage is that the language, "through images and symbols, gave us a view of the world, but it had a beauty of its own". This is the closest we come to an explanation of the cultural properties of language – the character of its images and symbols – but these too are a form of use. The issue is not whether the Kenyan child has a very particular and culturally specific social indoctrination, for clearly this upbringing may be very different from that of many English speakers. And it is certainly not to deny that a compulsory education in English for colonial children went hand in hand with learning a particular view of the world in which the local and the traditional were regarded as debased and primitive. The question is whether such a local cultural reality can be expressed in a language serving as such a consummate tool of cultural alienation. It is clear that as far as Achebe is concerned any language can be used creatively to convey a cultural reality through a range of techniques: the words, the music and rhythm of the language, and various other strategies that we will discuss later.

A subsidiary question raised by this link between language and culture concerns the ability of non-English speakers to effectively use the language. In his essay "The African Writer and the English Language" Achebe responds to Obi Wali's criticism that:

> until these writers and their Western midwives accept the fact that any true African literature must be written in African languages, they would be merely pursuing a dead end, which can only lead to sterility, uncreativity and frustration.
>
> (Achebe 1975: 60)

This is a version of Ngũgĩ's position – African writers will never reach their creative potential till they write in African languages. Achebe's response to this reiterates the point that a writer's use of a language can be as culturally specific as he or she makes it. If we ask *Can an African ever learn English well enough to use it effectively in creative writing?* Achebe's answer is yes. But the secret such a writer has at his or her disposal is a healthy disregard for its traditions and rules. All writers have a creative sense of the possibilities of language, but the non-English speaking post-colonial writer has the added dimension of a different mother tongue, a different linguistic tradition from which to draw. If we ask *Can he or she ever use it like a native speaker?* Achebe's answer is "I hope not." His point is as true today as it was then. The appropriation of English by post-colonial writers is not only possible but also extremely effective and enriches the language. "The price a world language must be prepared to pay is submission to many different kinds of use" (1975: 61).

What is at stake here is not whether the choice of language can revitalize some lost cultural essence or exorcise some colonial taint, but whether the use of English materially aids the process of decolonization. Does it substantially alter the audience addressed? Does it subvert the function of literature as a means of addressing an elite, controlled by its place in the social power structure? Does its use, therefore, challenge the institutional practices of the new ruling class in a genuinely subversive way? The answer to these questions will be very different in different societies, in Kenya as opposed to South Africa, in India or Singapore, and no one answer will serve for all. But it is clear that for writers such as Achebe the answer is yes.

"Writing in a colonial language alienates a writer from his or her culture"

Achebe approaches this question with remarkable directness. "Is it right that a man should abandon his mother tongue for someone else's?" he asks. "It looks like a dreadful betrayal and produces a guilty feeling." His answer has become famous in its simplicity: "I have been given this language and I intend to use it" (1975: 62). Although there will always be writers who write in their mother tongue, and it is good that they do so, Achebe sees great excitement in the possibilities for English use. His feeling about language, the sense that English was an alien language and reflected none of his experience, leads him to quote James Baldwin who wrote in the *London Observer*:

> My quarrel with the English language has been that the language reflected none of my experience. But now I begin to see the matter another way … Perhaps the language was not my own because I had never attempted to use it, had only learned to imitate it. If this were so, then it might be made to bear the burden of my experience if I could find the stamina to challenge it, and me, to such a test.

> (cited in Achebe 1975: 62)

This is a very astute perception of the relationship of writers to language. The problem with many users of a colonial language is the problem of *imitation*, which is very different from original *use*. This reiterates the point that language is a tool to be used and it is that use which can convey cultural specificity. Baldwin's statement has become one that Achebe repeats and which is true for all post-colonial writers; English can be "made to bear the burden of my experience". In some ways this sums up Achebe's view of his relationship to English, because it can be made to "bear the weight of my African experience". At base it is a refutation of the idea that culture is a property of language, a statement that language is a tool that can be used for many purposes. It is, significantly, the creative writer who can best show how the language can be used, how it can be made to bear the burden of a different cultural experience. This, indeed, is a primary value of post-colonial writing itself.

Elsewhere Achebe says:

> The price a world language must be prepared to pay is submission to many different kinds of use. The African writer should aim to use English in a way that brings out his message best without altering the language to the extent that its value as a medium of international exchange will be lost. He should aim at fashioning out an English that is at once universal and able to carry his particular experience … I feel that English will be able to carry the weight of my African experience. But it will have to be a new English, still in full communion with its ancestral home but altered to suit its new surroundings.
>
> (1989: 59)

"Of course," says Achebe, "it is true that the vast majority of people are happier with their first language than with any other. But then the majority of people are not writers" (59).

Language at the crossroads of cultures

Can a culture be pinned down to a particular set of beliefs, values and practices? Or, do cultures experience a perpetual process of internal change and transformation? Achebe describes it with the resonant phrase, "We lived at the crossroads of cultures". These crossroads have a dangerous potency "because a man might perish there wrestling with multiple-headed spirits, but also he might be lucky and return to his people with the boon of prophetic vision" (1975: 67–8). The metaphor of the crossroads doesn't fully indicate the extent to which cultures may become changed by the intersection. Indeed no culture is static, but is a constant process of hybrid interaction and change. It was always the case, but is becoming even more so, that subjectivities are mixed up. Rushdie claims that those who object most vociferously to the novel today are of the opinion that intermingling with a different culture will ultimately weaken and ruin their own. His *Satanic Verses* "celebrates hybridity, impurity, intermingling, the transformation of the new and unexpected combinations of human beings" (1991: 394). This is not an eccentric preference, hybridity is *how newness enters the world* (394).

Homi Bhabha uses the term the "Third Space" to describe this condition of dynamism, a space that emerges from the ambivalence of culture. This is the space of hybridity itself, the space in which cultural meanings and identities always contain the traces of other meanings and identities. Therefore, Bhabha argues, "claims to inherent originality or purity of cultures are untenable, even before we resort to empirical historical instances that demonstrate their hybridity" (1994: 37). To think of cultural identity we might return to Rushdie's example of cooking "with all our flavours leaking into one another" (1991: 394). A culture is like a cake that is baked out of many ingredients, none of which is *essential* to its identity. Consequently, a culture may be recognized in its general form, but its specifics, its ingredients, may change considerably. In time the general form of the cake may also change, as may its taste, but its identity will still be recognizable and generally coherent because it is represented in a particular way.

National and regional languages: Communication between different cultural groups

The debate about the need for an African *lingua franca* was vigorously pursued in the late sixties, with the advocacy of a new pan-African language such as Swahili. But Swahili is a hybridized language itself, the product of the colonial encounter of expansionist Islam with the East African indigenous languages and cultures and since it is not spoken widely in Western or even Southern Africa, support in these areas has been sporadic. Ngũgĩ is a fervent proponent of writing in indigenous languages but this receives equally heated opposition from writers such as Lewis Nkosi who sees crucial political benefit in writing in English. According to Achebe, English is, or will be, the language of national literatures (1975: 57). Although colonialism often divided a single ethnic group between several European powers, says Achebe (a division whose effects we see today in places like Rwanda), it also brought together many peoples and "gave them a language with which to talk to one another" (57). Nigeria, for instance, "had hundreds of autonomous communities ranging in size from the vast Fulani Empire founded by Usman dan Fodio in the North to tiny village entities in the East. Today it is one country".

Colonialism created immense disruption but it did provide the possibility for unity, even in resistance. "If it failed to give them a song, it at least gave them a tongue, for sighing" (57). It provided the possibility for interchange between a vast numbers of communities. Consequently there are not many countries in Africa today where the colonial language could be abolished and still have the facility for national communication. "Therefore," says Achebe, "those African writers who have chosen to write in English or French are not unpatriotic smart alecs with an eye on the main chance ... they are by-products of the same process that made the new nation states of Africa" (57). Rather than a culturally treacherous elite, writers in a colonial language represent in their own practice the developing culture of African states.

In his essay "Thoughts on the African Novel" Achebe asks:

> what is a *non-African* language? English and French certainly. But what about Arabic? What about Swahili even? Is it then a question of how long the language has been present on African soil? If so, how many years should constitute *effective occupation*? For me it is again a pragmatic matter. A language spoken by Africans on African soil, a language in which Africans write justifies itself.
>
> (Achebe 1975: 50)

At its base this issue stems from the problem of the homogenizing nature of the term 'Africa'. Achebe asks a question about language and identity which can be extrapolated into many cultures. What makes one language more appropriate than another? In the vast and complex continent of Africa what makes one language more African than another? Is it length of use? Indeed what is the validity of a term such as 'African language' or even 'Africa'?

Despite these arguments against the latent and incipient depictions of language (and the implications for subjectivity) in Ngũgĩ's position, his stance against English remains an extremely important political statement. Today the novelist accepts posts in the metropolitan academy and uses these positions as strategic points from which to publish novels in an English translated from Gikuyu. This is not to be unfaithful to his beliefs but to maintain an announcement of *difference*. This announcement is metonymic. It establishes a gap between his world and the world of his audience. But if we look at the production of post-colonial texts in English we can see that this establishment of a metonymic cultural gap is a fundamental feature of post-colonial writing.

***

In India, the tendency towards linguistic chauvinism has led, according to Braj Kachru, to the adoption of English as a relatively 'neutral' *lingua franca*. Although, obviously, a colonial language can never be historically or culturally neutral, it may act as a politically neutral compromise in the highly charged contest between India's regional languages.

> English does have one clear advantage, attitudinally and linguistically: it has acquired a *neutrality* in a linguistic context where native languages, dialects and styles sometimes have acquired undesirable connotations. Whereas native codes are functionally marked in terms of caste, religion, region and so forth, English has no such 'markers', at least in the non-native context. It was originally the foreign (alien) ruler's language, but that drawback is often overshadowed by what it can do for its users.
>
> (Kachru 1986 cited in Ashcroft *et al.* 2006: 272)

Because language is the way in which we have a world, the language itself often seems to embody something of the essence of our national or communal nature.

Paradoxically this assumption of 'essence' comes about because of the widespread use of a language in a particular community: the idea of essence relies on dispersal and the simple aggregation of use. This tendency towards essentialism has been the source of much argument amongst post-colonial writers. One of the key arguments about the use of a colonial language such as English is the assumption that the language both creates and limits one's experience of the world, that, for instance, the world of the non-English speaker is inaccessible to one who speaks only English. Language, on the other hand, because of its intense connection to the way we have a world, seems to offer and almost mystical entry into the soul of the colonizer. In 1959 the Malagasy poet Rabemanjara suggested that African writers

> have stolen from our masters this treasure of identity, the vehicle of their thought, the golden key to their soul, the magic Sesame which opens wide the door of their secrets, the forbidden cave where they have hidden the loot taken from our fathers and for which we must demand a reckoning.
>
> (Soyinka 1988: 89)

This "treasure of identity" has become a variegated and complex range of usages that sometimes owe more to the rules of a mother tongue syntax than to the grammar book. Increasingly, the apparent choice between reaching a world-wide audience by using English, and maintaining cultural integrity by refusing to do so, has turned out to be a false dichotomy.

The perpetuation of a standard written form has, curiously, been the very factor that has assisted the construction of cultural difference by creative writers through their use of English. This has become, perhaps, one of the major functions of the use of locally inflected Englishes in post-colonial societies. For these varieties of creative and literary language implicitly depend upon the existence of a comparatively stable written form, a relatively widespread global standard, to make their difference more obvious. This difference from a norm is the very thing that allows language itself to be the metonymy, the most potent signifier of cultural difference itself. This diversion from a norm is the very thing which makes post-colonial writing so powerful. For it is not merely the description of a different kind of cultural experience in a global language which allows the post-colonial society to liberate itself, it is the capacity to appropriate the language which gives breath to its voice. As Rushdie says:

> those peoples who were once colonized by the language are now rapidly remaking it, domesticating it, becoming more and more relaxed about the way they use it – assisted by the English language's enormous flexibility and size, they are carving out large territories for themselves within its frontiers.
>
> To take the case of India … . The children of independent India seem not to think of English as being irredeemably tainted by its colonial provenance. They use it as an Indian language, as one of the tools they have to hand.
>
> (Rushdie 1991: 64)

6   Language, culture and meaning
The Caribbean

There are many ways and many places in which Caliban appropriated Prospero's language, but none so striking as the land of the 'Canibals'. The political and cultural implications of English language use in the Caribbean produce a variety of English that is so fluid and dynamic – a continuum in fact – that it disrupts our ordinary views of how language works, and forces us to re-think the connection between language and culture. Edward Kamau Brathwaite's term for culturally specific forms of Caribbean English is 'nation language' which is heavily influenced by the African heritage in Caribbean cultures, a heritage in which African languages exist merely as traces:

> … it is an English which is not the standard, imported, educated English, but that of the submerged, surrealist experience and sensibility, which has always been there and which is now increasingly coming to the surface and influencing the perception of contemporary Caribbean people.
>
> …
>
> The poetry, the culture itself, exists not in a dictionary but in the tradition of the spoken word. It is based as much on sound as it is on song. That is to say, the noise that it makes is part of the meaning, and if you ignore the noise (or what you would think of as noise, shall I say), then you lose part of the meaning. When it is written you lose the sound of the noise, and therefore you lose part of the meaning.
>
> (1984: 271)

But the fact that it is accessible to other English speakers reveals a striking adaptability in the language, which forces us to ask the question, 'What exactly is English?' Once we dispense with the formal properties described by English grammar we encounter a strikingly malleable vehicle of expression. The contention that nation language somehow involves "a submerged, surrealist experience and sensibility" is really a way of talking about this malleability. The experience does not lie embedded in the language but in its use. 'Nation language' is one of the many ways that Caliban uses Prospero's language. Such language, its emergence, functions and cultural significance, can only be adequately understood as a social practice. Far from mimicking standard English, it "is like a howl, or a shout or a machine-gun or the wind or a wave. It is also like the blues" (311). Nation language is thus a lived, dynamic and changing phenomenon, not merely a linguistic structure.

The Creole continuum and language use

A better term, perhaps, for the complex of overlapping lects in the Caribbean is that of the 'creole continuum' developed by Bickerton and DeCamp. The theory states that the creole complex of the region is not simply an aggregation of discrete dialect forms but an overlapping of ways of speaking between which individual speakers may move with considerable ease. These overlapping "lects", or specific modes of language use, not only contain forms from the major languages "between" which they come into being, but forms which are also functionally – peculiar to themselves (Bickerton 1973: 642). Thus they are identifiable as stages on a continuum without being wholly discrete as language behaviours.

The theory of the creole continuum disrupts many traditional and structural ideas about language. It undermines static models of language formation, overturning those notions of language, which, either implicitly or explicitly, regard 'standard' English as a 'core'. Creole need no longer be seen as a peripheral variation of English. Those rules that develop as approximations of English rules are by no means random or unprincipled, and the concept of what actually constitutes 'English' consequently opens itself to the possibility of radical transformation. The Caribbean continuum is not the only example of the fluidity of language types. J.M. Arthur observes that:

> Aboriginal English is not really one dialect but a continuum, a series of 'Aboriginal Englishes'; at one end a language which differs in only a few words from other Australian speech, and at the other a language which has become so different from other Australian Englishes that it ceases to be Aboriginal English and becomes another language, called 'Kriol'.
>
> (Arthur 1997: 2–3)

The creole continuum provides the most vibrant post-colonial context for considering the fundamental political questions of language use, for this continuum consolidates many myths about the inherent cultural qualities of language. Jean D'Costa, the Jamaican children's author, says of Caribbean writers:

> Not for them the clear cut boundaries of bilingual or diglossia situations … For the writer within a large continuum, literary usage for expression *and communication* is almost a contradiction in terms …
>
> The (Caribbean) writer operates within a polydialectical continuum with a creole base. His medium, written language, belongs to the sphere of standardised language which exerts a pressure within his own language community while embracing the wide audience of international Standard English.
>
> (1983: 124)

She claims that if writers are to satisfy themselves, the local audience and that wider international audience then the conflicting demands of worldwide acceptability and local authenticity must be met. This is true for all English writing communities, but in a polydialectical community the challenge increases considerably in *degree*. The complex linguistic culture provides, at the same time, a rich source for imaginative and aesthetic experimentation. The writer in such a community has access to a range of 'lects' which may generate very different associations in native speakers and the wider literary reading public, and this makes the author's responsibility for meaning apparently more acute. A polydialectical culture such as that which exists in the Caribbean reveals that the interpenetrating complex of lects can have a central function in the development of a characteristic English idiom.

The concept of a Creole continuum is now widely accepted as an explanation of the linguistic culture of the Caribbean. Its general nature has been understood since Reinecke and Tokimasa (1934) and its specific application to the Caribbean (in particular, Jamaica) has been discussed over the past two decades (Le Page and DeCamp 1960; Alleyne 1963; Bailey 1966; DeCamp 1971; Bickerton 1973 and D'Costa 1983 and 1984). In essence the theory states that the creole complex of the region is not simply an aggregation of discrete dialect forms but an overlapping of language behaviours between which individual speakers may move with considerable ease. These overlapping isolects not only contain forms from the polar lects but forms that are also functionally peculiar to them (Bickerton 1973: 642). Thus they meet the paradoxical requirements of being identifiable as stages on a continuum without being wholly discrete as language behaviours.

The theory of the creole continuum reaffirms the notion of language as an adaptable practice and *its very existence* undermines the traditional project of post-Saussurian linguistics. As Chomsky states, "Linguistic theory is concerned primarily with an ideal speaker-listener, in a completely homogeneous speech community" (1965: 3). Orthodox linguistic theory deals exclusively in terms of static models of discrete languages and data not readily incorporated in such models is consigned to the "wastebasket of performance" (Labov 1969: 759). The creole continuum reminds us that a language is a human behaviour and consists of what people do rather than what models a linguistic theory can construct. In a similar way postcolonial writing reasserts that just as language is performed, so the rich plethora of constructions and neologisms introduced by writing in English continually reconstitutes that loaded political category 'English Literature'.

If all human speech is rule-governed then our theory must take all speech behaviour into account rather than consigning some examples to the 'too hard' basket. The result is a metatheory that takes linguistic variation as the centre rather than the periphery of language study. Instead of Chomsky's ideal speaker-listener, polydialectical theory reveals that the performance of speakers, and all the variations that must be taken into account, is the true subject of linguistics. The centre of this new perception is that variation itself is rule governed. "We thus assume," says Bickerton, "until the contrary can be proved … that all variation is rule-governed; consequently the linguist's task is to find the rules, however much these may conflict with theoretical preconceptions" (Bickerton 1973: 643).

The theory of the creole continuum therefore has particular utility in overturning the 'concentric' notions of language in which Standard English exists as a contributory core. Undermining as it does the static models of language formation, a linguistic theory that installs variation at the centre rather than the periphery of language study has important effects on the received pronouncements of literary theory.

Creole appears no longer a peripheral variation of English. Mesolectal rules, which develop as approximations of English rules, are by no means random or unprincipled (although a common principle in creole formation is the 'principle of least effort') and the concept of what English 'is' consequently opens itself to some revision. But whether we revise our model of English or not, it is indisputable that the extent of English literature becomes considerably increased to include all language which is communicable to an English speaker within an 'imaginative' written text. Elements of a very wide range of different lects contribute to form this discourse, the only criterion for their membership of 'English literature' being whether they are used or not.

Myths of meaning

The creole continuum leads to an heightened plasticity and transformability in the English text and provides a unique situation in which to consider the operation of meaning in appropriated language. In discussing some myths of meaning by looking at the Caribbean situation we will cover some of the ground already covered in the last chapter. But whereas offered a political argument for abolishing English as culturally inappropriate to the African writer, Jean D'Costa, herself a writer of English novels, gives a much more elaborate and 'linguistic' account of how a transformed English works. D'Costa's discussion of language variance in her writing is possibly the most sophisticated given by any post-colonial writer, but her explanation of the *effects* of the linguistic strategies she uses falls into some of the same traps into which many commentators on post-colonial writing fall. This discussion is therefore much more specific than the discussion of Ngũgĩ and is inspired, as may become clear, by Wittgenstein's explanation of meaning in *Philosophical Investigations* and *The Blue and Brown Books*. The question that dogs any examination of language variance is the question of meaning, specifically the possibility of a culturally specific or culturally opaque meaning. The discussion that follows may be summed up by the statement: "For a large class of cases – though not all – in which we employ the word 'meaning' it can be defined thus: the meaning of a word is its use in the language" (Wittgenstein 1975: #43).

In "Language Issues Facing Commonwealth Authors" (1984), D'Costa presents a cogent case for the cultural basis of polydialectical English. I will focus on this very articulate and still very topical essay to address some of the fundamental fallacies that accompany thinking about cross-cultural language use. But the essay is really only a springboard to an examination of how language in the cross-cultural text actually produces meaning. Simply stated, D'Costa's argument runs something like this: There are considerable challenges facing the writer in a poly-dialectical community because the essence of a culture is conveyed by its language (specifically the differences in language use) and to adequately communicate that culture one must get the language right while still enabling it to communicate to readers of standard English. The writer's task is not simply to manipulate the lexicon to make it accessible to the Standard English audience, but to introduce the multiple perceptions, systems of values, customs, experiences and attitudes of a culture in ways that are faithful to the original dialect, since these characteristics are inextricable from the language code. Stated like this, we could have no quarrel. But this position involves assumptions about cultural meaning, about the link between language and culture, that are extremely problematic and probably best conveyed by the statement 'the essence of a culture is conveyed by its language'. D'Costa's explanation of her own technical strategies are extremely cogent and illuminate very well the ways in which 'dialect' and other variant forms of usage offer a continually renewable source of energy to the English language. But implicit in her view of language is a sense of the ultimate incommunicability between cultures, an incommunicability that would undermine the very rationale of cross-cultural writing and, in consequence, D'Costa's own writing as well.

Some of the most common assumptions about language we could question are: (i) That meaning resides in language; (ii) That meaning emanates from the minds of speakers; (iii) That the meaning of writing proceeds from the author's mind; (iv) That language embodies or conveys the essence of a culture. These assumptions all concern the way language operates. The general principles of D'Costa's argument are sound and convincing. Language *is* culturally central and its identification with the uniqueness of cultures is profound. But we need to be very clear about the *nature* of the relationship between language and culture to understand the dynamism of post-colonial literatures.

(i) That meaning resides in language

The idea of the meaning of a word casts a spell over most of us who have cause to consider how language means. We see meaning as the invisible ontological parcel a word carries through life, and if we want to know what it is we go to a dictionary. The traditional empiricist view of language is that words have referents in the real world, and what a word refers to is what it means. But even a simple word like 'hot' in the English language has a number of meanings, depending upon how it is used. Indeed, these uses are the ways (and therefore what) the word means in certain circumstances. 'Hot' denotes sensations of touch and taste in its most common usage. But the word can also be used to refer to feelings of sexual arousal (hot to trot), a condition of peak performance (when you're hot you're hot), or indicate the imminence of an answer or discovery (now you're getting hot!). In some uses, such as 'hot stuff', it can accommodate itself to a range of purposes. When used to a child of two about to touch a hot tap (that's HOT!) it functions as a warning rather than the definition of a referent. After all, what could the referent be to a two year old? The tap? The water? The chromium sheen? The child will discover the 'meaning' of the word when she discovers the various intersecting uses of the term (see Wittgenstein 1975: #43).

This is crucial for cross-cultural writing, because if we believe that English words spoken in an English culture carry their referents around on their backs like loads of meaning, then we must be tempted to believe that the same word with a different meaning in another culture must somehow be referring to a different, or several conflicting referents, and is therefore inaccessible to anyone but a local speaker. The situation becomes exacerbated if we simply pluck words and phrases out of the context of their use and peer at them like objects as D'Costa does in the following passage:

> many lexical items have overlapping meanings in JC and SE ... often meanings may diverge utterly, and ... very different behavioural situations may be summoned up by what appears to be "ordinary English". The following are apparently well-formed English sentences:
>
> 1. My mother begged for me.
> 2. England is a big place.
> 3. You are an ignorant man.
> 4. She is a big woman.
>
> These sentences have clear dual meanings to the JC–SJE speaker. The first does not mean that my mother is a professional beggar acting on my instructions, but that she is an advocate pleading on my behalf for forgiveness. The second has nothing to do with the relative physical size of Jamaica and the British Isles, but expresses the psychological contrast between the megalopolis and the intimacy of Jamaican society. The third informs the JC–SJE speaker that 'you' are in a filthy temper, and much given to tantrums, while the fourth announces that 'she' is now a sexually mature adult, free to go her own way.
>
> (126)

Now we must first ask whether any of the focal words ('begged', 'ignorant', or 'big') in these sentences are operating in essentially different ways from the word 'hot'. The words are used differently in Jamaican Creole (JC), and Standard Jamaican English (SJE); this is a mundane fact. But the notion that these sentences offer 'dual' meanings to the JC–SJE speaker simply means that there are at least two possibilities for using these sentences as they stand here in this text. In fact we would have to say that there is no prohibition to these sentences being used in many more ways in either Jamaican Creole or Standard Jamaican English. The 'situational experiences', which may be 'summoned up' by the sentences, are not peculiar possessions of Caribbean English, or the Caribbean way of life, they are simply the situations in which the sentences may be used. In the written text these situations are textual situations. Words such as 'begged', 'ignorant', or 'big' may be used in just as great a variety of ways in any English code. The meaning possibilities of the sentences are not their possessions but the potentialities of their use by speakers and writers.

(ii) That meaning emanates from the minds of speakers

The issue at stake here is that of the communicability between cultures. How is a writer to communicate, for instance, the sense of 'she is a big woman' to the speaker of Standard English? The perception of this as a problem really stems from several misconceptions: first, there is an assumption that the word 'big' has only one meaning in 'Standard English'; second, there is an assumption that this meaning is present in the mind of the Standard English speaker, while the poly-dialectical speaker has dual or multiple meanings in her mind. But if the speaker of Jamaican creole understands which meaning is applicable when it is used, what prevents another English speaker from also perceiving how the sentences are used? The point is that this usage is no more the province of the Jamaican mind than the multiple meanings of the term 'hot' are the province of the 'Standard English' speaker's mind. But when we consider Bickerton's analysis of the creole continuum (1973) we see that the overlapping isolects forming a continuum are not necessarily held to exist in the speaker's mind at all, but are simply potential variations of use.

Of course, special techniques may well be required to quickly introduce another English speaker to this usage, but it is the usage being introduced, not the contents of another 'mind', neither individual nor collective. The four sentences quoted are not nearly as accessible as they would be when we saw how they were used in context. The challenges to polydialectical writers are clear and exciting, but they are by no means metaphysical.

Understanding does not involve the transfer of the contents of one mind to another, and yet the following passage seems to assert the primacy of the individual mind in the process of meaning something.

> Even the smallest minimal shift (e.g. 'She los' the money' vs. 'She lost the money') alters the kernel message in the writer's mind. The two sentences are distinct in the minds of native speakers: they evoke different attitudes and assumptions.
>
> (127)

Now what exactly might the 'kernel' in the writer's mind be? If we were to ask the writer what she meant by writing "los" rather than "lost", is it likely that she would recapitulate some kernel of meaning she had held in her mind at the moment of writing it? Surely the purpose of this abbreviation is not a kernel at all, but the horizon of possibilities that issue from the indication of a speaker of a certain class, in a certain culture, in a certain place? Such a method of signifying this horizon of possibilities in fact underlies any employment of English variants. If we were to ask the writer what she 'meant', her answer would not be a recapitulation but an explanation of its possibilities when she wrote "los".

That the two sentences may be distinct in the minds of native speakers is functionally irrelevant to the communication of meaning, for this distinction is accessible (though not necessarily automatic) through the way the different sentences are apprehended in discourse. Logically we cannot even talk about the minds of native speakers, for how do we know what is in their minds apart from what language can reveal to us? How do we *know* that differences in pronunciation invoke different attitudes and assumptions? Or even that different languages operate upon a different view of the world? How can we describe such a difference? Language is both the start and the finish of our experience of another mind or another world.

The crux of this problem of the linguistic uniqueness of cultures can be summed up in the fact that the same words and phrases will not summon up the same *associations* in a non-native speaker as they would in a native speaker. This is no doubt true, but *these associations are not the meaning* and they are of no importance in conveying meaning unless they are themselves made subjects in the text. Indeed, the problem for D'Costa only becomes a problem because her sense of an audience, as she explains it, focuses so firmly on the local community. In this event D'Costa's expectations about the associations of certain dialects interferes with her sense of the meaning of the text. For instance, in describing one of her novels she says:

> Throughout the novel there are many verbal signs ... which act as in-group markers to a child audience. These signs and cues are SJE expressions signalling experiences shared by all Jamaicans.
>
> (1984: 131)

Yet the only possible way to impute these shared experiences is from the evidence of a shared language. What she means by "in-group markers" pointing to "experiences shared by all Jamaicans" is simply the use of language that all Jamaicans use. No matter how 'in-group' these markers may be and no matter how convinced the author is that they signal shared experiences, the bottom line is that they are shared *language* and the imputed experiences that are 'marked' are irrelevant to the process of communication.

Despite the staggering array of attitudes and assumptions that may be evoked in the minds of speakers of a language, the one thing we can say with certainty is that to share a language is to share a way of talking about reality. When languages overlap as they do in a polydialectical continuum, that linguistic overlap can be called (metaphorically) a shared reality. A sharable language can therefore introduce a sharable reality. This is certainly not to say that just because two people share a language they share a complete set of attitudes and perceptions, but simply that that which *is* that which can be said. Cultures and peoples are different, the range of their experiences and knowledge, their perception and understandings unique and peculiar, and although language indicates this range of experience it does not *embody* it. The excitement of post-colonial writing is that the intersection of language is the focus of a momentous cultural sharing. The text is not a terrain over which words hump their individual and possibly conflicting swags of referents, but the scene of the shared practices of reading and writing.

(iii) That the meaning of writing proceeds from the author's mind

At one level the idea of the author's mind mediating the complexities of two different cultures is central to the allure and challenge of cross-cultural writing.

> The Caribbean writer confronts in his own mind the array of possible language forms which rise at the bidding of any single notion he may wish to express.
>
> (125)

> Even as I compose this sentence, I find myself responding to the pressure of alternative codes within the continuum.
>
> (127)

The impression one has of a cross-cultural writer is of a person living and writing on the knife-edge of translation, a process of writing as a creation and translation process in the one act of literary birth. No aspect of post-colonial literatures so imbues them with a sense of mystery and authority. It is not a translation, but a moment of interface, in the proper sense of the term, an 'inner translation'. We reach at this point the very heart of post-colonial literature. It seems to us that if we could understand this moment of incarnation at the point of interface of two cultures, we could understand everything there is to know about such writing.

But alas! The moment is an illusion. The mystery of cross-cultural writing is of vaster proportions than the mind of the author. Let us first try to consider what actually goes on in the writer's mind at the moment of creation. D'Costa says that *even as she writes this sentence she finds herself responding* to alternative pressures. Firstly, what response is possible other than the response to write something *meanable* according to the dictates of her preceding and prospective essay? When does she *find* herself under conflicting pressure if not in a retrospective consideration of the linguistic possibilities (possibilities which are hardly real and are quickly discarded by the demands of the writing)? It is not an arbitrary decision that decides her response; the context in which she is writing has already made the decision for her. The pressures on a writer present themselves as a range of choices and possibilities stretching out ahead of, rather than pushing the writer from behind. If she were writing dialogue the possibilities would be quite different. That the course already taken (in this case an analysis of polydialectical writing) determines what choices will be made and what possibilities discarded, means that the pressures are less multifarious than they seem, and this process is the process which pushes all writing ahead, in both style and content.

There can be no doubt that there is a great range of linguistic possibilities to be confronted by a writer, but what exactly does this confrontation entail? We could compare the process to the act of playing chess, in which, in each move, the player 'confronts' both the rules of chess and every possible move that might be made. Are the whole of the rules confronted in every move? Does the player contain the rules to be confronted 'in his mind' all the time, or just when he is making a move?

I think we are obliged to look closely at this and ask if there is any qualitative difference between the ways a polydialectical writer sorts the choices in her mind and the way a bilingual or monolingual writer makes this decision. There is no doubt that all writers make conscious decisions about their writing. In cross-cultural writing these decisions often concern (most often perhaps) the use of language. But in all writing, such decisions exist *outside* the mind, in the situation itself (and by situation I mean the linguistic history, the social conditions, the mode of writing, the expected audience and the asserted purposes of the activity). It is the text and the context that decide the choices, and the progression of writing (like the progression of the game of chess) which narrows these choices down. The writer of the cross-cultural text is limited, as any speaker or writer is limited, to a situation that is *meanable*.

(iv) That language conveys the essence of a culture

This is undoubtedly the most persistent misconception in considerations of cross-cultural writing, and is everywhere implied and stated. This is the basis of Ngũgĩ's complaint about English, but D'Costa's essay is valuable because she puts this essentialist fallacy in several ways. At one point she says, "my choices as a writer would seem to be limited to those ranges of experience *contained within* the internationally accepted registers of English usage" (1984: 125, my italics).

One would think that, being internationally accepted, these registers must be used to attempt to describe the experiences of people from a great number of cultures. It is unlikely that Standard English could therefore embody the essence of this variety of cultures, whether as a first or second language. So we are entitled to ask why and how dialect may do so. Nevertheless, it cannot be denied that the idea of the 'essence' of a culture is a concept that greatly exercises the cross-cultural writer:

> … expression … forces the writer … to attain new levels of usage that evoke the essence of this unique world.
>
> (123)

> … what can the writer do when faced with the need to express the multiple interrelated perceptions of a continuum culture?
>
> (129)

At first glance, this notion of the essence of a culture seems relatively harmless. We all know what is meant by the term. But is the notion of essence simply a loosely used metaphor, or does it lie at the heart of a profoundly erroneous assumption about language and culture? Would this essence, for instance, exist in every manifestation of culture? Would it exist in every instance of polydialectical speech? How exactly does a specific language convey this essence? Take, for example, a portion of a novel by D'Costa herself, which she quotes in her essay – "Cho! Nobody be ya in dis bush," Gerald replied scornfully, "Nobody nah hear me. Look up deh!" (133). Now how, exactly, does this dialogue of Gerald's evoke the essence of Jamaican culture? You might say this is unfair, taking the piece out of its context. But remember, it is the language that is supposed to 'evoke'. Yet what can it evoke? The dialect informs us that in this society some people speak differently from others. As the novel progresses we might discover that this dialect distinguishes its speakers as those who demonstrate other, possibly characteristic, traits of personality and attitude. It evokes what any such language might evoke – insouciance, a refusal to be bound by restrictions, an openness and freedom emanating from an oral discourse community. But these assumptions (if they are correct) hardly indicate the essence of Jamaican culture, nor can they even be regarded as distinctive.

The argument is not only with the contention that language conveys the essence of a culture, but also with the contention that a culture can have an essence. Wittgenstein discussed the problem of essence in terms of family resemblances. We may quickly see the family resemblance of different faces without identifying any single shared characteristic. Another way of seeing this is that a culture is very much like a rope. Many strands overlap to form the rope, but no one strand runs through its centre. We could observe a culture and say that it contained many distinctive features, but no single feature; no single 'strand' is present in every manifestation as essential to this culture distinct from all others.[1] Any one of these features may become a sign of the whole 'rope' and this is the way variants operate in cross-cultural literature, but no feature, or phenomenon or 'strand' can be said to be the essence of the culture.

There is an important and incontrovertible way in which polydialectical speech indicates the flavour or the character of a culture: the very complexity, the anarchic profusion of language (as it may seem to a monolingual speaker) is a compelling sign of a particular range of behaviours and (by imputation) of experiences within that culture. The variety of the languages, their dynamic interchangeability, and the ease with which they are used in alternation, indicates a society of similar variety, complexity and alternation. The one thing that remains certain is that the culture has many overlapping ways of talking about reality, ways that are indicated by the profusion of language registers that make up this very complex continuum.

---

1 See *The Brown Book* #87, *The Blue Book* #19, and *Philosophical Investigations* #67, #116; e.g. "What ties the ship to the wharf is the rope and the rope consists of fibres, but it does not get its strength from any fibre that runs through it from one end to the other, but from the fact that there is a vast number of fibres overlapping" (*Brown Book* #87, Wittgenstein 1961).

The use of language variants in the post-colonial text has an extremely important function. Such variants operate as signs for a view of reality for which some evidence is provided in the language itself. However, the mental image of the signified is immaterial to the operation of the sign, for the image is not a contingent feature of language, and the image could differ vastly if summoned up in speakers' minds without altering the operation of the sign – think of the possible images aroused by the word 'dog'. Therefore the function of dialect and the whole range of cultural signs, such as colloquialisms, idiom, slang and even pidgin and creole, when they are placed in the context of the dominant variant called 'Standard English', all operate in the same way. The associations aroused by the sign will differ for speakers and non-speakers, but they will differ for any two native speakers as well. Nevertheless, the metonymic function of the language variant still operates in the text for all readers. It does not convey the essence of a culture and it maintains no special privilege in communicating aspects of that culture but it does operate as a sign, just as the inscription of a range of dialects operates as a sign for the 'experience' of cultural complexity.

The fact that language is an *essential* tool in the human construction of the world seems to have led, in many cases, to the assumption that the essence of the world is somehow in that language. But the tools are neither the artist nor the art. Language shows us what perceptions and experiences may be considered to be peculiar to a society by showing the uses to which language may be put, it cannot be those experiences, nor, more to the point, can it cause them.

The importance of English variants is that they display the adaptability of the language to many different kinds of use. But in making these adaptations, post-colonial literatures have managed to relocate the 'centre' of the English language by *decentring* it. Hence the metropolitan norm of 'Standard English' has been shown to be what it always was – one variant among many, a king without clothes. Ultimately, the achievement of post-colonial literatures is not just linguistic, it is political. If language is an agent of social control, then the greater use of language variants must be a potential agent in social and political changes of varying degrees. For this reason, the need for writers to incorporate local language variants into their work is great. But if appropriate cultural expression is their aim, they had best not think that language would do all the work for them.

7 Caliban's books

Orality and writing

Remember
First to possess his books; for without them
He's but a sot as I am, nor hath not
One spirit to command

(III.ii.89–92)

When we talk about the use of language for empowerment, when we discuss the issue of language and authenticity, when we talk about the use of a dominant language in a global setting, we are talking mostly about writing. The power of writing in modern times stems from the ease with which writing lends itself to commodification. Books, writing, print, in their material presence, are more obviously exchangeable repositories of cultural capital. Obviously oral knowledge and skill works as cultural capital as well, but not as authoritatively in the post-Enlightenment reification of written discourse in the West. Writing assumed power over the oral in western society when the 'will to truth', as Foucault puts it, ensured that the 'enunciated' assumed precedence over the 'enunciation'. Once the power of the orator's discourse was overtaken by the 'will to truth', when the veracity of *what was said* assumed greater importance than the persuasiveness or eloquence of its delivery, the written text became privileged, as a means of fixing what was said. The conviction of the power of the written word in Western thinking becomes linked to its teleological notions of the 'improvement of mankind'. Lévi-Strauss, a consistent critic of the idea of historical progress, still asserted that the invention of writing made it possible to accumulate the knowledge of each generation as "working capital" for the next (Lévi-Strauss 1969).

When Caliban comes to write *his* books, when writers from an oral culture write in English, they are not simply dealing with two different languages – their mother tongue and the appropriated English – but two different ways of understanding what language is. This is not to say the 'oral' cultures are never without forms of inscription and forms of reading. The entire physical world is a 'text' to be read with varying degrees of subtlety. The example of tracking, of reading the country and the human inscriptions upon it, indicate the possibility that 'writing' in this more general sense of the textuality of place is endemic to the human experience and interpretation of the environment. Nevertheless language, to speakers in oral cultures, bears a very different relation to the world, as do these inscriptions themselves. For instance, words, uttered under appropriate circumstances, are assumed to have the power to *bring into being* the events or states they stand for. Such power can be seen in creation mythologies in which the Supreme Being is said to have formed the world out of chaos by uttering the names of the things within it.

In the language of oral cultures, words are granted a certain measure of control over the objects or situations to which they refer. Words are *sacred*. They have the *power* of the things they signify because they are imputed to *be* the things they signify. Language embodies the seamless connection between people and their environments. This type of language culture is distinguished by the general absence of metaphor, but the nature of representation itself is different. Words are concrete and the relation between the word and the thing is characterized by analogy and embodiment, or 'presentation', rather than by representation. Thus the concepts of soul, mind, time, courage, emotion or thought are intensely physical, as in the languages of Australian Aboriginals, South Pacific and African peoples.

An interesting survival of this unity of word and referent can be seen in Hebrew in the form of the Jewish phylactery, pieces of written text worn on the head and arm – the word of God objectified as physical presence. The phylactery is not merely the representation of the wearer's closeness to the strictures of the Law, but the Law *itself* in its actual, unambiguous and power-laden presence. Rather than an indication of the power of the writing, this is a specific demonstration of the power of the word as it exists in the oral culture being conferred on the written inscription. This is because the word is not a sign of the Law in this case, but its embodiment. Similarly Arabic is the only language in which the Koran can be written (as was Latin for the medieval Bible) because Arabic is believed to be the language of God, not merely a representation but an embodiment.

A consequence of this is the importance of the link between the word and the physical breath. The 'breath' remains the sign of the tangible reality of words. Oral myths are the fundamental means of communicating history, traditions, morality, customs and values. They are life giving and they can only be maintained by continual repetition. The anthropologist A.P. Elkin found that these oral myths in Aboriginal clans must be inculcated, indeed, breathed into, all members of the tribe, and this is done in a very literal manner by constant repetition through infancy and childhood.

> Most striking of all, however, is the teaching of the sacred chants to the newly initiated … in Arnhem Land, the elders grip the young fellow, and vigorously sing the chant into his very mouth, so that after several such 'treatments', it becomes part of him.
>
> (Elkin 1946)

The breath is the metonym of language, the tangible link between words and world, the sign of their material embodiment of meaning.

Often, the co-extensivity of the body with the world and the personal potency of the objects with which it is familiarly connected seem to play a greater part than language. Maurice Leenhardt, the missionary anthropologist in New Caledonia expressed his profound surprise at the assurance of his old friend and informant Boesoou that it was not the notion of the spirit, but of the body that the missionary had brought them (Clifford 1982: 172). Notions of spirit were completely compatible with the Melanesian view of the interpenetration of man and reality. The really new concept was of the body as 'set apart' from a world external to it. In such a society the symbolic power of parts of the human body such as excreta, hair, nail parings, skin, spittle, domestic utensils and a whole host of objects and artifacts, play a central role in procedures to affect or influence the individuals to whom they are connected.

This is because, although they may seem symbolic, such objects are dramatically *metonymic* in the sense that they are possessed of the essence of the individual. They are not simply the parts that 'stand for' or represent, the whole person, they *are* the whole. These non-verbal symbols appear to contradict the function of language in magical processes, but in fact they are given their potency precisely because they are employed with the accompaniment of spells and incantations, which are necessary to accord them the requisite power. Without the metaphoric power of language their potential symbolic functions remain unrealized. In being given verbal labels, the objects themselves become a form of language. The reason magicians spend so much time choosing objects and actions as surrogate words, when spoken words themselves have magical potential, is that objects become a more permanent and more manipulable *form of words*.

Leenhardt's encounter with his informant is an encounter with the distant past of European languages themselves, in which words were hieratic. The move from the oral phase, where this *is* that, to the metonymic phase where this is *put for* that, comes in the European world with Plato, when words begin to be the outward expression of an inner reality, and language a verbal imitation of something now conceived of as beyond the subject. The impact made by Greek culture on a large part of the world means that European society emerges with a view of language and mind founded on a separation of subject and object. Language never regains the sacredness of pre-Socratic times but for many centuries language still remains the province of the elect. With the invention of printing in the fifteenth century and again in the rationalist philosophy of the eighteenth century the separation of language from the world in European culture is complete. In the philosophy of the Enlightenment the subject is exposed to the impact of an objective world and, as Locke puts it, words signify nothing but the "ideas in the minds of those who use them". Printing, which inscribes speech in its most iconic form, frees language from the constraints of utterance in one sense, allowing greater narrative freedom, but at the same time restricts and concretizes the word in a way which makes the text available to all classes. The language which has ascendancy today is the language of signification, which is particularly useful, not only for describing an 'objective' universe, but for constituting that universe as itself 'objective'. Language defines what the mind 'discovers' about the reality which is 'already there'.

The objectivity of European languages, since the eighteenth century, has exerted a specifically hegemonic pressure by claiming veridical fidelity in descriptions of the world, and a special objectivity in the description of other cultures. This 'scientific' assumption that the world is 'simply there' results in the modern language of ethnography by which individuals (anthropologists) 'describe' the realities of other cultures. As Clifford Geertz has put it, we set up models of reality, structures that are held to explain all the phenomena over which we can place them, and think that we are describing what is 'factually' there.

By using a language that constitutes reality as objectively given, ethnographic texts precipitate the cultures they purport to describe; they frame and delimit them; they give the illusion of the possibility of absolute knowledge where there is no such possibility. The scientific languages are particularly dangerous in constructing universal realities and it may be that the *literary* text generated in formerly oral cultures such as those in Papua New Guinea may be a powerful way to overcome this kind of cultural incorporation. It is against this process of incorporation that the post-colonial text works to recreate reality and to recreate the discourse of literature itself.

Oyewùmí discusses the difference between Yoruba and Western languages such as English:

> The tonality of Yorùbá language predisposes one towards an apprehension of reality that cannot marginalize the auditory. Consequently, relative to Western societies, there is a stronger need for a broader contextualization in order to make sense of the world. For example Ifá divination, which is also a knowledge system in Yorùbá, has both visual and oral components. More fundamentally, the distinction between Yorùbá and the West symbolized by the focus on different senses in the apprehension of reality involves more than perception – for the Yorùbá, and indeed many other African societies, it is about 'a particular presence in the world – a world conceived of as a whole in which all things are linked together'. It concerns the many worlds human beings inhabit – it does not privilege the physical world over the metaphysical.
>
> (Oyewùmí 1997: 14)

The perception of a more inclusive approach to the senses in the oral cultures reminds us that the dominance of vision in western societies emerged at about the same time as the emergence of the demotic status of writing.

Myths of orality

In a vigorous debate conducted in the journal *Transition* in 1975, Wole Soyinka took the *bolekaja* critics, Chinweizu *et al.* to task for various misapprehensions which underlay their somewhat hysterical rejection of poetry which seemed to them to be inauthentic, not 'truly' African, including Soyinka's. His essay, rejecting the "Neo Tarzanism" of critics such as these, has become famous for its lucid presentation of the dilemma which essentialist and negritudinist critics must negotiate:

> An earlier published essay by Chinweizu ("Prodigals, Come Home", *Okike* No. 4) defines the troika's concept of the African poetic landscape with its flora and fauna – "a landscape of elephants, beggars, calabashes, serpents, pumpkins, baskets, towncriers, iron bells, slit drums, iron masks, hares, snakes, squirrels … *a landscape portrayed with native eyes to which aeroplanes naturally appear as iron birds*; a landscape in which the animals behave as they might behave in Africa of folk-lore, animals presented through *native* African eyes" (my italics) … I am not at all certain how this proves more acceptable than the traditional Hollywood image of the pop-eyed African in the jungle – 'Bwana, bwana, me see big iron bird.' My African world is a little more intricate and embraces precision machinery, oil rigs, hydro-electricity, my typewriter, railway trains (not iron snakes!), machine guns, bronze sculpture etc., plus an ontological relationship with the universe including the above listed pumpkins and iron bells.
>
> (Soyinka 1988: 293–4)

The problem Soyinka addresses reaches deep into discussions of post-colonial cultural production. But a key to this argument by Chinweizu *et al.* is the preference for the simple orality of the African oral tradition, over 'heavy', 'tongue twisting' and 'difficult to articulate' contemporary poetry. At the centre of this complaint is a myth about the oral tradition, an assumption that only the simplest and most jejune words, rhythms and sounds, what Soyinka calls "one-dimensional verses on cassava and yam" (294), characterise its traditions.

But in oral traditions we may find those characteristics often associated with written and even modernist poetic production:

> The musicality of poetic recitations of the Yoruba people, for example, is *not* the bland mono-rhythmic smoothness advocated by our critics; it is often staccato and deliberately so. Themes are abandoned, recovered, merged with a new arbitrary inclusion under the deft, inspired guidance of both reciter and accompanist. The stark linear simplicity of translations should never be permitted to obscure the allusive, the elliptical, the multi-textured fullness of what constitutes traditional poetry, especially *in recital*. And those who read the original lines in cold print do *hear* it, and the generous intricacy of rhythm and structure.
>
> (Soyinka 1988: 296)

Soyinka's argument is against the kind of nativism which simply accepts the binary between colonizer and colonized established by imperial discourse. The oral tradition is not necessarily, if ever, simplistic, 'primitive' either in content or form. The espousal of a kind of nativist simplicity in contradistinction to the 'heavy complexities' of written poetry is a recapitulation of the colonial stereotype.

Orality and the English text

The power of language to embody its referent in oral cultures has a common thematic place in much post-colonial literature and there are many descriptions of the sacred power of words. Gabriel Okara says in *The Voice*:

> Spoken words are living things like cocoa-beans packed with life. And like the cocoa-beans they grow and give life. So Okolo turned in his inside and saw that his spoken words will not die. They will enter some insides, remain there and grow like the corn blooming on the alluvial soil at the river side.
>
> (Okara 1964: 110)

Language becomes an activity with a tangible force and manifests the actual capacity of fertility and growth. The Guinean novelist Camara Laye describes his father at work as a goldsmith:

> Although my father spoke no word aloud, I know very well that he was thinking them from within. I read it from his lips, which were moving while he bent over the vessel. He kept mixing gold and coal with a wooden stick which would blaze up every now and then and constantly had to be replaced. What sort of words were those my father was silently forming? I don't know – at least I don't know exactly. Nothing was ever confided to me about that. But what could these words be but incantations?
>
> (Laye 1959: 25)

But most interestingly, beside the goldsmith, a sorcerer works, whose use of language is intimately and creatively involved in the process of the smith's work:

> Throughout the whole process his speech became more and more rapid, his rhythms more urgent, and as the ornament took shape, his panegyrics and flatteries increased in vehemence and raised my father's skill to the heavens. In a peculiar, I would say immediate and effective, way the sorcerer did in truth take part in the work. He too was drunk with the joy of creation, and loudly proclaimed his joy: enthusiastically he snatched the strings, became inflamed, as if he himself were the craftsman, as if he himself were my father, as if the ornament were coming from his own hands.
>
> (1959: 30)

A similar, though subtler, process occurs in Ngũgĩ's *A Grain Of Wheat*, when Gikonyo repairs the handle of Mumbi's panga.

> He drove the plane (he had recently bought it) against the rough surface, peeling off rolls and rolls of shavings. Gikonyo saw Mumbi's gait, her very gestures in the feel and movement of the plane. *Her voice was in the air as he bent down and traced the shape of the panga on the wood. Her breath gave him power ...* [emphasis added]

New strength entered his right hand. He brought the hammer down, up, and brought the hammer down. He felt free. Everything, Thabai, the whole world, was under the control of his hand. Suddenly the wave of power broke into an ecstasy, an exultation. Peace settled in his heart. He felt a holy calm; he was in love with all the earth.

(Ngũgĩ 1967: 71)

Even though imagined, the voice and breath of Mumbi become incorporated in the process of creation. The co-extensive reality of language and world is focused in the act of creation through which Gikonyo feels he has control of the earth itself. Even more, Gikonyo is in love with the whole earth, primarily through the reality of Mumbi's voice in the process of crafting an object which connects him to his lover. This passage goes beyond the explicit embodying power of language to show the single fabric of his reality in which the interconnection between language, creative action and the world of creation is constant.

Orality and objectivity

The English language, geared as it has become, to constituting an objective world, renders events conceived in the metaphoric world-view as 'objective' and unqualified fact. An example of this occurs in the Nigerian writer I.N.C. Aniebo's *The Journey Within*, when Ejiaka remembers the time when her sisters had confessed to being *ogbanje*. These are spirit children who come to dwell for a time in the human world in the form of successive children reborn to the same family. Thus a couple whose children are continually dying will suspect that an *ogbanje* has taken hold of their childbearing and they will attempt to expel it to the spirit world by finding the *ogbanje* symbols which the child has hidden to retain its links with the world. The most interesting aspect of Ejiaka's experience is that her sisters confessed to being *ogbanje*:

> Ejiaka had been ten years old when the younger of her two sisters revealed the secret pact they had made prior to being born into the world.
> Her sisters had been ill for days with acute malaria when the elder confessed they were *ogbanjes* loath to leave the world because they had not known it would be so good. Under her direction the family hearth, the vegetable farm, the roots of the tallest coconut tree and the oldest iroko tree, were frantically dug up. But their symbols were not found.

(Aniebo 1978: 219)

Eventually an *ogbanje* hunter is called in, who discovers the symbols, removes them and enables the girls to live normal lives thereafter. Western readers might be surprised by the total lack of irony or scepticism with which these events are recorded. There is no allusion to the psychological processes that might lead the sisters to make such a confession, no indication that Ejiaka's memory has embellished the events, no indication that these events are somehow metaphoric of a particular cultural reality. The occasion is concrete. It simply *is*. This is a strikingly clear example of how a different 'way of seeing' can be incorporated into the English text without making any concessions at all to the expectations of the contemporary reader. In this way both cultural difference and the perception of the nature of that difference can exist side by side in the text.

Orality and naming

The embodying power of language is particularly true for names, which in oral cultures substantiate the objects or persons they name. To know the name of a being or thing is to have some degree of control over it. On the other hand naming also incarnates the being and can be particularly dangerous when speaking of the dead since naming the person would summon the departed spirit, with possible fearful consequences. Ngũgĩ describes this power in the name through the refusal of the Gikuyu to speak the name of a greatly feared District Officer: "They spoke of him with awe, called him Tom or simply 'he' as if the mention of his full name would conjure him up in their presence" (Ngũgĩ 1967: 211).

The absence of a name for a major character is therefore of obvious significance. In Ayi Kwei Armah's *The Beautyful Ones Are Not Yet Born* the protagonist is referred to simply as 'the man', signifying his feeling of ephemerality in a world where corruption and venality is the norm, where shady dealing is the 'national sport' and where to feel that bribery is somehow wrong is to alienate oneself from family, friends and loved ones. He finds it

> more and more difficult to justify his own honesty. How could he, when all around him the whole world never tired of saying there were only two types of men who took refuge in honesty – the cowards and the fools? Very often these days he was burdened with the hopeless, impotent feeling that he was not just one of these, but a helpless combination of the two.
>
> (Armah 1968: 59)

The man's namelessness is a sign of his nothingness in the sight of the world around him. Because he cuts himself off from the aimlessness, decay and corruption of the world, he denies himself a name in that world. Namelessness signifies the profoundest state of alienation. Not only cut off from the society around him, he is cut off from his own history and any sense of moral focus by which to give his own feelings of right and wrong some reference point. The result is a feeling that he is not only nameless but has *no being*.

In Aniebo's *The Journey Within*, when Ejiaka is praised effusively by a strange old lady who comes to her door, she lies to protect her name, and hence, herself:

'What is your name?'

'Mary', Ejiaka lied. The profuse prayer had put her on her guard.

'Mary? You are a Christian?'

'No. Are Christians the only ones that answer Mary?'

'Don't you know? Mary is the mother of the Christian god.'

'My husband gave me the name. I did not know it had any meaning or that it is that of the mother of the Christian god.'

'It is good that you are not a Christian because I would not have told you what I am going to tell you now. I am Nwaigwe of Agbenu. I am one who sees … '

(Aniebo 1978: 214)

Names are extremely important in this novel and Ejiaka's spontaneous decision to name herself 'Mary', the most 'Christian' of names, is deeply ironic because it is the old woman's links with traditional soothsaying which are to be of benefit to Ejiaka and which point out the wisdom of Ejiaka's refusal to adopt 'alien' Christianity. Ejiaka's continued links with traditional life are that which motivates her to protect her name in the first place. The fact that people *are* their names means that in Aniebo's novel the naming of characters seems somewhat heavy handed.

But the names embody the thematic point of the story; the comparative evaluation of traditional and western or 'Christian' life and values. There is 'Ejiaka', who maintains her traditional lifestyle, 'Nelson', her husband, who is traditional but who succumbs to the rise in social status and job prospects which church membership entails, 'Christian' the "black man whose roots were no longer in the soil" and 'Janet', his wife, whose children all die (presumably because her sincere Christian beliefs have severed the links with the soil and with tradition which would nourish them). The process of naming is the most potent realization of the power of language in much African literature. In the 'metaphoric' culture, the individual is the name. Language is not separated from the 'objective' world, nor is the world caused by language. Language is the world.

This process of naming takes on a particular importance in modern works. In Papua New Guinean writer Nora Vagi Brasch's *Which Way Big Man*, the satirical naming of the characters: Gou Haia (Go higher), Sinob Haia, Chuck Braggin-Crowe, Professor Noual, might seem a fairly obvious device to the English reader. But the names have an important metonymic force that is not unrelated to the function of names in oral society. The characters not only represent aspects of the social deterioration of modern capitalist society, but in a curious way they embody them.

Naming is particularly important in all post-colonial societies because the names of beings and objects are the particular signs of the cultural space within which things have their being. It is therefore central to the process of colonization, as names that are more or less inappropriate are called into the service of the language's reconstitution of the alien cultural reality. These terms may have nothing to do with the 'experience' of a colonized people because they are so different from the ways in which the world is habitually described by that people (not because the uniqueness of the experience is somehow essentially constitutive of the language). In Australia's case the invaded language was that of the Australian Aborigines. But longer association with the environment by the European inhabitants led to a variant of English that also tended to reveal the inappropriateness of the original English names. The terms of an invading language are tools chosen for their suitability to a different kind of environment and need to be superseded and modified to become culturally 'appropriate'.

The power of colonial naming and mapping to control space is preceded by the power of names in indigenous cultures. Naming predicates an assumption of ownership and for this reason language assumes great importance in the establishment of colonial place. Very often these names referred to a far away metropolitan centre rather than to the experienced place. But the appropriateness or inappropriateness of language, particularly of names, is not a function of some inherent fidelity between the object and the word, but a function of the appropriateness of the normal use of the word to a different environment. The process of using English in a location other than its cultural home, is a use (at least in the beginning) that is in some sense metonymic, since the word is used to stand for objects and experiences that may not correspond to their normal usage. In this sense the words are representatives of the location of their normal use, and they act to appropriate perceived experience to the situation of this use. The post-colonial text, negotiating as it does the space between the textual language and the lived space, becomes a continual process of reclamation, as a cultural reality is not so much posited as reclaimed from the appropriating dominance of English.

Using English

While the sacred power of language assumes the status of a theme in much African, Pacific and indigenous literature the interesting question remains as to what extent this concrete property in the mother tongue intervenes in the use of English. Even at the superficial level a different resonance in the language can be discerned in those literatures in English that draw their energies from a first language of an oral culture. To students of literature the effect is of a controlled economy of diction that often appears overly simple at first reading. Rather than a matter of overt technique, however, the English of the text appears to ascribe more metaphoric resonance to the words themselves, more 'embodiment' of their subject than might immediately appear in the western novel.

Another effect on English writing is the influence of orality on the rhythms of the written language, as may be seen in a passage from Achebe in which he describes the reactions of parents to a child who exhibits characteristics of a previous child who had died:

> Edogo's mind was in pain over the child. Some people were already saying that perhaps he was none other than the first one. But Edogo and Amoge

never talked about it; the woman especially was afraid. Since utterance has the power to change fear into living truth they dared not speak before they had to.

(Achebe 1964: 12)

This passage is particularly interesting because not only does it use the rhythms of the Igbo language, it demonstrates the text in the process of negotiating the conceptual gulf between the Igbo sense of the power of language where "utterance has the power to change fear into living truth", and the English text in which this is conveyed, where words are representations. The language of the novel, with its adapted African rhythms, becomes metonymic of the culture it is describing. It stands for the difference of Igbo culture without actually circumscribing it, and becomes a sign standing for experiences that are ultimately incommunicable. Language operating in this way achieves something a simple translation could never achieve.

Consequently, we find a language that lays stress on metrical regularity and tonal cadence. The character's "mind was in pain", the metre smoothed out by the 'n' sound and carried into the next sentence. Instead of "perhaps he was the same", we find the more formal and attenuated "perhaps he was none other than the first one", in which the 'n' sound again carries the rhythms generated in the first sentence. The Igbo language has an eight-vowel system in which harmony is essential and this harmony is reflected in the harmony of the English consonants. This, allied to the African 'mode', which uses both proverbs and what we might call a 'proverbial diction', produces a text with a distinctive character.

Language operating in this way achieves something a simple translation could never achieve: it foregrounds the various forms of language use in the text and constructs difference in two ways. On the one hand the linguistic features simultaneously install and bridge a cultural gap between African subject and English-speaking reader by replicating the rhythms of oral language in literary English. On the other, the reader, simply by opening the 'African novel', makes an unspoken commitment to accept this formal, highly structured, metrically measured and tonally smooth writing as African English. This dialectic is the essential feature of the literature of linguistic intersection.

Meaning and the text

One salient question raised by the operation of literary writing in oral cultures is the nature of meaning itself. Okara coins an apt image of futility when he says of his hero Okolo: "Nobody sees what he sees. His talking seems to him like throwing words away like one throws money into the river" (1964: 51). Words are much more potent than money however, even if just as concrete:

> Money may be lost forever but words, teaching words, are the same in any age. Some of these teaching words are as true today as they were centuries

ago. They may be given different meaning to suit the new times but the root is the same.

(Okara 1964: 52)

We might say that people interpret things differently, but to Okolo, the meaning and the potent concrete reality of the words are different things.

Although words have a tangible ontological authenticity, a *presence*, their meaning is still a function of use in context, that is, words still function in a text in the same way whatever their cultural provenance. Although words are their referents, so to speak – concrete embodiments – they can still be used in different ways. This is the clear implication of Okolo's thought that teaching words "may be given different meaning to suit the new times". The words have a powerful concrete presence, but they can be used in different ways to obtain new meanings as is demonstrated by Okara's use of the word 'insides'. Their sacred embodying power simply means that they are much more potent when they are used and must be couched in a cushioning and sometimes elliptical 'proverbial' mode (characteristic of African speech in particular).

The following sentences from *The Voice* occur at the beginning of the novel: "Okolo had no chest, they said. His chest was not strong and he had no shadow" (23). To the western reader this seems clearly metaphoric, but it is less clear exactly what the tenor of the metaphor might be. The meaning must be determined from the place of the sentence in the opening paragraphs:

> Some of the townsmen said Okolo's eyes were not right, his head was not correct. This they said was the result of his knowing too much book, walking too much in the bush, and others said it was due to his staying too long alone by the river.
>
> So the town of Amatu talked and whispered; so the world talked and whispered. Okolo had no chest, they said. His chest was not strong and he had no shadow. Everything in this world that spoiled a man's name they said of him, all because he dared to search for *it*. He was in search of *it* with all his inside and with all his shadow.
>
> (23)

Now we see that Okolo is 'other-worldly', detached, vague, and disengaged from the manly and respectable pursuits expected of him. "Knowing too much book" conveys an element of treachery in his forsaking an oral past for the 'book', the sign of a modern and specifically English culture.

Words may function in discourse in different ways. But beyond and behind these differences meaning depends upon the situation in discourse. The power of some languages to so erase the gap between the tenor and vehicle of a metaphor that the object and word become ontologically conflated, does not alter the actual process of meaning itself. The word, which, in English, is 'simply' a word, until it is employed in certain specified ways in discourse, may be a much more complex and potent vehicle in an oral language, but it cannot *mean* until it also is employed in the language in some way.

Orality and imagery

The development of Western science and epistemology in the Newtonian world, where the cosmos is taken to be something essentially seen, establishes visual perception itself as the analogue of knowledge. Walter Ong (1982: 125) claims that if we assume that everything in cognition hangs on vision, nothing works, for though vision may be the *sensus maxime cognoscitivus* (the primary cognitive sense) under one aspect, under another and more profound aspect understanding is allied with the word and the world of sound, which is the sensory habitat of the word. Ong's argument is for the spoken word as a primordial figure of understanding, a foundation for knowing, characteristic of oral cultures. While Ong and his followers never properly recognize the need to defend the universal assumptions of his theory of orality, and, as a result has been criticised for washing out cultural difference (see Schmidt 1985) his theory has an historical importance in reinstating orature over literature.

One argument of his theory is that using visual perception as the prime analogue of knowledge robs the process of its temporal element, and, as a related consequence, obliterates the subject. In oral cultures the subject is installed in equal prominence with the object. Oral narrative belongs to no one individual yet each telling is uniquely the orator's own, and in a special sense the object has no sensory existence until brought into being by a subject. Above all, the diachronic element of understanding retains its primary importance in a culture where the 'known' unfolds orally. The voicing of the word emphasizes the temporal nature of understanding, oratures do not limit consciousness to the aural. On the contrary, when oral cultures engage the written word in English, the full sensory range of the processes of consciousness are allowed play and result in an imagery which completely overturns the western adherence to the visual.

An excellent example of this occurs in *The Beautyful Ones Are Not Yet Born*, in which Armah uses the full range of sensory images to convey metaphors of the corruption and decay of Ghanaian society at the time, when the official propaganda for self-sacrifice on behalf of the nation masked the actual venality and greed of individuals. The state of things is starkly symbolised in the fate of a friend of the protagonist's, who, in a vain search for purity tries all manner of mystical paths, but dies, and is found to be eaten away by worms. "And so," says the man, "what did this dead rot inside his friend not have to do with his fear of what was decaying outside of himself?" (1968: 56).

A bus journey taken by the unnamed protagonist is described in the following long passage, demonstrating the commitment to the non-visual in Armah's depiction of the corruption around him, the way this depiction works metaphorically, and how it relies on the *movement* of knowledge.

> In one or two places the eye that chooses to remain open can see the weird patterns made by thrown wrecks of upended bicycles and a prewar roller. Sounds arise and kill all smells as the bus pulls into the dormitory town. Past the big public lavatory the stench claws inward to the throat.

Sometimes it is understandable that people spit so much, when all around decaying things push inward and mix all the body's juices with the taste of rot. Sometimes it is understandable, the doomed attempt to purify the self by adding to the disease outside. Hot smell of caked shit split by afternoon's baking sun, now touched by still evaporating dew. The nostrils, incredibly, are joined in a way that is most horrifyingly direct to the throat itself and to the entrails right through to their end. Across the aisle on the seat opposite, an old man is sleeping and his mouth is open to the air rushing in the night with how many particles of what? So why should he play the fool and hold his breath? Sounds of moist fish frying in open pans of dark perennial oil so close to the public lavatory. It is very easy to get used to what is terrible. A different thing; the public bath, made for a purification that is not so offensive. Here there is only the stale rotten soap suds merging in grainy rotten dirt from everybody's scum, a reminder of armpits full of yellowed hair dripping sweat down arms raised casually in places of public intimacy.

(Armah 1968: 46–8)

The retreat from vision accentuates the temporal nature of understanding. By using the descriptive vehicle of the bus ride the essentially oral culture in which the experience is grounded maximizes certain functional effects on the range and intensity of the imagery. The man retreats from the visual by simply laying his head back and closing his eyes. The first sense is one of touch as "the air that rushes in comes like a soft wave of lukewarm water". It is possible to know where one is "because the air brings these places to the open nose". Knowledge is immediately released from vision though the writing echoes the visual in its similes of knowledge: "smells hit the senses like a strong wall". The senses are involved in the progressive and temporal movement of experiences when one sense takes over from another: "Sounds arise and kill all smells as the bus pulls into the dormitory town"; smell moves to taste: "Past the big public lavatory the stench claws inward to the throat". Conversely, the movement of senses, which connect the outside to the inner man (a physical association which represents the spiritual) is reversed in the bodily functions through which the inner man adds to the ordure: "decaying things push inward and mix all the body's juices with the taste of rot. Sometimes it is understandable, the doomed attempt to purify the self by adding to the disease outside. Hot smell of caked shit split by afternoon's baking sun". Man is thus involved in a cycle of filth, disease and decay from which there is apparently no escape.

Armah's world is profoundly dystopian because neither the body nor the natural world provides a focus against which the corruption of the post-war, postcolonial Ghanaian society can be judged. Pervasive decay characterizes the everyday stench of the town arranged around its central rubbish dump. The body's natural functions produce the matter that becomes a metaphor for the inner life of individuals. Excreta and detritus are the people who exude them, and these contribute to an outer life overwhelmed by corruption. The images of decay and filth are a peculiar trope, neither fully metonymic, since the images are such obvious signs of the corruption in the society, nor fully metaphoric, since they are the extensions of the individuals themselves, a kind of existential property which signifies both the inner and outer life. The smells and tastes have their visual correlates, but these are unnecessary to the experiences, which, in themselves, affirm the place of the subject in the world. "The nostrils, incredibly, are joined in a way that is most horrifyingly direct to the throat itself and to the entrails right through to their end," says the man. Where the visual may seem to propose the separation of subject and object, the 'fuller' sensation of experience through smell, touch and taste connect the subject to the world, and particularly to the continual process of consumption and evacuation which links man's inner life to the filth around him. The contention here is admittedly conjectural, but it seems that an oral background sensitizes the writer to the full range of imagery because there is a far stronger relationship between language and the senses. The passage above is only one example and instances of the extensive use of sensual imagery in western literature are multifarious, but in general this capacity for evoking an imagery that explores the full range of sense experience is less well developed in visual, literate cultures where the visual sense predominates.

The music of writing

One obvious way in which the oral transforms the written text is through the sound and rhythm of the language in the writing. The rhythm of the proverb-laden language of African writing, particularly Igbo, can be seen in some of the passages above. In dialogue we find an even more pronounced entry of the voice into the writing. But sometimes the sound of the language captures the writing so comprehensively that it defies reading, and must be heard. Interestingly, this is particularly the case with poetry and prose from the creole continuum of the Caribbean. James Berry's Caribbean Proverb Poems are a case in point.

Caribbean Proverb Poems

Dog morning prayer is, Laard
wha teday, a bone or a blow

Tiger wahn fi nyam pickney, tiger sey
he could-a swear he woz puss
If yew cahn mek plenty yeyewater
fi funeral, start early morning

(Donnell and Welsh 1996: 383)

There are at least two major strategies at work here. The first is one we will discuss further in Chapter 9 – the inclusion of untranslated words, in this case ones that need a glossary: 'nyam' means 'eat', 'pickney' means 'child' and 'yeye' means 'eye'. The use of these words creates a distance from the reader of the English text that installs cultural difference. The 'different' words become metonymic of that difference. But the other feature of the poem is that it virtually drags the written word into the zone of the oral. This is a poem that needs to be *heard*. A prosaic translation would be:

> A dog's morning prayer is 'Lord what will it be today, a bone or a blow?'
> 'If Tiger wants to eat a child he says he could have sworn it was a cat.'
> If you can't cry plenty of tears at a funeral, start early in the morning.

This translation might capture the proverbial sense of the lines but obviously much is lost in the sound, which gives the *feel* of the creole culture, and the sense of insouciance that gives the proverbs their particular character. Significantly, this strategy is more prevalent in Caribbean Creole, a language that is inflected with the orality of its development but doesn't arise from an oral culture as such, but is rather a cultural continuum that includes literary language at some point.

Lines such as Berry's wrestle with the written text in a struggle that leaves the uncommitted reader stranded. But the sound of the language can still impress itself as needing to be heard without creating quite so much distance. In Linton Kwesi Johnson's "Street 66", a poem that impresses its orality, emerging as it does from the creole continuum:

> de room woz dark-dusk howlin softly
> six-a-clack,
> charcoal lite defyin site woz
> movin black;
> de soun woz muzik mellow steady flow,
> an man-son mind jus mystic red,
> green, red, green … pure scene.
>
> no man would dance but leap an shake
> dat shock thru feelin ripe;
> shape dat soun tumblin doun
> makin movement ruff enough;
> cause when de muzik met I taps,
> I felt de sting, knew de shock,
> yea had to do an ride de rock.

The third stanza launches into the music of the vernacular voice:

> outta dis rock
> shall come
> a greena riddim
> even more dread
> dan what
> de breeze of glory bread.
> vibratin violence
> is how wi move

rockin wid green riddim
de drout
an dry root out

(Donnell and Welsh 1996: 374)

The language of the poem appropriates the writing for its own purposes, not just transforming the written form but adapting it to a voice whose very presence in writing creates the sense of cultural difference within the shared language. In this way the oral doesn't just enter the text but wrestles it to the ground.

The oral flavour of Caribbean creole seems particularly suited to the musical modality of poetry and the music often comes with a sense of mischief as in Valerie Bloom's poem "Language Barrier":

Jamaica language sweet yuh know bwoy,
An yuh know mi nebba notice i',
Till tarra day one foreign frien'
Come spen some time wid mi.

An den im call mi attention to
Some tings im sey soun' queer,
Like de way wi always sey 'koo yah'
When we really mean 'look here'.

(Thieme 1996: 580)

But the musical quality is not limited to Caribbean poems. In Nissim Ezekiel's "Very Indian Poems in Indian English", a mild parody of Indian English actually comes in lines whose oral quality is compelling.

Some people are not having manners
this I am always observing,
For example the other day I find
I am needing soap

For ordinary washing myself purposes
So I'm going to one small shop
Nearby in my lane and I'm asking
For well known brand of soap

(Ezekiel 1989: 268)

The affectionate representation of Indian English, which Ezekiel makes no attempt to hide, produces a poem that is musical rather than mocking, humorous rather than satirical. This is because the *sound* of the lines is appealing.

The observation of the passage from an oral language to writing prepares us for the discussion of literary language in the following chapters. First, writing is not an artifact presented to the reader as a 'work', but a dialogue in which writer and reader participate as 'dialogically' as they do in conversation. Second, language variance in the 'demotic' English text, does not transport the writer's culture metaphorically into the text, but operates as a metonym of difference. In this metonymic function lies the secret of how post-colonial writers can produce a text in English that is true to the cultural identity from which they write. As we have seen many times, cultural meaning is not embodied in language, either in the mother tongue or the adopted English. But by strategies of language variance the difference of the originating culture is inscribed metonymically in the putatively shared language. While writing might be accused of 'colonizing' the voice, the oral returns to usurp literature in the post-colonial text. Post-colonial literatures thus become a form of decolonizing transformation.

8   How books talk

When Caliban enters the world of Prospero's language, when he comes to write his own books and appropriate the power they embody, how will those books talk? To answer this we must first ask how Caliban is to arrive at meaning in Prospero's language, how he will use writing. But how does writing communicate? How can Caliban produce his own books, his own source of magic power? The answer to this lies at the heart of the practice of writing: Caliban uses writing, as all writers do, by entering into dialogue. The written text is a social situation. That is to say, it has its existence in something more than the marks on the page, namely, the participations of social beings whom we call writers and readers, and who constitute the writing as communication of a particular kind, as 'saying' a certain thing. When these participants exist in different cultures, as they do in post-colonial writing, two issues quickly come to the forefront: can writing in one language convey the reality of a different culture? Or, conversely, is writing linguistically bound to a particular culture? One of the most persistent misconceptions about this activity is that the meaning of writing is an *a priori* to be uncovered; existing either as a function of the language, or the inscription of something in the mind of the writer, or the reconstruction of the reader's experience. Indeed, the very term 'meaning' tends to infer some objective content which is the end point of reading. This problem in metaphysics is itself a problem of language.

The 'objective' meanings of writing come about through a process of 'social' accomplishment between the writing and reading participants. This is because meaning is a social fact which comes to being within the discourse of a culture, and social facts as well as social structures are themselves social accomplishments. If we focus the 'meaning event' within the usage of social actors who present themselves to each other as functions in the text, and see that cultural 'distance' is privileged at the site of this usage, it resolves the conflict between language, reader and writer over the 'ownership' of meaning. The social accomplishment of textual meaning occurs despite the cultural distance between writer and reader. This contention engages, head-on, the fact that people in different cultures may well live in totally different, and even incommensurable worlds: different worlds of experience, expectation, habit, understanding, tradition. The constitutive theory of meaning does not underestimate this. Rather it assesses how meaning can nevertheless be accomplished between writing and reading participants.

Clearly the notion of the text as dialectical, even dialogical, accomplishment requires some clarification since our assumption of the 'givenness' of texts (and hence, very often, the fixity of their meaning) is supported at the very least by their physical tangibility. To the question, "How do you mean?", we could say that the *meaning* of a word is *meant* by the person who utters it and is *taken to mean* something by the person who hears it. Often it seems that the history of European literary theory has been an arena in which all of these participants – the language, the speaker or writer, and the hearer or reader – have been locked in a gladiatorial contest over the ownership of meaning. But on closer examination we can see that all three 'functions' of this exchange participate in the 'social' situation of the written text. The constant insistence of that discourse which operates through hybridity and marginality is that writing is a social practice.

Meaning is a social accomplishment involving the participation of the writer and reader functions within the 'event' of the particular discourse, hence we may refer to the achievement of meaning as a 'situated accomplishment'. It is easy to see the understanding reached in conversation as a 'situated accomplishment' for the face-to-face interaction enables a virtually limitless adjustment to the flow of talk. A conversation has a life of its own beyond the intentions of the conversants. The central feature of such activity is *presence*, the speaker and hearer communicating by being 'present' to each other. Yet if we think about it, even in the most empathetic exchange the speaker and hearer are never fully present to one another. The experience of one conversant can never *become* the experience of the other, and in this sense, what we call the 'mind' is a retrospective and largely hypothetical construct which we infer from what is 'revealed' in language. So the psychological 'distance' which might seem to characterize interlocutors from different cultures can be seen to be a feature of all communication. The experience aroused by a word, the associations it evokes, may be very different in people *within* a culture – the experiences aroused in men and women by particular words, for instance – but this does not prevent meaning occurring. Meaning and understanding of meaning can occur because the language encodes the reciprocity of the experiences of each conversant. It is the situation, the *'event'* of this reciprocal happening which 'tells', which 'refers', which 'informs'.

The example of conversation alerts us to the extent and the limitation of the structuring activities of individuals in any social situation. Speakers are not totally free agents, for that would be to deny the effects of society, culture, and history upon them and the situation in which they are acting. But neither are they purely cyphers for broader social forces. The situation, with all its attendant antecedents operates in conjunction with, rather than *upon*, the participating individuals. And though these individuals can direct or unleash the potentialities of the antecedents affecting the situation, they cannot change them. The apparently simple example of a casual conversation clearly demonstrates the complex array of structuring participations in the social event. But it is the 'event', the *situation* of its structure and structuring participations, rather than the contingent intentions or psychological states of speakers, which imparts a direction and a meaning to the conversation. The situation of textual meaning occurs, we might say, within the 'third space of enunciation', although this is appropriating Bhabha's term for a slightly different purpose.

The discursive 'event', the site of the 'communication', therefore becomes of paramount importance in post-colonial literatures because the 'participants' are potentially so very 'absent' (both culturally and psychologically). Indeed, unlike spoken discourse, the central problematic of studies of writing is *absence*. It is not so easy to see the *written* meaning as the situated accomplishment of participants because the message 'event' occupies the apparent social fissure between the acts of writing and reading, the discursive space in which writer and reader as social actors never meet. Whether the writing is a newspaper article, instructions for the assembly of a model aeroplane, or a philosophical treatise, the writer and reader have access to each other only through the mutual construction of the text within certain linguistic and generic parameters. That distance between minds which seems to be compensated for in the spoken conversation by the situation of the dialogue, appears to elude writing.

How meaning is constructed in the writing by its absentee users becomes a critical question, and is made much more prominent by post-colonial writing, in which writer and reader might have ranges of experience and presuppositions which may not be expected to overlap greatly, if at all. Post-colonial literatures bring an additional perspective to this discussion by accentuating this phenomenon of *distance*: they present us with writers and readers far more 'absent' from each other than they would be if located in the same culture; they present a situation which in some cases (because literary writing is so alien to some cultures) provides a totally ambivalent site for communication. One qualification to this may be that sharing an imperial system of education and cultural patronage, with similar curricula, readers, and other cultural 'guides' used throughout Britain's empire, considerably ameliorates this distancing within the post-colonial world. But even in the monoglossic settler cultures the sub-cultural distancing which generates the evolution of variant language shows that the linguistic cultures encompassed by the term 'English' are vastly heterogeneous.

The face-to-face situation of spoken discourse is replaced by the distancing of the writing system, a distance which frees the meaning from the constraints of speech and creates a vehicle which at once confirms and bridges the absence of writers and readers. As writing, the message event is not merely a different physical mode, but a different ontological event.

> Inscription alone … has the power to arouse speech from its slumber as sign. By enregistering speech, inscription has as its essential objective … the emancipation of meaning … from the natural predicament in which everything refers to the disposition of a contingent situation. This is why writing will never be simple 'voice painting' (Voltaire). It creates meaning by enregistering it, by entrusting it to an engraving, a groove, a relief, to a surface whose essential characteristic is to be infinitely transmissable.
>
> (Derrida 1978: 12)

By freeing language from the contingent situation, writing, paradoxically, gives language its greatest permanence, whilst, at the same time, giving meaning its greatest volatility because it opens up wider horizons of meaning. Writing does not merely inscribe the spoken message or represent the message event, it *becomes* the new event. Nor is it merely the inscription of thought without the medium of speech, for such thought is only accessible as a putative associate of the event. Post-colonial literatures reveal this most clearly when their appropriation of English, far from inscribing either vernacular or 'standard' forms, create a new discourse at their interface. Post-colonial writing *represents* neither speech nor local reality but constructs a discourse which may intimate them. This distinction ought to be made as clearly as possible. While writing is a new ontological event it does not cut itself off from the voice. The inscription of the vernacular modality of local speech is one of the strategies by which a 'marginal' linguistic culture appropriates the imported language to its own conceptions of society and place. This discourse also questions the Derridian conclusion that writing is infinitely transmissible and hence infinitely interpretable. Infinite transmissibility assumes a totally homogeneous world. It elides the political and cultural limits of interpretation and subsumes all writing into a universalist paradigm which is essentially that of the metropolitan centre.

This concurs with Said's view of the worldliness of texts. The key challenge for Said is to negotiate between two attitudes to the text that in different ways misrepresent how texts have a being in the world. On the one hand the classical realist position sees the text as simply referring to the world 'out there'. Such a view fails to take into account the ways in which language mediates and determines what is seen in the world. On the other hand a structuralist position sees the world as having no absolute existence at all but as being entirely constructed by the text. This view would not allow for any non-textual experience of the world, nor, potentially, for any world outside the text. Said negotiates these extremes by claiming that the text (and by this we can mean speech, pictures and all other forms of texts) is important in negotiating our experience of the world, but the worldliness and circumstantiality of the text, "the text's status as an event having sensuous particularity as well as historical contingency, are considered as being incorporated in the text, an infrangible part of its capacity for conveying and producing meaning" (Said 1983: 39). This means that the text is crucial in the way we 'have' a world, but the world does exist, and that worldliness is constructed within the text. The text has a specific situation which places restraints upon an interpreter, "not because the situation is hidden within the text as a mystery but because the situation exists at the same level of surface particularity as the textual object itself" (1983: 39). The text does not exist outside the world, as is the implication in both the realist and structuralist positions, but is a part of the world of which it speaks, and this worldliness is itself present in the text as a part of its formation.

Texts are in the world, they have various kinds of affiliation with the world, and one of their functions as texts is to solicit the world's attention, which they do in a number of ways. Many texts incorporate the explicit circumstances of their concretely imagined situation. In writers such as Gerard Manley Hopkins, Joseph

Conrad and Oscar Wilde, the "designed interplay between speech and reception, between verbality and textuality, *is* the text's situation, its placing of itself in the world" (Said 1983: 40). But it is in the example of post-colonial texts that the worldliness of the text itself becomes most urgent and most explicit. Through metonymic processes which we shall examine below, post-colonial texts insist their worldliness.

However, such worldliness is extremely contentious for much contemporary theory. In fact, this problem begins with structuralist linguistics which tends to reify the linguistic code. In Saussure's distinction between *langue* and *parole, langue* is the code or set of codes on the basis of which a speaker produces *parole*, a particular message (Saussure 1916). While *langue*, the description of the synchronic systems of language, is the object of a linguistics, the *parole*, the language in use, the intentional message, focuses a study of language on its actual operation. Now *parole* is precisely what Saussure's *Course in General Linguistics* (1916) is *not* about, and ever since its publication, linguistics, the handmaiden of structuralism, has bracketed the message in order to concentrate on the code, in which it is primarily interested.

A post-colonial approach to linguistics however, like the theory of the creole continuum, redresses this imbalance by focusing on the message, reinstating the *parole* as the operation of the code in social life. This has the consequence of re-establishing the 'margins' of language as the substance of theory. Language has its only practical existence in the *parole* within which the usage of members, rather than a linguistic structure, determines meanings. This becomes particularly true of English in which the notion of a standard 'code' is dismantled by the continuum of practices by which the language is constituted.

This constitutive approach radically modifies the most fundamental tenets of Saussurian theory, namely:

(a) That in a semiotic system there are *differences* but no substantial existence. No entity belonging to the structure of the system has a meaning of its own; the meaning of a word, for example, results from the opposition to the other lexical units of the same system.

(b) That all systems are closed, without relation to external, non-semiotic reality.

(Saussure 1916: 71–140)

While it is certainly true that meaning is not necessarily determined by the external relation of a sign and a thing, meaning *is* determined within the *message* rather than in the abstract system of language. Consequently, the message event marks the terrain of meaning for the written work, for only the message event gives currency to language within the relations of social beings. Neither the mental lives of speakers and writers, nor the objects of their talk can usurp this fundamental concern.

The recognition of the importance of the message event reassesses traditional approaches to meaning such as those in speech act theory (Austin 1962). While we can inscribe the propositional content of a speech act we cannot, for instance, inscribe its illocutionary force. Such force is carried in the situation of the message. The illocutionary and perlocutionary force of the sign THIS WAY → are embodied entirely in its character as sign and the social conventions surrounding its role. Similar conventions surround and determine the forms of different kinds of writing, particularly those we call 'literary'. The illocutionary force of these texts similarly cannot be *conveyed* by means of grammar, italics, punctuation, but rather actualized constitutively in the conventional practice – the situation – of the reading. The writing 'event' thus becomes the centre of the accomplishment of meaning, for it is here that the system, the social world of its users and the absent 'participants' themselves, intersect.

We can see how important the message event becomes in cross-cultural literatures. Nothing better describes to us the distance traversed in the social engagement which occurs when authors write and readers read. But it is clear that the distances *are* traversed. Writing comes into being at the intersection of the sites of production and consumption. Although the 'social relationship' of the two absent subjects is actually a function of their access to the 'situation' of the writing, it is in this threefold interaction of situation, author function, and reader function that meaning is accomplished. If meaning is locked into any one of these factors; if it is controlled by either the sender, the receiver, or the medium itself, then language becomes untransformable.

Language

We may now examine more closely the contending claims in the struggle for the dominance of meaning. The first of these is language which is commonly held to embody or contain meaning either by direct representation or in a more subtle way by determining the perception of the world. Language which exists in the complex, hybrid and constantly changing environment of post-colonial interchange inevitably rejects the assumption of a linguistic structure or code which can be characterized by the colonial distinction of 'standard' and 'variant'. All language is 'marginal', all language emerges out of conflict and struggle. The post-colonial text brings language and meaning to a discursive site in which they are mutually constituted, and at this site the importance of usage is inescapable.

Although the view is rarely expressed by anyone conversant with languages in different cultures that language 'represents' or 'reflects' an autonomous reality, it is probably the most ubiquitous Western assumption about the operation of language because our sense of how words mean operates within a discourse in which the world (the object) is irremediably separated from the speaker (the subject). The Cartesian separation of subject and object, the separation of the consciousness from the world of which it is conscious, is the schema which still underlies the modern Western episteme with its passion for 'scientific' objectivity and its tendency to see the world as a continuum of technological data. Such a view is possibly the most crucial factor separating Western society from those societies in which much (though not all) post-colonial literature is generated. The view of language which this schema installs is best represented by the theories of 'reference' which dominated Anglo-empiricism in the earlier part of this century, but which still hold sway in most empirical philosophies. According to this view words have referents in the real world, and what a word refers to is, for all intents and purposes, what it means.

But words are never so simply referential in the actual dynamic habits of a speaking community. Even the most simple words like 'hot', 'big', 'man', 'got', 'ball', 'bat', have a number of meanings, depending on how they are used. Indeed, these uses are the ways (and therefore what) the word means in certain circumstances. A word such as 'bat' can operate as a noun with several referents, a verb describing several kinds of actions and probably several other ways as well. Many other words, such as 'bush' (which has hundreds of meanings in post-colonial societies), reveal that the meaning of words is also inextricably tied to the discourse of place. Post-colonial literature has continually shown both the importance of this discourse and the inescapable linking of meaning to the usage within the event.

Language cannot, therefore, be said to perform its meaning function by reflecting or referring to the world in a essential or immutable way, and thus meanings cannot remain exclusively accessible to those speakers who 'experience their referents', so to speak. We have looked at this in relation to polydialectical writing in Chapter 6. The central feature of the ways in which words mean things in spoken or written discourse is the situation of the word. In general, one may see how the word is meant by the way it functions in the sentence, but the meaning of a word may require considerably more than a sentence for it to be adequately situated. The question remains whether it is the responsibility of the author in the cross-cultural text to employ techniques which more promptly 'situate' the word or phrase for the reader. While post-colonial writing has led to a profusion of technical innovation which exists to span the purported gap between writer and prospective reader, the process of reading itself is a continual process of contextualisation and adjustment directly linked to the constitutive relations within the discursive event.

An alternative, determinist view which proposes that language actually constructs that which is perceived and experienced by speakers is less problematic for post-colonial literature. Edward Sapir proposed what was at the time an exciting and revolutionary view that what we call the 'real' world is built up by the language habits of a group, and that the worlds in which different societies live are quite distinct, not merely the same world with different labels attached (Mandelbaum 1949: 162). The central idea of Whorf and Sapir's thesis is well known. It proposes that language functions not simply as a device for reporting experience, but also, and more significantly, as a way of defining experience for its speakers.

> [T]he linguistic system (in other words, the grammar) of each language is not merely a reproducing instrument for voicing ideas but rather is itself the shaper of ideas, the program and guide for the individual's mental

activity, for his analysis of impressions, for his synthesis of his mental stock in trade ... We dissect nature along the line laid down for us by our native languages. The categories and types that we isolate from the world of phenomena we do not find there because they stare every observer in the face; on the contrary, the world is presented in a kaleidoscopic flux of impressions which has to be organised in our minds – and this means by the linguistic system in our minds.

(Whorf 1952: 5)

But even this more attractive view of the link between language and the world may give rise to a number of objections from constitutive theory. Clearly, language offers one set of categories and not another for speakers to organize and describe experience, but to assume that language *creates* meanings in the minds of speakers misconceives the way in which meaning is constituted in discourse. While it is quite clear that language is more than a 'reproducing instrument for voicing ideas' (for what do thoughts or ideas look like apart from their expression in language?) the same objections can be applied to the idea of language as the 'shaper' or 'programmer' of ideas. Such ideas are still inaccessible apart from language.

To possess a language is to possess a technique, not a 'firmly bounded system of knowledge' about the world, therefore it is tautological to say that one speaker 'sees' the world in the same way as another because they share a language – they share a technique; the 'seeing' is embedded in the practice. To speak of language as 'shaping' ideas also logically leads to the identification of one particular 'shaping' with a particular language, or more commonly, with the use of language in a particular place. This sort of identification leaves itself no conceptual room to cope with the phenomenon of second language use or vernacular linguistic variance, for it is only in the most metaphorical sense that we can talk about a speaker 'seeing' a different world when he or she speaks in a second language. The key to this problem is the habitual way in which we tend to conflate experience and meaning. We think that because one person cannot have the same *experience* as another they cannot understand each other's *meaning*. But, as we saw, even speakers in the same culture can never have exactly the same experience of language, yet this does not stop them communicating.

But it is the situation of the 'meaning event' rather than the linguistic system in the speaker's mind in which the 'obligatory terms' of language are structured. For instance, Whorf's discovery that Inuit languages have a variety of words for 'snow', thus suggesting they see the world differently from non-Inuits, overlooks the fact that skiers of all languages have a similar variety of words for snow, but could hardly be said to see the world differently in the way Whorf means. The meaning and nature of perceived reality are not determined within the minds of the users, nor even within the language itself, but within the use, within the multiplicity of relationships which operate in the system. Margaret Atwood makes an interesting reference to a North American Indian language which has no noun-forms, only verb-forms. In such a linguistic culture the experience of the world remains in continual process. Such a language cannot exist if language is either anterior or posterior to the world but reinforces the notion that language inhabits the world, *in practice*. The semantic component of the sentence is contained in the syntax: the meaning of a word or phrase is its use in the language, a use which has nothing to do with the kind of world speakers 'have in their heads'.

What the speaker 'has in mind', like a linguistic system or culture, or intentions or meanings, are only accessible in the 'retrospective' performance of speaking. The categories which language offers to describe the world are easily mistaken to shape something in the mind because we naturally assume that like the rules of chess, we hold the linguistic system 'in our minds', in advance of the world. But language is co-extensive with social reality, not because it causes a certain perception of the world, but because it is inextricable from that perception.

The fallacy of both the representationist and culturally determinist views of language may be demonstrated by a brief example. In *The Voice* (1964) Gabriel Okara attempts to develop a 'culturally relevant' use of English by adapting Ijaw syntax and lexical parameters to English. This exercise specifically demonstrates the importance of the situation of the word in the discourse by giving rise to lexical items that have various meanings depending on how they are employed in the text. A significant example of this is the use of the terms 'inside' and 'insides', which are employed in a variety of ways in the novel.

> … "Listen. Asking the bottom of things in this town will take you no place. Hook this up with your little finger. Put it in your inside's box and lock it up." (36)
>
> "Your teaching words do not enter my inside." (36)
>
> You must leave this town. It will pain our insides too much to see you suffer. (48)
>
> But Okolo looking at them said in his inside that his spoken words would only break against them as an egg would against a stone. (48)
>
> "These happening things make my inside bitter, perhaps more bitter than yours." (48)
>
> "How can I change my inside?" he said. (49)
>
> "I see in my insides that your spoken words are true and straight. But you see it in your inside that we have no power to do anything. The spirit is powerful. So it is they who get the spirit that are powerful and the people believe with their insides whatever they are told. The world is no longer straight … So turn this over in your inside and do as we do so that you will have a sweet inside like us." (49)

In these passages, it would be possible to gloss these uses of "inside(s)" as 'emotions or feelings', 'self-referentiality', 'outlook on life', personality, intellectual perception, understanding, intellectuality, 'heart' and 'mind'. But to do so would be to interpret Okara's words and contain them rather than allow their meaning to be determined by their place in the sentence. The term 'sweet inside' is dense with metaphoric possibility, connoting all the characteristics of a harmonious and congenial spirit. We may make some very clear deductions from these passages about the holistic nature of self in Ijaw culture, of the notion of the 'inside' as that which responds to everything which is 'other' or 'outside' (and, on further reading, of the notion of the 'inside' and 'outside' as coextensive). But it would be erroneous to believe that this sense of self is the central component in the communication of the meaning of the term 'inside(s)' when used in the novel. This is because the word does not have some 'essential' meaning, unique to Ijaw and experientially inaccessible to members of another culture; the meaning of the word is that composite of uses which emerges in any reading. 'Inside' is not a metaphor for 'the Ijaw sense of self', when used in these ways in the novel. It is a metaphor for 'self', and may give rise to the possibility of many meanings: 'mind', 'will', 'spirit' or 'emotion', according to the ways in which it functions in the text.

Given this deployment of the word in its situation, the 'meaning' of the term "inside(s)" becomes virtually limitless, and many more senses of the term could be compiled from this one novel. "Our father's insides always contained things straight" (50); "everybody's inside is now filled with cars and money" (50); "he remained talking with his inside until sundown" (51); "My inside has become hard" (53) or "You are indeed a child in your inside" (55). Clearly, the notion of a referent for the term "inside(s)" apart from its application in the context of discourse ceases to have any meaning. The 'objective' and 'universal' state represented by the word does not exist. Such a metaphoric use of language may or may not be indicative of language use in Okara's native Ijaw, but this is immaterial to the function of the word in the English text and to its ability to mean in the same way as it does in Ijaw.

This shows the creative potential of intersecting languages when the syntactic and grammatical rules of one language are overlaid on another, and of the way in which cross-cultural literature reveals how meanings work. In a consumption of the text, which is divorced from any knowledge of what is being represented, the field of intersection, the literary work, is the field within which the word announces its purpose. Similarly, in whatever way the prolixity of the word 'insides' is linked to the Ijaw perception of the world, this function cannot be limited to the understanding of the Ijaw consciousness. The 'world' as it exists 'in' language is an unfolding reality, which owes its relationship to language to the fact that language interprets the world in practice, not to some imputed referentiality.

Meaning exists, therefore, neither before the fact nor after the fact but *in the fact*. Language constitutes reality in an obvious way: it provides some terms and not others with which to talk about the world. Because particular languages provide a limited lexicon they may also be said (metaphorically) to 'use' the speaker, rather than vice versa. But the worlds constituted in this way do not become fixed composites in the speaker's mind, a set of images that differs, by definition, from the set in the mind of the speaker of a different language. Worlds exist by means of languages, their horizons extending as far as the processes of neologism, innovation, tropes and imaginative usage generally will allow the horizons of the language itself to be extended. Therefore the English language becomes a tool with which a 'world' can be textually constructed. The most interesting feature of its use in postcolonial literature may be the way in which it also constructs difference, separation and absence from the metropolitan norm. But the ground on which such construction is based is an abrogation of the essentialist assumptions of that norm and a dismantling of its imperialist centralism.

The reader function in the writing

If the written text is a social situation post-colonial texts emphasize the central problem of this situation, the 'absence' of those 'functions' in the text which operate to constitute the discursive event as communication: the 'writer' and 'reader'. The Author, with its vision and intentions, its 'gifted creative insight', has historically exerted the strongest claim upon the meaning of writing. But the concept of the author is quite alien to many post-colonial cultures and is really a quite recent phenomenon in European culture. The need to ground discourse in an originating subject was the need to accord it the status of a possession. Speeches and books were assigned real authors only when someone had to be made responsible for them as possessions and subject to punishment first as transgressing religious rules and later as transgressing or affirming the rules of property ownership (Foucault 1977: 124–5). To attain this social and legal status the *meaning* had to be a product attributable to a subject. Consequently, the immense and complex forces of which the text was a product could be conveniently located in an originating mind.

This should assist us to find some balance in assessing the author's place in the 'production' of the text. We have made an important start by rejecting the notion that meaning is a mental act, a sort of picture which the author translates into words or vice versa. But how *does* the non-English speaker, for instance, mean anything in English? Firstly, the writer, like the language, is subject to the *situation*, in that he or she must say something *meanable*. This does not mean the language cannot be altered, used neologistically and creatively, but the non-English writer becomes limited *as any speaker or writer is limited*, to a situation in which words have meaning. Take the example of a verse from the poem by the Caribbean poet Linton Kwesi Johnson:

> di lan is like a rack
> slowly shattahrin to san
> sinkin in a sea of calimity
> where fear breeds shadows
> dat lurk in di daak
> where people fraid fi waak
> fraid fi tink fraid fi taak
> where di present is haunted by di paas

(Donnell and Welsh 1996: 375)

While the poem transcribes the sound of the local dialect, its orthography still 'constructs' a reader for whom its variations pose no serious obstacle. Rather, the code variations become a part of the enjoyment of the poem. When we say that the writer is limited to a situation in which words have meaning, the word 'situation' refers to something of extremely wide range. It is, at its simplest, the place of the word within a meanable context, the grammar or rules which make the context meanable, but it is also a continuously unfolding horizon which ever more finely articulates the meaning. This is not to say that some post-colonial writing is not much more inaccessible to the reader, but this inaccessibility is part of a strategy of difference. Literature, and particularly narrative, has the capacity to domesticate even the most alien experience. It does not need to *reproduce* the experience to construct the meaning. This principle applies to even the most recondite culturally specific terms. Although there is no word in English, for instance, which has the associations of *mana* (oneness with the world) in Polynesian or *Tjukurrpa* (the 'Dreaming') in Pintjantjatjara, there is no insurmountable conceptual difficulty in articulating their associations.

One could go further than this to say that the author is subject not only to the situation of discourse but to the reader as well. The reader is present, as a *function*, in the writing of the text. Thus the relationship between these social forces and the text is the same as that between the linguistic system and the 'text' of a particular world view: neither causal nor representative, but co-extensive. Within the framework of these social antecedents, the writer and reader functions are as 'present' to each other in the acts of writing and reading as conversants are in conversation. The reader may be present in the writing at a conscious level, in the author's sense of an audience, of a purpose for writing, but it is not necessarily so specific. To detect the presence of the reader function in the writing let us first think clearly whether the act of writing can ever exclude the simultaneous act of reading. That moment of writing in which the self is objectified is also the moment of a reading in which the other is constituted. It is the other, even when the other is oneself which confers objectivity on the writing, constitutes it as written. In this sense, as Sartre says, the others "were already present in the heart of the word, hearers and speakers awaiting their turn" (Sartre 1972: 494). The requirement of meanability itself implicates the reader function. The space within which the writer meets the reading other is neither one culture nor another, neither one language nor another, but the *parole*, the situation of discourse.

The writer function in the reading

Just as readers 'write' the text because they take it to mean something, and just as the reader function is present in the writing as the focus of its meanability, so the author is present in the reading. Again, this is firstly true at a conscious level, where the reader accepts the convention that the author is telling him or her something through the text. Readers respond to the text as 'telling' them something because such ways of using language as this literary text represents come within the rules for the activity of 'telling'. But one cannot 'tell' others anything that they do not incorporate or 'tell themselves'. The mind is active in knowing. Whether a child learning a language or a scientist 'observing' an 'objective' universe, knowing is conducted within the *situation* of horizons of expectations and other knowledge. In reading, a horizon of expectations is partly established by the unfolding text, while the horizon of other knowledge (actually other texts), a *relevant* horizon of other knowledge, is established by exploration.

The reader constructs the other dialogic pole of discourse because speaking is a social act. But readers do not simply respond to the convention of the authoring other, they responds to the 'intentionality' of the work itself, quite apart from any imputation of an Author. The work is a way of seeing and responding, a way of directing attention to that which is 'given to consciousness'. It is more accurate to say that the reader sees according to, or 'with', the text rather than 'sees it'. This orientation to the intentionality of the text occurs whether there is an actual author or not.[1] We can deduce from this that the intentionality of the text can be *put for* the direction of the author's consciousness. Thus interpretation is never univocal but the reader is subject to the situation, to the rules of discourse and to the directing other as the author is subject to them.

As with language, our natural assumption about understanding is that it must be a discrete experience, that there must be characteristic experiences of understanding when we 'understand' which have corresponding identifiable mental correlates. Consequently how could we 'understand' a writer, even writing in a common language, who has a profoundly different experience of the world? But we can test this assumption that understanding is an identifiable experience. Take the example of a bricklayer who uses the term 'Brick!' to his helper as an elliptical form of the phrase 'Pass me the brick'. Neither he, nor the helper need to translate the word 'Brick!' into the phrase every time it is used, in order to understand it. The word operates perfectly well as a communication within the exchange and it is its use and the continuation of the job which locates the understanding of the word 'Brick' as an order. The same process applies when English variants, neologisms and borrowings are situated in the written English text. As with most words there may be many possible uses but it is the use in this situation which locates the meaning. When I understand what another person says, I am not required to have their mental images nor when they communicate meaning are they obliged to transfer to the listener the 'contents' of their mind, nor any of the mental images and associations which may be aroused by that language.

The particular facility of writing which uses English as a second language, and invites the reader into the mental and emotional horizon of the 'other' culture, is to bridge this gap, to reveal that understanding is a function of the linguistic situation. The dialectic of writer and reader functions within this situation is particularly significant. Such writing re-emphasises the constitutive nature of the meaning event and the varied nature of the usage in which meaning is accomplished. Yet, curiously, there is an element in such literature which introduces a

---

1 I discovered this in an experiment conducted at the Australian National University. Participants were offered progressive lines of separate poems selected randomly in the belief that they were progressively reading a single poem. Respondents of high professional competence revealed great ingenuity in interpreting the 'poem' and in all cases directed their response to a constructed intentionality generally identified as 'the poet'.

gap of a different kind. By stressing the distance between the participating writers and readers, the text prevents itself from being so transparent that it is absorbed into the dominant milieu of the reader of English. Such writing, while it provides a path for cultural understanding that overcomes the exclusionary effect of anthropological explanation, also questions easy assumptions about meaning and its transmissibility, and actively re-installs the reality of its own cultural difference in quite explicit ways.

Dialogism

The observation of the constitutive nature of the text alerts us to the dialogue that occurs at the meeting point of the writer and reader functions. Indeed 'dialogue' is what the post-colonial text is all about. This dialogue is reflected in another form of dialogic discourse, which Bakhtin calls 'heteroglossia'. Bakhtin is particularly interested in the novel because for him the novel form provides a particularly rich medium for the many-voiced appearance of different languages.

> For the novelist working in prose, the object is always entangled in someone else's discourse about it, it is already present with qualifications, an object of dispute that is conceptualized and evaluated variously, inseparable from the heteroglot social apperception of it. The novelist speaks of this "already qualified world" in a language that is heteroglot and internally dialogized. Thus both object and language are revealed to the novelist in their historical dimension, in the process of social and heteroglot becoming.
>
> (Bakhtin 1981: 330)

The significant thing about this is that Bakhtin is talking about a putatively monoglossic text, unhampered by issues of cultural communication. For him, such text is already heteroglossic, already engaged in dialogue *within* the text, a dialogue, which to all intents and purposes, is a *cross-cultural* dialogue between 'belief systems'. In addition, the novel unifies its language and its world: "For the novelist, there is no world outside his socioheteroglot perception – and there is no language outside the heteroglot intentions that stratify that world" (330). Thus we might say that the novel is already a function of the meeting of many languages, all of which come with their own belief systems, a meeting that bodies forth fully the world of the novel: "Incorporated into the novel are a multiplicity of 'language' and verbal-ideological belief systems ... kept primarily within the limits of the literary written and conversational language" (1981: 311). The speech of Dostoyevsky's narrators, for instance, who are themselves characters, "is always *another's speech* (as regards the real or potential direct discourse of the author) and in *another's language*" (1981: 324).

This leads to non-direct speaking – "not *in* language but *through* language, through the linguistic medium of another" (324). In effect, Bakhtin arrives at the same point that Benjamin reaches in his discussion of translation in the next chapter. But whereas Benjamin sees translation as unfaithful because language itself is unfaithful, Bakhtin counters the myth of authentic, "faithful" language with the term "heteroglossia". All literary language is already multi-voiced, the author's 'intentions' already refracted through the multiple belief systems of the dialogic text. But consequently, the dialogue between author and narrator opens the way to consider all language as a multi-voiced space of translation. All forms involving a narrator

> signify to one degree or another by their presence the author's freedom from a unitary and singular language, a freedom connected with the relativity of literary and language systems; such forms open up the possibility of never having to define oneself in language, the possibility of translating one's own intentions from one linguistic system to another, of fusing 'the language of truth' with 'the language of everyday,' of saying 'I am me' in someone else's language, and in my own language 'I am other'.
>
> (314–15)

The dual dynamic of saying 'I am me' in another's language and 'I am other' in my own language captures precisely the dual achievement of the second language writer. For such a writer, while emphasizing the way in which the space between author and reader is closed within the demands of meanability, also demonstrates in heightened form, the writer's negotiation of the forces brought to bear on language.

> Every concrete utterance of a speaking subject serves as a point where centrifugal as well as centripetal forces are brought to bear. The processes of centralization and decentralization, of unification and disunification, intersect in the utterance; the utterance not only answers the requirements of its own language … but it answers the requirements of heteroglossia as well; it is in fact an active participant in such speech diversity.
>
> (1981: 272)

For the post-colonial writer these forces are the forces of a culturally ossified way of seeing and the heteroglossia of a world readership.

As the Australian poet and activist Judith Wright says, "there are other ways of seeing and perceiving, and of relating ourselves to the world, if we can only break out of that trap [i.e. of seeing constructions of language as reality] and find them" (Salter 1989: 9–10). One of the preeminent advantages of cross-cultural writing in English is the capacity to translate ways of seeing into the 'bilingual' text without making any concessions to the 'way of seeing' of the reader. This is because the text is already a heteroglot profusion of ways of seeing. But it is also because the post-colonial text manages to extend Bakhtin's view of dialogue with the discovery that *true dialogue can only occur when the difference of the other is recognized.*

Post-colonial writing, by stressing the distance between the participants, re-emphasises the constitutive nature of the meaning event and the complex nature of the usage in which meaning is accomplished. But the most interesting possibilities of this theory are provided by the way in which it distances itself from the tendency of European theory to establish universal laws and principles. Post-colonial writing questions assumptions about meaning and its communicability and privileges the conception of writing as a social act conceived within the fusion of culture and consciousness.

9   Translation and Transformation

To establish his identity, Caliban, after three centuries, must himself pioneer into regions Caesar never knew.

(C.L.R. James)

I have crossed an ocean
I have lost my tongue
from the root of the old one
a new one has sprung
(Grace Nichols, "Epilogue")

The dialogue Caliban enters when he appropriates Prospero's language and writes his own books means that he communicates with an audience who would otherwise not understand him. But he communicates on his own terms, for Caliban's books reveal something profound about dialogue – true dialogue can only occur when the difference of the other is recognised. The language with which Caliban enters into dialogue is transformed, and so to some extent is the reader. For the 'dialogue in difference' that characterises post-colonial writing necessarily produces a different reader – a translated reader, just as it produces a translated/translating writer.

However, this dialogue also involves Caliban recognising the difference of the other when he *translates* books from his own vernacular. Translation has become one of the most prominent issues in post-colonial studies over recent years. The debates about translation in the field have revolved almost solely around the translation of vernacular texts into English. But the kind of 'inner translation' that occurs when writers write in a second language, could be the point at which Translation Studies and Post-Colonial Studies meet. The argument of this chapter is that Translation – the movement of text from a source language to a target language – and Transformation – the reshaping of text in a target language by the cultural nuances of a source language – have come to overlap in post-colonial literatures (although their distinctiveness should still be recognised). This intersection of translation and transformation occurs because the context of the post-colonial writer is profoundly transcultural: the postcolony is the archetypal contact zone. Interpretation is a feature of all translation but in the post-colonial situation, where books are written in English, translation and transformation are co-existent. Whether a text is translated from the vernacular into English, or a vernacular writer writes directly in English, similar kinds of dialogic transformations occur in the writing process.

The problem is not that translation and transformation are seen as incompatible in Translation Studies. Far from it: most discussion on Post-Colonial Translation overlooks this intersection, by treating post-colonial writing in English as if it were translation.[1] This underplays the brilliant creativity often deployed in post-colonial writing in English. It fails to recognise that the absence of an 'original' text in the vernacular makes the post-colonial writing in English a paradigmatic demonstration of the productive instability of language itself. The relationship is that of a continuum rather than a binary. Maxine Hong Kingston, the Asian American novelist, says that her first novel was a 'translation' in the sense that she felt like a translator, putting into English that text which was conceived in Chinese. But *Trip Master Monkey* was an example, she claims, of her speaking in her own Chinese American voice an appropriated and syncretic tongue. However the point about transformation is not simply that it transforms the writer's original medium of communication into English, but much more importantly, it transforms Standard English into something else. Even *more* significantly, perhaps, it is not merely the *language* that is transformed, but in a subtle way both writer and reader are transformed in the cultural engagement represented by post-colonial literatures.

The merging of the concepts of translation and transformation can be found in a provocative metaphor proposed by the Brazilian Oswald de Andrade – that of cannibalism (Bassnett and Trivedi 1999: 4) In his *Manifesto Antropofago in 1928* he suggested that only by devouring Europe could the colonized break away from what was imposed upon them: "And at the same time, the devouring could be seen as a violation of European codes and an act of homage" (5). The metaphor of consumption suggests that in post-colonial contexts translation takes on a very different form. Devouring the colonizer could be framed in terms such as 'appropriation' as it was first introduced in *The Empire Writes Back*. Translation, in the post-colonial context occurs both inside and between the colonizing and colonized languages, all of which can be seen to occupy the Third Space of Enunciation.

The Third Space of translation

The myth, against which I have been arguing in this book, that cultural identity is somehow embodied, 'hard-wired', in language, would present insurmountable problems to translation if it were true. If our language 'is us', as we tend to assume, how can our cultural identity be translated? But cultural identity is not so much the

---

1 Many chapters in Bassnett and Trivedi's *Post-Colonial Translation* actually deal with the transformative strategies of writing in English. The opening essay by Maria Tymoczko directly appropriates post-colonial writing to translation studies by claiming that literary translation "is an *analogue* of post-colonial writing" (Bassnett and Trivedi 1999: 20).

problem here as the concept of identity itself. If we agree with Lacan that the word 'I' does not refer to a subject that preexists it, but rather the place of, the 'use' of the 'I' in the sentence produces the subject, we can see that the *position* of the subject can vary. As Stuart Hall suggests in his essay "Cultural Identity and Diaspora" (1990), we should not think of subjectivity alone but of subject *positions*. We can think of these subject positions as 'articulations' that occupy the 'Third Space' of enunciation, which is the space of language itself. The variable operation of subject positions is so clearly apparent in the transcultural space of post-colonial society that translation and transformation merge to become related processes.

The concept of language as *itself* somehow a 'Third Space', a vehicle that is by its very nature interstitial, is suggested in Sherry Simon's discussion of the hybridity and self-doubt characteristic of much contemporary Quebec writing:

> These doubts increasingly take the form of the cohabitation within a single text of multiple languages and heterogeneous codes. In this case, translation can no longer be a single and definitive enterprise of cultural transfer. Translation, it turns out, not only negotiates between languages, but comes to inhabit the space of language itself.
>
> (Simon 1992: 174)

In other words, language itself is transformative, a space of translation. Translation no longer negotiates between languages, for language *is itself* the site of ceaseless translation. And the critical discovery here (a discovery Samuel Johnson made centuries ago, as we saw in the Introduction) is that language – this site of translation – is continually and productively *unstable*.

When Samuel Beckett published his poetry to include his own facing-page translations he bemused and challenged readers with the apparent 'disloyalty' of the translations from the original French. What Beckett was doing was signifying the space of unintelligibility that exists in the interstices of all languages. His 'translations', in effect, signified his view of the untranslatability of language. Because language is never a simple correspondence between signs and referents, a simple translation of reality into words, we may say that *all* language occupies the Third Space of enunciation in its provisionality and untranslatability. This is the space that post-colonial writers inhabit between the imperial and vernacular cultures. But it is one version of the interstitial space that all language occupies.

In his classic essay "The Task of the Translator", Walter Benjamin rejects the notion that translation can or should be faithful to the original text, for "the task of the translator … may be regarded as distinct and clearly different from the task of the poet. The intention of the poet is spontaneous, primary, graphic; that of the translator is derivative, ultimate, ideational" (1969: 76–7). Benjamin's point is that it is language that presents the 'problem'. Poets are doomed to be unfaithful to experience just as translators are doomed to be unfaithful to the poet, because language itself is 'unfaithful'.

Commenting on Benjamin's essay, Paul de Man posits that, like history, critical philosophy and literary theory – all derivative activities, all translations disarticulate, they undo the original, they reveal that the original was always already disarticulated. They reveal that their failure, which seems to be due to the fact that they are secondary in relation to the original, reveals an essential failure, an essential disarticulation that was already there in the original. They kill the original, by discovering that the original was already dead.

(2000: 84)

This has profound implications for the assumption that identity resides in one language and is only adequately expressed in that language. The bilingual writer discovers "the inability of one language to assimilate perfectly the experience that is already imperfectly embedded in the other. The bilingual writer therefore suffers doubly from the failure of both languages to articulate a double self" (McGuire 1992: 3).

The complaint that a colonial language is inauthentic to local identity assumes that there can be such an 'authentic' language. But what if *all* writers find themselves subtly displaced from language in one way or another? This is certainly the implication of Benjamin's essay. Post-colonial writers have the added experience of being unfaithful to two languages both of which can only ever be 'unfaithful' to experience. Unfaithfulness is the hyperbole that identifies the instability of language. But perhaps even 'instability' is not quite the right word. All language is *horizontal* in that it offers a horizon of representation to experience – all representation intimates a 'something more' in the horizon of the statement. Within this horizon of possibilities language can never be perfectly 'faithful' to experience, for experience itself functions in concert with, rather than prior to, language. Without resorting to Whorfian determinism, we can say that the language does not reflect but invents, or 're-presents' the experience. So the post-colonial writer does not exist in a state of suffering and loss, but of an expanded and fluid capacity to recreate experience.

One can therefore never write exactly what one 'intends'. The meaning, as we have seen, does not exist *before* the linguistic exchange, but *in* it. Benjamin disperses intention completely: "all suprahistorical kinship of languages rests in the intention underlying each language as a whole – an intention, however, which is realized only by the totality of their intentions supplementing each other: pure language" (1969: 74). His point here is that all writing is already a translation of this "pure language", what he calls "*reine Sprache*", or, to put it another way, translation elevates the original into pure language: "the language of a translation can – in fact, must – let itself go, so that it gives voice to the *intentio* of the original not as reproduction but as harmony, as a supplement to the language in which it expresses itself, as its own kind of *intentio*" (1969: 79). There is no metalanguage or transcendental signifier because

[t]his movement of the original is a wandering, an errance, and a kind of permanent exile if you wish, but it is not really an exile, for there is no homeland, nothing from which one has been exiled. Least of all is there

something like a *reine Sprache*, a pure language, which does not exist except as a permanent disjunction that inhabits all languages as such, including and especially the language one calls one's own. What is one's own language is the most displaced, the most alienated of all.

(1969: 92)

The term *"reine Sprache"* – "pure language" – is ironic then, because it can never be realized. It is the utopian horizon of all communicability. The vessel of pure language, to use Benjamin's well-known metaphor, is eternally fractured, and translation is but a reenactment of this fragmentation, the emblem of its own failure to be primary.

In this absence of a pure language, not only post-colonial writing, but perhaps *all* writing, may be a form of perpetual translation. Salman Rushdie's response to the supposed inferiority of cross-cultural writing is that something is gained in translation:

The word 'translation' comes, etymologically, from the Latin for 'bearing across'. Having been borne across the world, we are translated men. It is normally supposed that something always gets lost in translation; I cling, obstinately, to the notion that something can also be gained.

(1991: 17)

This makes post-colonial writing a powerful extension of the theory of translation, as post-colonial theorists of translation have been quick to recognise. The post-colonial writer faces in two directions, so to speak. The decision he or she makes is not just how to write 'between languages', but how to make language perform this 'bearing across' (indeed, to 'bear' this particular 'cross') within itself: how to be both 'source' and 'target'.

The routes of translation

Three forms of transaction are possible in the context of post-colonial writing: the translation of a vernacular text into English (by colonizer or colonized); the translation of an English text into a vernacular language; and the production of an English text by a bilingual writer. In turn, these three processes develop a much greater number of overlapping possibilities depending on readership, publication, the linguistic skill or creative ability of the translator or writer, who is doing the translating, and the relative transparency of the vernacular language. Take readership, for instance: in most cases where post-colonial writers choose to write in English, they are choosing their audience – a global audience of English speakers. But in the case of India they will be writing to an audience of Indian English speakers as well, for whom glosses and explanations will only irritate. Trying to please both these audiences may result in pleasing neither. The identity of the audience will also depend greatly on the publisher; on marketing capacity; and on production values (such as the quality of editing processes and of materials such as paper). Where linguistic or creative skill is concerned the task is to reproduce in a target language, whether in translation or original, the cultural nuances of particular vernaculars, which requires not just linguistic knowledge, but considerable creativity. This task may be all but impossible to achieve in an aesthetically satisfying way with some languages.

These difficulties explain why translation has usually been regarded as inferior to the original. Robert Frost, for example, claimed that, "poetry is what gets lost in translation". Translation has also been marked by metaphors of gender (Simon 1996). In 1603 John Florio said that all translations were defective since they were considered to be women (Simon 1996: 1). The classic example of this is the well-worn cliché that 'translations are like women: they can be beautiful or faithful but not both'. It is an easy step to move from these dismissive metaphors to see the colony itself as a woman to be wooed, a child to be instructed, a 'translation' or 'copy' of the colonizing culture, and therefore inferior to the original. Indeed, the issues of translation, authenticity, simulation and originality, not to mention 'literary value', are closely bound up in discussions of translation.

Extreme reactions to the denigration of translation have demanded the cessation or radical reduction of translation into dominant cultural systems. However, conversely, the translation of vernacular texts into English has been seen to be a strategy of political resistance and even cultural survival. This is particularly so in South Asia, where the translation of vernacular texts contests what some believe to be an anglo-centric focus of post-colonial cultures. Indian English, according to G.J.V. Prasad, is a language born in and of translation, one that occupies the space of translation (Prasad 2002: 44). This refers to the fact that India is a land of hundreds of languages in which linguistic chauvinism and dominance are hotly contested issues, and where the translation between regional languages has itself been an endemic feature of Indian culture. "Our languages and cultures are part of an extended family," says Prasad (47). 'Indian culture' is a perpetual dynamic flow, a profusion of movement and translation, between languages, between cultures and regions.

Translation and power: Translating into English

The use of translation as a means of domination occurs in many ways in imperial discourse but I want to discuss two: the issue of Naming that comes to prominence in imperial cartography; and the question of cultural sensitivity in legislative and other state documents that re-interpret cultural concepts. Names *of* places are names *in* language and are the most powerful means of cultural incorporation. Names invoke ownership, because to have the power to name is to have the power of possession. Naming is a form of translation because it inserts the named object or location – translates it – into a particular cultural narrative. The scientific naming of a region's climatic, geological, topographical and geographical features inserts it into the more consuming global narrative of modernity itself. This power of language to appropriate the physical environment is one with which post-colonial peoples must always contend. Whatever the sense of inherent or cultural 'belonging' to place indigenous inhabitants may have, it is clear that place may be 'controlled', by being familiarized and domesticated through language.

Brian Friel's Translations

The Irish playwright Brian Friel focuses on just this link between colonial naming and power in his play *Translations* (1981). Set in the Donegal hedge-school of Baile Beag in 1833, the play describes the process by which an Ordnance Survey undertaken by the British Army proceeds to 're-map' the area by substituting English names for the original Gaelic place names. This re-naming symbolizes the sweeping social changes that ensued at that time, but the renaming of colonized place manifests the true subtlety and power of imperial discourse. The headmaster of the hedge-school, Hugh, reports that Captain Lancey, the leader of the ordnance survey "voiced some surprise that we did not speak his language" (25). To Lancey the survey is what the government white paper says it is; the provision of "up-to-date and accurate information on every corner of this part of the Empire" (31) and a means of "equalizing taxation" and advancing "the interests of Ireland". The naming process itself is completely arbitrary.

This arbitrariness demonstrates that it is the discourse of renaming, of translation, rather than the particular names themselves that matter. Friel's description of the ways in which places are renamed shows that the very arbitrariness is a comprehensive dismissal of the value or meaning of any previous reality in the colonized place. In effect, Irish land becomes a translated place, *reconstructed* by imperial power.

Owen:	Now. Where have we got to? Yes – the point where that stream enters the sea – that tiny little beach there. George!
Yolland:	Yes. I'm listening. What do you call it? Say the Irish name again?
Owen:	Bun na hAbhann.
Yolland:	Again.
Owen:	Bun na hAbhann.
Yolland:	Bun na hAbhann.
Owen:	That's terrible George.
Yolland:	I know, I'm sorry. Say it again.
Owen:	Bun na hAbhann.
Yolland:	Bun na hAbhann.
Owen:	That's better. Bun is the Irish word for bottom. And Abha means river. So it's literally the mouth of the river.
Yolland:	Leave it alone. There's no English equivalent for a sound like that.
Owen:	What is it called in the church registry?
Yolland:	Let's see … Banowen.
Owen:	That's wrong. (*Consults text.*) The list of freeholders calls it Owenmore – that's completely wrong. Owenmore's the big river at the west end of the parish. (*Another text.*) And in the grand jury lists its called – God! – Binhone! – wherever they got that. I suppose we could Anglicise it to

Bunowen; but somehow that's neither fish nor flesh. (*Yolland closes his eyes again.*)

Yolland: I give up.

Owen: (*At map.*) Back to first principles. What are we trying to do?

Yolland: Good question.

Owen: We are trying to denominate and at the same time describe that tiny area of soggy, rocky, sandy ground where that little stream enters the sea, an area known locally as Bun na hAbhann ... Burnfoot! What about Burnfoot?

Yolland: (*Indifferently.*) Good, Roland. Burnfoot's good.

(II.i.1–34)

This is an astute description of the way in which a translation, a renaming, fractures the link between language and place at the very point of its central claim: the point at which it is supposed to be providing a description. The arbitrariness of the ultimate naming is an ironic subversion of the scientific posturing of the survey, and a demonstration of the way in which imperial discourse provides a constitutive grid over the local reality, which reconstitutes it according to the requirements of the map rather than any requirements of habitation or personal experience. "Bun na hAbhann", "Owenmore", and "Binhone" are names that operate in different social and material contexts. The translation of the place-name into the arbitrary "Burnfoot", plucked from nowhere but the lexicon of English, accords an authority by simple virtue of its inscription on the authorized text of the survey map. The name itself is metonymic of the authority of the imperial discourse, which commissions the map.

The Treaty of Waitangi

This translation into imperial discourse is not limited to geographical names. More subtle and far reaching perhaps have been those uses of language that operate in practical terms to order the moral and political world of the colonized. This power is nowhere more obvious than in the linguistic sleight of hand performed by the British in the Treaty of Waitangi: On 6 February 1840 forty-six Maori chiefs from the northern regions of New Zealand 'signed' a document written in Maori called "Te Tiriti o Waitangi", "The Treaty of Waitangi". In doing so, according to the English versions of that document, they ceded to Her Majesty the Queen of England "absolutely and without reservation all the rights and powers of Sovereignty" which they themselves individually exercised over their respective territories. That act of assent became the substantive ground of British sovereignty over New Zealand. (Mackenzie 1985: 9). It hinged on the interpretation of a word that described Maori relationship with the land.

D.F. Mackenzie explains the situation in the following way: In all the English versions of the treaty the chiefs "cede to Her Majesty the Queen of England, absolutely and without reservation, all the rights and powers of Sovereignty". The question here is what the English meant and the Maori understood by the word 'Sovereignty'. In other words, what was being named? Did it mean that the chiefs gave up to the Crown their personal power and supreme status within their own tribes, or was it only something more mundanely administrative, like 'governorship'? In fact the word used by Henry Williams to translate 'Sovereignty' was precisely that: *kawanatanga*, not even a translation but a transliteration of 'Governor' (*kawana*) with a suffix to make it abstract. What he significantly omitted in translating 'Sovereignty' (which the Maori were being asked to surrender) was the genuine Maori word *mana*, meaning personal prestige and the power that flowed from it, or even the word *rangatiratanga*, meaning chieftainship, the very words used in 1835 to 1839 to affirm Maori sovereignty over New Zealand .... By choosing not to use either *mana* or *rangatiratanga* to indicate what the Maori would exchange for "all the Rights and Privileges of British subjects", Williams muted the sense, plain in English, of the treaty as a document of political appropriation. Had any Maori heard that he was giving up his *mana* or *rangatiratanga* he could never have agreed to the treaty's terms (McKenzie 1985: 41–2).

This treaty is based on a simple but far-reaching deception embedded in the translation of the word 'sovereignty'. In this instance the naming process involved not a place on the map, but a concept, the concept of sovereignty. This concept was about place because the words *mana* and *kawanatanga* conceived entirely different relationships with place and the (re)*naming* operated at the same time as a process of *erasure*. The act of re-naming, deceptive though it was, was a crucial aspect of the exertion of colonial power in New Zealand.

***

Another issue hovering around this question of cultural power is the dependence of translations of vernacular texts on publishing networks. The outcome of such dependency may be the circulation of abridged, bowdlerized and generally inadequate versions. A classic example is the Macmillan edition of Tagore's novel *Gora* which has been the only access to the original text for the better part of a century. But it is an abridged version replete with stylistic solecisms ranging from Victorian English to British colloquialisms. The inadequacy of such translations shows that:

> it is possible for a translator to impose an ideological design on the text or modify/inhibit the rhetorical play of the text. It goes without saying that the translator as a model reader can set the source language text into cultural motion or bring it to stasis.
>
> (Mukherjee 2002: 152)

It is a translation truism that translation is best made *into* one's own language rather than out of it. But this leaves a text such as *Gora* exposed to the colonial or Orientalist prejudices of the English translator, an exposure that will inevitably bring the source text to 'cultural stasis'. The solution is clearly the translation of vernacular texts by increasingly skilful bilingual Indian translators.

Translation and empowerment: Translating out of the vernacular

Fortunately, translation into English is not only performed at the behest of the colonizer nor only as an exercise of colonial power. The translation of vernacular texts into English – in South Asia particularly – is increasingly seen as a means of cultural empowerment. Vigorous traditions of writing in Indian languages existed before and continue to exist after colonization, and their translation and publication challenges colonial power relations and their publishing systems. Although translation of this kind appears to privilege English, the translation of a large number of indigenous novels into English opens up a potentially huge readership both in the post-colonial countries themselves and the world. Such a cultural resource becomes, through translation, a vehicle of cultural communication, and perhaps a mode of cultural survival.

Translations of post-colonial texts face the same theoretical issues as all translations: Who is the 'author'? Is translation interpretation? Should the translator strive for literalism or aestheticism? What is more important – substance or essence? But the Indian situation is complicated not only by a plethora of vernaculars, but also varieties of English. "Thus the task for the translator," says Prasad, "is to create an Indian domesticity as well as maintain relational distance between the texts from different languages" (Prasad 2002: 47). He compares the editorial policies in two collections of Indian stories. Rimli Bhattacharya, in *Katha Prize Stories 1*, states that her aim is to retain differences to demonstrate the heterogeneous nature of India and Indian languages and literatures: "This means choosing the local language term even if there was an 'Indian' word available for it" (Bhattacharya and Dharmarajan 1991: 12). Clearly, Indian translation requires different strategies because the sub-cultural differences in the source text are manifold. By retaining the local term, says Prasad "you are not simply adding local colour, you are demonstrating ways in which the languages/cultures have differentiated themselves from each other" (2002: 48). Another collection of stories, on the other hand, falls short because in omitting stories that the editors judge to be difficult to translate, "they are still thinking in and thinking of Standard English, not any kind of Indian English" (2002: 48).

Nevertheless the translator's work consists of continual choices about which idiomatic expressions to leave. Uma gives the example of the Telegu word *asidhaaraavratam*, a ritual in which a sword is placed between a husband and wife to ensure abstinence. "Should we translate it as 'the ritual of the sword line' and leave it like that for the reader to interpret, or give a footnote to the literal translation, or leave the original expression and give a footnote, or find a near English equivalent?" (Uma 2002: 94). In the end they used the English expression 'be on guard'. But the choices about culturally specific words have an important function: the text must negotiate the space between intelligibility and cultural specificity, a space in which the post-colonial text in English comes into being. Writers and translators must choose the particular balance of vernacular and translation to convey cultural difference at the same time as they ensure intelligibility.

Of course in the case of poetry, the task of producing a translation that is 'true' to the original either culturally, poetically or aesthetically is virtually impossible for any language. The cliché about fidelity or beauty is nowhere more obvious than in translations of poetry. The sense of the poem cannot be separated from its materiality – its music, sound, rhythm, metre, and its structure, the look of the lines on the page – and these are notoriously difficult to transfer across languages although they constitute the very *poesis* of the poem. The distance between post-colonial vernaculars and English may be greater than that between other lan-guages and very often the option chosen is not transliteration but *transcreation*. Although Tagore translated many of his poems into English he always insisted that they should be read in Bengali because

> my English translations are not the same. Each country has its symbols of expression, so when I translate my work I find new images and presently new thought and finally it is something almost entirely new. The funda-mental idea is the same but the vision changes. A poem cannot be trans-lated, it can only be relived in a different atmosphere.
>
> (1916)

This perception allowed Tagore considerable creative freedom in his transla-tions of other Bengali poems. In one instance he captured a forty-line Bengali poem in ten lines of English, a remarkable exploitation of the creative potential of the language, but one in which he was not constrained by the need for any literal fidelity (Ray 2002: 84–6).

The problem that seems to haunt translation is the extent to which cultural identity can be 'borne across' a linguistic divide. The question of identity takes on a very active cast when we get down to the practicalities of word choice. G.J.V. Prasad describes the way in which R.K. Narayan, one of the masters of Indian English literature, goes through a translation process to produce his English text. Strictly speaking, Prasad is describing Narayan's *transformation* of English, but he offers a case for the similarity between the kinds of decisions the South Indian writer and (say) a translator of South Indian texts might make in addressing dif-ferent audiences. Narayan, says Prasad,

> struggles like all good translators to construct his world. His struggle is mainly because he cannot fully identify his audiences. He is writing for a western audience for sure, but he is also going to be read across India, and really he is a Tamilian writing for people like him, people to whom he should speak in English with the same kind of humour. So who[m] should he be thinking of in his choice of words? Thus in the same sentence he can address all three audiences – "He had donned a white khaddar cap, a long new jibba, and a dhoti, and had a lace upper cloth on his shoulders" (*Maneater of Malgudi* 1990: 113). 'Khaddar' was understood across India as the cloth of the national movement, but what about 'jibba'? This is a

Tamilian name for what would be called a 'kurta' in the north. And if he can say 'jibba' why can't he say 'veshti'? Why does he have to use the north Indian 'dhoti'? Is it because 'dhoti' would be understood across India, including among his Tamil audience.

(Prasad 2002: 49)

This is a very clear demonstration of the practicalities of word choice as the writer 'constructs' a variable audience. We might also suggest that 'dhoti' is a word more likely to be known by non-Indian English speakers. So there is constant give and take as the writer includes enough to familiarize readers of various audiences, but withholds enough to communicate cultural specificity. This, we discover, is a fusion of translation and transformation, the 'metonymic gap', which we will examine later. But interestingly, the cultural specificity here is not just Indian, but south Indian. Narayan may not have a 'problem' at all in identifying his audiences as Prasad suggests, but brilliantly employs a balance of familiar and specific words to communicate *both* meaning and cultural specificity to different audiences. Prasad admits as much when he quotes Narayan's observation that what he and his contemporaries attempted

[m]ay have seemed "an awkward translation of a vernacular rhetoric, mode or idiom. But occasionally it was brilliant (Narayan 1979: 22)." This translation and transformation of English, he goes on to say in the same passage, served his "purpose admirably, of conveying unambiguously the thoughts and acts of a set of personalities, who flourish in a small town called Malgudi (supposed to be) located in a corner of South India" (1979: 22).

(52)

Narayan demonstrates here that in the practical business of choosing words, glossing some and leaving others, writing by post-colonial writers intimates a kind of third language that originates in the overlap of the vernacular voice and the colonial language. But he also demonstrates something generally overlooked in discussions about language and cultural identity – the interaction of writer and reader *functions* in the text that we discussed in the previous chapter. The writer constructs an audience, not just a cultural location or a self.

Translation into vernacular language

The translation of English texts into vernacular languages can produce the same kinds of problems of cultural transmission. Translating Seamus Heaney's poem "Digging" into Telegu, M. Sridhar found that the sense of lines such as "He rooted out tall tops, buried the bright edge deep/ To scatter new potatoes that we picked/ Loving their cool hardness in our hands" could be translated, but of course not their associations. It is arguable whether any non-Irish reader could fully engage the deep cultural associations of such lines. But this is, in a sense, the function of the poem, to draw the reader towards that deep substratum of cultural experience. Such an experience does not need to be experienced to be understood by the reflective reader.

But the most fascinating consequence of the translation of English texts into vernacular languages is the effect they may have on the vernacular *literatures* themselves. While Ngũgĩ wa Thiongo's decision to write in Gikuyu makes a political point about colonial languages, the writer appropriates the novel form to do so, a form that had not existed in the Gikuyu language. This doesn't just empower, but could be said to *create* the Gikuyu novel. The impact of translation is, of course, most obvious in those languages that have a long literary tradition such as South Asian regional languages. This is a point at which deep traditions of literature can be read in a post-colonial way – the vernacular literatures can be regarded as 'post-colonial' because they have been affected, through translation, by colonial contact – changed and hybridized, not by the actions of the colonizers but by the appropriation of native speakers. Just as post-colonial writers appropriate the dominant language for cultural empowerment, to 'seize the means of representation', so the translated English literature was often a means of revivifying local literatures that might have become moribund. At first glance this might seem to be a paternalistic assumption of the superiority of the English literature. But in fact the translation of English texts by linguistic nationalists themselves demonstrates the transformative power of appropriation. On one hand the influence of English created imitative forms in Indian languages, but at the same time this influence provoked entirely new forms. Bengal was the most intense point of colonial influence in India. "It was the force of this influence, however, that provided the impetus for renewed forms of Bengali narrative, and in particular the emergence of the novel in Bengali" (Das 1986: 41). As with colonized cultures throughout the British Empire, not only language but linguistic *forms* were appropriated in a process of cultural self-assertion.

A fascinating example of this is the work of B.M. Srikantaiah discussed by Viswanatha and Simon (1999). Srikantaiah was a Kannada speaker from the state of Karnataka, in South India, where a large body of religious and mythological narrative had existed for many centuries. By the time of colonial contact the literature produced in the language was entirely derivative, with very little link to contemporary life (166), but translations by missionaries and administrators first helped Kannada literature break away from these archaic forms. "The modern Kannada short poem came into being around 1838 through the invocation poems translated by Christian missionaries" (167). Following this came textbooks of poems and stories translated for school children. A.B. Srikantaiah made the point that, "There are two ways to develop our mother tongue. Either the native language should be strong within itself. When that is not so, we have to gain this strength through translations" (cited in Viswanatha and Simon 1999: 168).

The work of B.M. Srikantaiah in the first decades of the twentieth century considerably increased the impetus of this early work. Srikantaiah, who became an ardent linguistic nationalist, wrote a collection of poems, criticism and a series of essays on the development of Kannada literature.

But his most influential intervention was the translation of three plays: an adaptation of a tenth-century Kannada epic; an application of the story of

Sophocles' *Ajax* to a character in the Mahabarahta; and a translation of Aeschylus' *The Persians*. These three examples demonstrate three different writing/translation strategies for which there are three different Sanskrit terms: *roopaanta* (changing the shape); *anu-vada* (something that follows after); and *bhashanthara* (changing the language). It was the first, the transformation of indigenous material into a contemporary mode that had a lasting impact on Kannada literature. The transformation here was one of form rather than language but it had a comparable impact on the indigenous culture as the appropriation of English by Indian writers to produce post-colonial literature. But whereas the English texts empower the local culture by speaking to a potential global audience, the transformation of ancient literary traditions with modern genres may revivify the local literature, representing the integrity and distinction of the culture to an audience of modern Kannada speakers.

Transformation: The language of post-colonial literatures

Clearly the transcultural environment of the post-colonial society offers considerable opportunity to observe an overlap between translation and transformation. But I think it is a mistake to simply call post-colonial writing 'translation' as some critics have done. The writer of a post-colonial text has many more opportunities to direct the development of the text; more freedom to decide the types of audience for whom the text is written; more opportunity to make original creative decisions. As Benjamin put it, "the intention of the poet is spontaneous, primary, graphic; that of the translator is derivative, ultimate, ideational" (1969: 76–7). The movement from source language to target language is much more subtle, if indeed one can even call it a movement, for the transformation occurs in the target language under the creative influence of a source language. The post-colonial writer has none of the standard problems of translation: Who is the author? Is it faithful or beautiful? Can a comparable word or concept be found? Although, as the discussion of Narayan above shows, the author must make very specific decisions about which word to use where, those decisions are the author's to make and not demanded by an original text.

When such a writer enters the productive space of language he or she can be said to create a new language. *The Empire Writes Back* (2002) calls this language "english" as opposed to English. Edward Kamau Brathwaite, as we have seen, calls it 'nation language', and compellingly describes the ways in which the character of language, not just the orthography and grammar, can be transformed. "English it may be in terms of some of its lexical features," he says, "But in its contours, its rhythm and timbre, its sound explosions, it is not English" (1984: 13). This is particularly true of poetry in which the sound and the form become an inextricable part of the meaning: "the noise that it makes is part of the meaning, and if you ignore the noise (or what you would think of as noise, shall I say) then you lose part of the meaning" (1984: 17).

We find something of this in Brathwaite's poem "Caliban" in which the second stanza takes the form of the limbo.

And
Ban
Ban
Cal-
iban
like to play
pan
at the Car-
nival;
pran-
cing up to the lim-
bo silence
down
down
down
so the god won't drown
him
down
down
down
to the is-
land town
…

Ban
Ban
Cal-
iban like to play
pan
at the Car-
nival;
dip-
ping down
and the black
gods call-
ing, back
he falls
through the water's
cries
down
down
down

where the music hides
- him
down
down
down
where the si-
lence lies.

(Brathwaite 1969: 35)

The first thing we notice is the writerly form of the poem that seems to perform the limbo dance. Caliban, the model of the Caribbean subject, makes one
of his many appearances, but the limbo dance has a dense cultural meaning. As
Wilson Harris explains (1981) the limbo is a form of history, a performance of the
crossing of the Middle Passage – it enacts the movement in the black hold of the
slave ship, across the Atlantic to the New World. This is just one structural form
among several in the poem and clearly Brathwaite asks the poetic language – the
written word on the page – to do more than represent as it performs its own
limbo. The language has both the 'noise' and rhythm of the limbo dance and of
nation language as it performs this quintessential act of memory in the person of
Caliban.

The function of the language is to operate as a metonym of culture, and in
Brathwaite's formulation, to operate as a metonym for race as well. Very often the
two are conflated. Brathwaite's contention is that Standard English creates a disjunction between language and experience in the Caribbean. The writer intervenes to produce a transformed English, moulded and shaped by the effects of the
creole continuum. The Caribbean is the site of some of the most exciting
linguistic developments in post-colonial literatures. But similar developments may
be found in writing from all post-colonized cultures, whatever the nature of their
colonization or language background. All language groups, even those called
'monoglossic', may show linguistic peculiarities as significant as those in more
complex linguistic communities. The world language called English is a continuum of 'intersections' in which the speaking habits in various communities have
intervened to reconstruct the language. This 'reconstruction' occurs in two ways:
on the one hand, regional English varieties may introduce words which become
familiar to all English speakers, and on the other, the varieties themselves produce
national and regional peculiarities which distinguish them from other forms of
English.

The metonymic gap

The discovery we make in Brathwaite's poetry is that the language is metonymic
of the culture, that is, linguistic variation stands for cultural difference. This sets
up what can be called a 'metonymic gap' – the cultural gap formed when writers
(in particular) transform English according to the needs of their source culture.
This occurs when they insert unglossed words, phrases or passages from a first

language, when they use concepts, allusions or references that may be unknown to the reader, when they code switch, or when they transform the literary language by adherence to vernacular syntax or rhythms. Such variations become synecdochic of the writer's culture – the part that stands for the whole – rather than representations of the world, as the colonial language might. Thus the inserted language 'stands for' the colonised culture in a metonymic way, and its very resistance to interpretation constructs a 'gap' between the writer's culture and the colonial culture. Being constructed, this gap is very different from the gaps that might emerge naturally in a translation. The local writer is thus able to represent his or her world to the coloniser (and others) in the metropolitan language, and at the same time, to signal and emphasise a difference from it. In effect, the writer is saying, "I am using your language so that you will understand my world, but you will also know by the differences in the way I use it that you cannot share my experience".

The metonymic gap is a central feature of the transformation of the literary language. The writer concedes the importance of *meanability*, the importance of a situation in which meaning can occur, and at the same time signifies areas of difference which may lie beyond meaning, so to speak, in a realm of cultural experience. The distinctive act of the cross-cultural text is to inscribe *difference* and *absence* as a corollary of cultural identity. Consequently, whenever a 'strategy of transformation, is used, that is, a strategy which appropriates the dominant language and inflects it in a way that transforms it into a cultural vehicle for the writer, there is an installation of difference at the site of the meaning event. In this sense such strategies are directly metonymic of that cultural difference which is imputed by the linguistic variation. In fact they are a specific form of metonymic figure – the synecdoche.

The technique of such writing demonstrates how the dynamics of language change are consciously incorporated into the text. The metonymic gap is always *inserted* in the text in a particular way: whether by allusion, dialogue or language variance. The critical feature of this for our purpose, is that the strategies of transformation, by opening up a metonymic gap, are a *refusal* to translate. While they produce a communicable text, they remind us of the untranslatability of language. So in answer to the question of how post-colonial writers resolve the argument about the connection between language and identity, they do it by avoiding it altogether, raising *difference* to prominence instead. All of the strategies below operate metonymically in this way and in so doing they distance themselves even further from translation, because the process of transformation is also, subtly, a process of withholding complete transparency.

Strategies of transformation in post-colonial writing

Clearly, it is in the language that the curious tension between communicating and holding something back is most evident and this tension occurs in all forms and regions of post-colonial writing. In the Foreword to his novel *Kanthapura* Raja Rao explains the particular tasks viewed by the writer in conveying cultural specificity in a different language:

> The telling has not been easy. One has to convey in a language that is not one's own the spirit that is one's own. One has to convey the various shades and omissions of a certain thought-movement that looks maltreated in an alien language. I use the word 'alien', yet English is not really an alien language to us. It is the language of our intellectual make-up – like Sanskrit or Persian was before – but not of our emotional make-up. We are all instinctively bilingual, many of us writing in our own language and English. We cannot write like the English. We should not. We cannot write only as Indians.
>
> (Rao 1938: vii)

Such writing is, in effect, an ethnography of the writer's own culture. The post-colonial writer, who creates a life 'between two languages', stands already in that position that will come to be occupied by an interpretation. As we saw in the last chapter the writer writing in a second language is the reader/translator, uniting meaning and 'spirit', emphasizing the Third Space that is language itself. Editorial intrusions, such as the footnote, the glossary, and the explanatory preface, where these are made by the author, are a good example of this. Situated outside the text, they represent a reading rather than a writing, primordial sorties into that interpretative territory in which the Other (as reader) stands.

Glossing

Parenthetic translations of individual words, e.g. 'he took him into his obi (hut)', are the most obvious and most common authorial intrusion in cross-cultural texts. Although not limited to cross-cultural texts such glosses foreground the continual reality of cultural distance. But the simple matching of 'obi' and 'hut' is not quite satisfactory because the Igbo word 'obi' is more specifically 'a hut owned by a family which is used for the reception of guests rather than for sleeping'. If simple reference does not work even for simple objects, it is even more difficult to find a referent for more abstract terms. Glossing has become far less prevalent in contemporary writing, but it is useful for showing how simple referential bridges establish themselves as the most primitive form of metonymy.

Untranslated words

The technique of leaving some vernacular words untranslated in the text is a more widely used, and a more politically canny, device for conveying the sense of cultural distinctiveness, because glossing gives the translated word, and thus the 'receptor' culture, the higher status. Refusing to translate words not only registers a sense of cultural distinctiveness but also forces the reader into an active engagement with the vernacular culture. The refusal to translate is a refusal to be subsidiary. The reader gets some idea about the meaning of these words from the subsequent conversation, but further understanding will require the reader's own expansion of the cultural situation beyond the text. Hence the absence of translation has a particular kind of metonymic function.

Cultural difference is not inherent in the text but is inserted by such strategies. By developing specific ways of both constituting cultural distance and at the same time bridging it, the text indicates that it is the 'gap' rather than the experience (or at least the concept of a gap between experiences), which is created by language. The absence of explanation is therefore first a sign of distinctiveness and also ensures that meaning is not a matter of definition but of active engagement. In the passage – "The day he had come to show her husband sample suitings, he slipped nearly breaking his neck. He had learnt since then to walk like an *ogwumagada*" (Aniebo 1978: 35) – we do not need to know exactly what an *ogwumagada* is to know that its walk is significant, that he must walk carefully, with caution, foot after foot. In fact, *ogwumagada* means 'chameleon' in Igbo. Although we can locate the meaning of the word, more or less, by its location in context, the word itself confirms the metonymic gap of cultural difference.

Interlanguage

The refusal to translate words seems a successful way to foreground cultural distinctions, so it would appear even more profitable to attempt to generate what might be called an 'interculture' by the fusion of the linguistic structures of two languages. Amos Tutuola published his first novel in 1952 with a language that seemed to do just this:

> I was a palm-wine drinkard since I was a boy of ten years of age. I had no other work more than to drink palm-wine in my life. In those days we did not know other money except COWRIES, so that everything was very cheap, and my father was the richest man in town.
>
> (Tutuola 1952: 7)

Tutuola's work has been the centre of controversy since it was published. It was simultaneously read by English critics as a delightful post-Joycean exercise in neologism, and rejected by many African critics as simply an inaccurate plagiarizing of traditional oral tales. But Tutuola's style may fruitfully be described by the term 'Interlanguage', a term coined by Nemser (1971) and Selinker (1972) to characterize the genuine and discrete linguistic system employed by learners of a second language.

The concept of an interlanguage reveals that the utterances of a second language learner are not deviant forms or mistakes, but rather are part of a separate but genuine linguistic system. Bearing no relation to either source or target language norms, they are potentially the basis of a potent metaphoric mode in cross-cultural writing. It may well be that Tutuola, in the early years of the post-war African novel, located the most primal form of language variance. If this is so, Tutuola's work may not be the mere linguistic aberration it has sometimes been dismissed as, but an important and early example of a diglossic formation in post-colonial literature. In this sense Tutuola's 'interlanguage' may be seen as paradigmatic of all cross-cultural writing since the development of a creative language is not a striving for competence in the dominant tongue, but a striving towards appropriation, in which the cultural distinctiveness can be simultaneously overridden/overwritten.

Syntactic fusion

Tutuola's novels uncovered a widely held assumption that alien worldviews might come closer if their linguistic structures were somehow meshed. This was, as we have seen, more obviously and self-consciously the project of Gabriel Okara's attempt in *The Voice* to marry the syntax of his tribal language, Ijaw, to the lexical forms of English. But syntactic fusion is much more common in post-colonial writing as a less overt feature of the linguistic material. A multilingual society like Papua New Guinea, for example, provides a rich source for syntactic variation.

In Kumula Tawali's play *Manki Masta* the influence of pidgin on the language of the play emerges in the way in which the inadequate English of the 'bush kanaka' follows pidgin syntax. When Poro says "Masta, me ... me want work for houseboy for you" (1972: 3) his English is a direct translation of the pidgin – "Mi laik wok long hausboi long yu", just as his "Yessa, masta I have some wantok (friends) there" (1972: 3) is a rendering of the pidgin, "Yessa, masta, mi get sampela wantok longhap ia". Syntactic (and orthographic) fusion can signify difference in a number of ways, but as an example of the metonymic gap it is difference that is inserted by the language rather than identity. The fascinating thing here, of course, is that difference is constructed in reference to another *learned* language. Pidgin bears not a cultural, but an historical and political reference to difference, Melanesian *tok pisin* being the mode of an emergent 'National Culture' in PNG.

Predictably, the literature of the Caribbean continuum provides the widest range of possibilities of syntactic variation. The following passage from St Lucian poet and playwright Derek Walcott's poem "The Star-Apple Kingdom" is a subtle demonstration of the way in which poetry can hover in the tension between the vernacular and the standard by alternating one with the other:

> Man, I brisk in the galley first thing next dawn,
> brewing li'l coffee; fog coil from the sea
> like the kettle steaming when I put it down
> slow, slow, 'cause I couldn't believe what I see:
> where the horizon was one silver haze,
> the fog swirl and swell into sails, so close,
> that I saw it was sails, my hair grip my skull,
> it was horrors, but it was beautiful.

(Walcott 1977: 10)

The adaptation of vernacular syntax to standard orthography makes the rhythm and texture of vernacular speech more accessible.

Code-switching and vernacular transcription

Perhaps the most common method of inscribing alterity by the process of appropriation is the technique of switching between two or more codes, particularly in the literatures of the Caribbean continuum. The techniques employed by the polydialectical writer include variable orthography to make dialect more accessible, double glossing and code switching to act as an interweaving interpretative mode, and the selection of certain words which remain untranslated in the text. All these are common ways of installing cultural distinctiveness in the writing. But probably the most distinctive feature of the Caribbean novel is the narrator who 'reports' in Standard English, but moves along the continuum in the dialogue of the characters.

> 'The moment you start reading to me you does make me feel sleepy. I know some people does feel sleepy the moment they see a bed.'
> 'They is people with a clean mind. But listen, girl. A man may turn over half a library to make one book. It ain't me who make that up, you know.'
> 'How I know you ain't fooling me, just as how you did fool Pa?'
> 'But why for I go want to fool you, girl?'
> 'I ain't the stupid little girl you did married, you know.'
> And when he brought the book and revealed the quotation on the printed page, Leela fell silent in pure wonder. For however much she complained and however much she reviled him, she never ceased to marvel at this husband of hers who read pages of print, chapters of print, why, whole big books; this husband who, awake in bed at nights, spoke, as though it were nothing, of one day writing a book of his own and having it printed!
>
> (Naipaul 1957: 85)

Naipaul's novel *The Mystic Masseur* is not only a typical example of the interspersion of Standard English and Trinidadian dialect, but a masterful demonstration of the function of writing to accord power, a sign of the power invested in the colonial language itself.

Such code switching can be vibrantly evocative in drama. In Jimmy Chi and Kuckles' Aboriginal play *Bran Nue Dae* the interpolation of a chorus and the variation between different forms of English give an impression of productive instability to the language. From the group who greet the central character, Willie:

LUCY   Hey Rosie, he wanna sit wit you!
ROSIE   Who?
LUCY   Willie

ROSIE   He stalebait
SALLY ANNE   He deadly boy. He come from Lombadina
BERNADETTE   He bin Perth for Schooling, Rossmoyne

(Gilbert 2001: 324)

This is followed by the German accent of Father Benedictus which is mimicked by Willie after stealing sweets from the tuckshop.

WILLIE   Yah it is gut to eat at der Lord's table. First ve haff made an inventory ov der spoils. (*He holds the black book up*) Den ve haff to partake of der fruits ov our labours. Thankyou Lord –

(Gilbert 2001: 325)

The chorus of the congregation is sung in standard English:

There's a new day dawning
And it's wiping out the tears
With the task unfolding
With the passing of the years

(326)

This highly energetic play is almost frenetic in its code switching but it gives a strong and celebratory sense of the fluid and inventive dimensions of Aboriginal culture. The choral structure and the use of dance and song allow the audience into the play, so to speak, while the code switching maintains their status as spectators.

Code switching is a feature of novel after novel in West Indian literature. Merle Hodge's *Crick Crack Monkey* (1970) is a particularly rich source of examples of the strategy, but the following passage from de Lisser's *Jane's Career* (1913) also demonstrates the ease with which the writer in the polydialectical continuum may move from one code to another:

'So this is the way you use me yard!' was her greeting to both the young women. 'Tou bring you' dirty friends into me place up to twelve o'clock at night and keep me up and disgrace me house. Now don't tell me any lie! ...'

Sarah knew that Mrs Mason may have heard but could not possibly have seen them, since only by coming into the yard could she have done that. She therefore guessed that the lady was setting a trap for her ...

'Y'u know, Miss Mason,' she protested, 'y'u shouldn't do that. It's not because I are poor that you should teck such an exvantage of me to use me in dat way; for y'u never catch me tellin' you any lie yet, ma'am ...

(de Lisser 1913: 53)

The space between languages

The Aboriginal poet Lionel Fogarty uses a range of strategies within a single poem to create the metonymic gap within the English text. In the following poem untranslated words, creolized syntactical forms and ethno-rhythmic prose all serve to draw readers into the poem through the rhythms of a lullaby yet hold them at an invisible edge of Aboriginal culture.

Joowindoo Goonduhmu

Ngujoo nye muyunube
Little black buree
You must respect golo
You must praise to junun
You must seek love with googee
little black buree hear your
song 'nuyeeree munu juwoon'
The gendergender
will bring the message
The googuhgu
will laugh when you cry sad
to make your world happy
Gugun gugun buree 'gukoore doongge'
Wake up little buree your
old gulung boome
all gnumgnin to
love mooroon gunggen ge
Oh little buree goonduhmu sing
goonduhmu the feelings of
gurring ina narmee, gurring ina narmee
nha gun goon na nhorn goo
yea little buree our binung love
your sounds in the boorun
now miremumbeh and
monu goondir helps
little black gukoore your gumee
loves you. Even mumu love you

(Fogarty 2002)

By stretching the 'Englishness' of the poem to the very limit, a limit so extensive that the poem is filled to excess with the words, rhythm and sound of the Aboriginal language, the poet arrives at, or at least gestures towards, that zone of untranslatability that all aesthetic objects occupy. The poem seems to build itself around cultural difference. But despite the apparent resistance of the poem to a reading it is quite accessible to the reader of English because the poet has moved the Aboriginal voice towards the target language in at least two major ways. First, the transcription of the Aboriginal words in roman script situates the sound of the words in the English text. In this respect the poem maintains the musical quality of poetic form but it moves further towards English by situating the Aboriginal words in English syntax. Thus "You must respect golo/ You must praise to junun" enacts the process of teaching as the mother communicates the figures that are important in Aboriginal society. The sense of the sentence is accessible though the individual words remain untranslated. The text resists at the level of vocabulary but 'concedes' – translates – at the level of script and syntax. Thus the metonymic gap is maintained while the spirit and sense of Aboriginal values are communicated. The reader is introduced to, but stands at the edge of, a spiritual world the vast difference of which can be demonstrated even if it cannot be experienced.

In this case the transformation of English in the production of the poetic object demonstrates the political accessibility of a space beyond translation, a space of presence that exists prior even to the structures of meaning on which a translation, either inner or outer, must rely. The poem is in the form of a lullaby, as if to show that poetic language itself is a zone of pure potentiality. In this way, rather than conclude the discussion of the relationship between translation and transformation, it stands as a signpost to a road travelling deeper into the third space of language itself.

Epilogue

The future that Shakespeare neither wrote nor imagined for Caliban has been one of extraordinary energy and creativity. While Prospero went off to retirement in Milan, Caliban proceeded to use Prospero's language to change the world. In doing so he revealed something about language and something about the agency of the colonized, about the human capacity to prevail. But even more than that he showed that the transformation of language, like the writing of literature, is a utopian project, one that extends beyond cursing. Transformation is the strategy of possibility, infused with the hope for a different kind of future. It is this hope that energises post-colonial writing.

Bibliography

Achebe, Chinua (1964), *Arrow of God*, London: Heinemann.

Achebe, Chinua (1975), *Morning Yet on Creation Day*, London: Heinemann.

Achebe, Chinua (1989), "Politics and Politicians of Language in African Literature", in G.D. Killam (ed.) *Historical and Cultural Contexts of Linguistic and Literary Phenomena*, Guelph: University of Guelph.

Advisory Committee of the Imperial Education Conference (1923), *Report*, London: HMSO.

Alleyne, M.C. (1963), "Communication and Politics in Jamaica", *Caribbean Studies*, 3 (2): 22–61.

Aniebo, I.N.C. (1978), *The Journey Within*, London: Heinemann.

Aristotle, *Rhetoric*, 111, 1410.

Armah, Ayi Kwei (1968), *The Beautyful Ones Are Not Yet Born*, London: Heinemann.

Arteaga, Alfred (1994), *An Other Tongue: Nation and Ethnicity in the Linguistic Borderlands*, Durham, NC: Duke University Press.

Arthur, J.M. (1997), *Aboriginal English: A Cultural Study*, Melbourne: Oxford University Press.

Arthur, J.M. (1999), "The Eighth Day of Creation", *Journal of Australian Studies*, June 1999: 66–72.

Arthur, J.M. (2003), *The Default Country: a Lexical Cartography of Twentieth-Century Australia*, Sydney: UNSW Press.

Ashcroft, Bill (1987), "Language Issues Facing Commonwealth Writers", *Journal of Commonwealth Literature*, 12 (1): 99–118.

Ashcroft, Bill (1989), "Constitutive Graphonomy: a Post-colonial Theory of Literary Writing", *Kunapipi*, 11 (1): 58–73.

Ashcroft, Bill (2001a), *Post-Colonial Transformation*, London: Routledge.

Ashcroft, Bill (2001b), *On Post-Colonial Futures: Transformations of Colonial Culture*, London: Continuum.

Ashcroft, Bill (2001c), "Language and Race", *Social Identities*, 7 (3): 311–28.

Ashcroft, Bill, Gareth Griffiths and Helen Tiffin (1989), *The Empire Writes Back: Theory and Practice in Post-Colonial Literatures*, London: Routledge.

Ashcroft, Bill, Gareth Griffiths and Helen Tiffin, eds. (1995), *The Post-Colonial Studies Reader*, London: Routledge.

Ashcroft, Bill, Gareth Griffiths and Helen Tiffin (1998), *Key Concepts in Post-Colonial Studies*, London: Routledge.

Ashcroft, Bill, Gareth Griffiths and Helen Tiffin, eds. (2006), *The Post-Colonial Studies Reader*, 2nd Edition London: Routledge.

Assad, Talal (1973), *Anthropology and the Colonial Encounter*, New York: Humanities Press.

Austin, J.L. (1962), *How to do Things with Words*, Oxford: Clarendon.

Awoonor, Kofi (1971), *Petals of Blood*, London: Heinemann.

Azaryhu, Maoz and Arnon Golan (2001), "(Re)naming the Landscape: the Formation of the Hebrew Map of Israel 1949–1960", *Journal of Historical Geography*, 27 (2): 178–95.

Bailey, Beryl L. (1966), *Jamaican Creole Syntax*, Cambridge: Cambridge University Press.

Bakhtin, Mikhail (1981), *The Dialogic Imagination: Four Essays* (ed. Michael Holquist, trans. Caryl Emerson and Michael Holquist), Austin: University of Texas.

Balutansky, Kathleen M. and Marie-Agnès Sourieau, eds. (1998), *Caribbean Creolization: Reflections on the Cultural Dynamics of Language, Literature, and Identity*, Gainesville: University Press of Florida; Barbados: The Press University of the West Indies.

Barthes, Roland (1971), 'From Work to Text', in Rick Rylance (ed.) *Debating Texts*, Milton Keynes: Open University [1987].

Bassnett, Susan and Harish Trivedi (1999), *Post-Colonial Translation: Theory and Practice*, London: Routledge.

Beaglehole, J.C. (1955), *Journals of Captain James Cook*: Vol 1: *The Voyage of the Endeavour*, Cambridge: Cambridge University Press for Hakluyt Society.

Benjamin, Walter (1969), "The Task of the Translator", *Illuminations* (trans. Harry Zohn), New York: Schocken.

Bennett, Meredith (1982), "The Poet as Language Maker: Sri Chinmoy", *New Literature Review*, 10: 13–22.

Berger, P. and H. Kellner (1964), "Marriage and the Construction of Reality", *Diogenes*, 46: 1–24.

Bhabha, Homi (1984), "Representation and the Colonial Text: Some Forms of Mimeticism", in Frank Gloversmith (ed.) *The Theory of Reading*, Brighton: Harvester.

Bhabha, Homi (1994), *The Location of Culture*, London: Routledge.

Bhattacharya, Rimli and Geeta Dharmarajan (1991), *Katha Prize Stories: The Best Short Fiction*, Vol. 1, New Delhi: Katha.

Bickerton, Derek (1973), "On the Nature of a Creole Continuum", *Language*, 49 (3): 640–69.

Bloom, Harold (1988), *William Shakespeare's*, The Tempest, New York: Chelsea House.

Bolt, Christine (1971), *Victorian Attitudes to Race*, London: Routledge.

Bourdieu, Pierre and Jean-Claude Passeron (1977), *Reproduction in Education, Society and Culture* (trans. Richard Nice), London: Sage.

Brady, F. and W.K. Wimsatt, eds. (1977), *Samuel Johnson: Selected Poetry and Prose*, Berkeley: University of California Press.

Brantlinger, Patrick (1988), *Rule of Darkness: British Literature and Imperialism 1830–1914*, Ithaca, NY: Cornell University Press.

Brathwaite, Edward Kamau (1969), *Islands*, Oxford: Oxford University Press.

Brathwaite, Edward Kamau (1971), "Rehabilitations", *Critical Quarterly*, 13 (3): 175–83.

Brathwaite, Edward Kamau (1974), "The African Presence in Caribbean Literature", *Daedalus*, 103 (2): 73–109.

Brathwaite, Kamau (1976) *LX the Love Axe/1: Developing a Caribbean Aesthetic*, Leeds: Peepal Tree Press.

Brathwaite, Edward Kamau (1984), *History of the Voice: the Development of Nation Language in Anglophone Caribbean Poetry*, London: New Beacon.

Brew, J.O., ed. (1968), *One Hundred Years of Anthropology*, Cambridge, MA: Harvard University Press.

Brydon, Diana (1984), "Re-writing *The Tempest*", *World Literature Written in English*, 24 (2) (Autumn): 74–89.

Buffon, Comte de (1812), *Natural history general and particular, by the Count de Buffon: the history of man and quadrupeds* (trans. William Wood), London: T. Cadell Readex Micr Reprints [1968].

Carter, Paul (1987), *The Road to Botany Bay*, London: Faber.

Chapman, Michael (1996), *Southern African Literatures*, London: Longman.

Chomsky, Noam (1965), *Aspects of the Theory of Syntax*, Cambridge, MA: MIT Press.

Clifford, James (1982), *Person and Myth: Maurice Leenhardt in the Melanesian World*, Berkeley: University of California Press.

Cresswell, Tim (1996), *In Place/Out of Place: Geography, Ideology and Transgression*, Minneapolis: University of Minnesota Press.

Cresswell, Tim (2004), *Place: a Short Introduction*, Oxford: Blackwell.

Cronon, W. (1995), "The Trouble with Wilderness, or, Getting Back to the Wrong Nature", in W. Cronon (ed.) *Uncommon Ground: Toward Re-inventing Nature*, New York: W.W. Norton, 69–90.

Crystal, David (1997), *The Cambridge Encyclopaedia of Language*, Cambridge: Cambridge University Press.

Cudjoe, Selwyn R. (1993), *Eric Williams Speaks: Essays on Colonialism and Independence*, Wellesley, MA: Calaloux.

Cudjoe, Selwyn R. (1998), "Eric Williams and the Politics of Language", *Callaloo*, 24 (4): 753–63.

Daniel, Samuel (1599), *Musophilus: Containing a General Defense of Learning*, in *The Oxford Edition of Samuel Daniel*, Oxford: Oxford University Press [1999].

Das, Kamala (1986), *Kamala Das: a Selection, with Essays on Her Work*, ed. S.C. Harrex and V. O'Sullivan, Adelaide: CRNLE.

Dasgupta, Sanjukta (2004), *First Language*, Kolkatta: Dasgupta.

Davies, John (1994), *A History of Wales*, Harmondsworth: Penguin.

D'Costa, Jean (1983), "The West Indian Novelist and Language: a Search for a Literary Medium", in Lawrence D. Carrington (ed.) *Studies in Caribbean Language*, Society for Caribbean Linguistics, St Augustine, Trinidad: University of the West Indies.

D'Costa, Jean (1984), "Expression and Communication: Literary Challenges to the Caribbean Polydialectical Writers", in Language Issues Facing Commonwealth Authors: a Symposium, *Journal of Commonwealth Literature*, 19 (1): 123–41.

D'Costa, Jean (1985), "Expression and Communication: Literary Challenges to the Caribbean Polydialectical Writers", in Language Issues Facing Commonwealth Authors: a Symposium, *Journal of Commonwealth Literature*, 19 (1): 121–43.

de Lisser, Herbert G. (1913), *Jane's Career*, London: Collins [1971].

de Man, Paul (1980), *Allegories of Reading*, New Haven, CN: Yale University Press.

de Man, Paul (2000), "'Conclusions' on Walter Benjamin's 'The Task of the Translator', Messenger Lecture, Cornell University, March 4, 1983", *Yale French Studies*, 97, *50 Years of Yale French Studies: a Commemorative Anthology Part 2: 1980–1998*: 10–35.

DeCamp, David (1971), "Towards a Generative Analysis of a Post-Creole Speech Continuum", in Dell Hymes (ed.) *Pidginisation and Creolisation of Languages*, Cambridge: Cambridge University Press.

Deleuze, Gilles and Felix Guattari (1972), *Anti-Oedipus: Capitalism and Schizophrenia* (trans. Robert Hurley, Mark Seem and Helen R. Lane), Minneapolis: University of Minnesota Press [1987].

Deleuze, Gilles and Felix Guattari (1980), *A Thousand Plateaus: Capitalism and Schizophrenia* (trans. Brian Massumi), Minneapolis: University of Minnesota Press [1983].

Derrida, Jacques (1978), *Writing and Difference* (trans. Alan Bass), London: Routledge.

Dewey, James (1920), *Democracy and Education*, New York: Macmillan.

Donnell, Alison and Sarah Lawson Welsh (1996), *The Routledge Reader in Caribbean Literature*, London: Routledge.

Dreyfus, Hubert L. and Paul Rabinow (1982), *Michel Foucault: Beyond Structuralism and Hermeneutics*, Brighton: Harvester.

Eliade, Mircea (1959), *The Sacred and the Profane*, New York: HarperCollins.

Elkin, A.P. (1946), *The Australian Aborigines*, Sydney: Angus and Robertson [1974].

Eoyang, E.C. (1994), "'Seeing with Another I': Our Search for Other Worlds", in Arteaga (1994): 93–112.

Eri, Vincent (1970), *The Crocodile*, Harmondsworth: Penguin.

Eze, Emmanuel Chukwudi, ed. (1997), *Postcolonial African Philosophy: a Critical Reader*, Oxford: Blackwell.

Ezekiel, Nissim (1989), *Collected Poems 1952–1988*, Delhi: Oxford University Press.

Fabian, Johannes (1982), *Language and Colonial Power*, Berkeley: University of California Press.

Fairclough, Norman (1989), *Language and Power*, London: Longman.

Fanon, Frantz (1952), *Black Skin White Masks* (trans. Charles Lam Markmann), London: Paladin [1968].

Fanon, Frantz (1959), *Studies in a Dying Colonialism* (trans. H. Chevalier), Harmondsworth: Penguin [1965].

Fanon, Frantz (1961), *The Wretched of the Earth*, Harmondsworth: Penguin.

Fanon, Frantz (1964), *Towards the African Revolution* (trans. Haakon Chevalier), New York: Grove [1967].

Fishman, Joshua A., Andrew W. Conrad and Alma Rubal-Lopez, eds. (1996), *Post-Imperial English: Status Change in Former British and American Colonies, 1940–1990*, Berlin: Mouton de Gruyter.

Florio, John (1603), *The Essays of Montaigne* (trans. John Florio; introd. George Saintsbury), New York: AMS [1967].

Fogarty, Lionel (2002), "The Poetry of Lionel Fogarty, Selected by Coral Hull", *Thylazine: the Australian Journal of Arts, Ethics and Literature*, 5. http://www.thylazine.org/archives/thyla5/lf.html (accessed 27 May 2008).

Foucault, Michel (1977), "What Is an Author", in *Language, Counter-Memory, Practice*, Oxford: Blackwell.

Foucault, Michel (1980), "Lecture Two: 14 January 1976", in *Power/Knowledge: Selected Interviews and Other Writings* (ed. Colin Gordon), New York: Pantheon [1976].

Foucault, Michel (1982), "The Subject and Power", in Dreyfus and Rabinow 1982: 208–26.

Frame, Janet (1962), *The Edge of the Alphabet*, New York: Braziller.

Freeman, Edward Augustus (1879), "Race and Language", in Edgar Thompson and Everett Hughes (eds.) *Race: Individual and Collective Behaviour*, New York: Free Press [1958].

Friel, Brian (1981), *Translations*, London: Faber.

Fry, Northrop (1982), *The Great Code: the Bible and Literature*, New York: Harcourt Brace Jovanovich.

Furphy, Joseph [Tom Collins] (1903), *Such Is Life*, Sydney: Angus & Robertson [1975].

Gandhi, M.K. (1910), "Hind Swaraj or Indian Home Rule" (Ch.1 trans. M.K. Gandhi), Gujarat Columns of *Indian Opinion* 11th and 18th Dec 1909. http://www.soilandhealth.org/03sov/0303 critic/hind%20swaraj.pdf (accessed 27 May 2008).

Gates, Henry Louis, ed. (1986), *Race, Writing and Difference*, Chicago: University of Chicago.

Geraghty, P. (1984), "Language Policy in Fiji and Rotuma", in *Duivosavosa: Fiji's Languages: Their Use and their Future*, Bulletin of the Fiji Museum, 8, Suva: Fiji Museum.

Gilbert, Helen, ed. (2001), *Postcolonial Plays: an Anthology*, London: Routledge.

Glissant, Edouard (1989), *Caribbean Discourse: Selected Essays* (trans. Michael Dash), Charlottesville: University of Virginia Press.

Glissant, Edouard (1997), *Poetics of Relation* (trans. Betsy Wing), Ann Arbor: University of Michigan Press.

Greenblatt, Stephen (1990), *Learning to Curse: Essays in Early Modern Culture*, New York: Routledge.

Grove, Richard (1995), *Green Imperialism: Colonial Expansion, Tropical Island Edens and the Origins of Environmentalism 1600–1860*, Cambridge: Cambridge University Press.

Hall, Stuart (1990), "Cultural Identity and Diaspora", in Jonathan Rutherford (ed.), *Identity: Community, Culture, Difference*, London: Lawrence & Wishart.

Hansen, P.H. (1995), "Albert Smith, the Alpine Club, and the Invention of Mountaineering in Mid-Victorian Britain", *Journal of British Studies*, 34: 300–24.

Harris, Wilson (1981), "History, Fable and Myth in the Caribbean and the Guianas", in Hena Maes-Jelinek (ed.) *Explorations: Talks and Articles 1966–81*, Aarhus: Dangaroo.

Harris, Wilson (1999), "Creoleness: the Crossroads of a Civilization?", in A.J.M. Bundy, *Selected Essays of Wilson Harris: the Unfinished Genesis of the Imagination*, London: Routledge: 237–47.

Heidegger, Martin (1975), *Poetry, Language, Thought* (trans. and introd. Alfred Hofstadter), New York: Harper & Row.

Hilliard, F.H. (1957), *Short History of English Education in British West Africa*, London: T. Nelson.

Hirson, Denis (1996), "Denis Hirson interviewed by Robert Berold', *New Coin*. www.rhodes.ac.za/institutes/isea/newcoin/docs/96/i96may.htm (accessed 16 June 2004).

Hobson, J.A. (1902), *Imperialism* (introd. by Philip Siegelman), Ann Arbor: University of Michigan [1965].

Howard, Shane (1982), 'Solid Rock (Sacred Ground)', on the album "Spirit of Place" by *Goanna*, W.E.A. 600127, Sydney.

Hulme, Peter (1986), *Colonial Encounters: Europe and the Native Caribbean 1492–1797*, London: Routledge.

Jahn, Janheinz (1968), *A History of Neo-African Literature*, London: Faber.

Jakobson, Roman and Morris Halle (1956), *Fundamentals of Language*, The Hague: Mouton & Co.

Jensen, M. (1988), *Passage from India: Asian Indian Immigrants in North America*, New Haven, CT: Yale University Press.

Johnson, Samuel (1756), "Observations on the Present State of Affairs 1756", in Donald Greene (ed.) *The Yale Edition of the Works of Samuel Johnson*, Herman Liebert *et al.* (eds.) 16 vols, New Haven, CT: Yale University Press [1977], 10: 188, 186.

Johnstone, B. (1990), *Stories, Community and Place: Narratives from Middle America*, Bloomington: Indiana University Press.

Jones, H.M. (1964), *O, Strange New World*, New York: Viking.

Jones, Thomas Jesse (1922), *Education in Africa*, New York: Phelps-Stokes Fund.

Joyce, James (1964), *The Portrait of the Artist as a Young Man*, New York: Viking.

Kachru, Braj (1990), *The Alchemy of English: the Spread, Functions and Models of Non-Native Englishes*, Oxford: Pergamon.

Kachru, Braj (2005), *Asian English: Beyond the Canon*, Hong Kong: Hong Kong University Press.

Kant, Immanuel (1764), *Observations on the Feeling of the Beautiful and Sublime* (trans. John T. Goldthwait), Berkeley: California University Press [1960].

Karmi, Ghada (2004), *In Search of Fatima: a Palestinian Story*, London: Verso.

Kasaipwalova, John (1971), "Betel-nut is Bad Magic for Aeroplanes", in G. Powell (ed.), *Through Melanesian Eyes*, Melbourne: Macmillan [1987].

Kingsley, Mary (1897), *Travels in West Africa: Congo Français, Corisco and Cameroons*, London: Macmillan.

Kirby, Kathleen M. (1993), "Thinking Through the Boundary: the Politics of Location, Subjects, and Space", *Boundary 2*, 20 (2): 173–89.

Kroestch, Robert (1974), "Unhiding the Hidden: Recent Canadian Fiction", *Journal of Canadian Fiction*, 3 (3): 43–5.

Labov, William (1969), *The Social Stratification of English in New York City*, Washington, DC: Centre for Applied Linguistics.

Lamming, George (1960), *The Pleasures of Exile*, Ann Arbor: University of Michigan [1992].

Laye, Camara (1959), *The African Child* (trans. James Kirkup), London: Fontana. (First published in English as *The Dark Child* 1955.)

Le Page, Robert and David DeCamp (1960), *Jamaican Creole*, London: Macmillan.

Lee, Dennis (1977), *Savage Fields*, Toronto: Ananse.

Leenhardt, Maurice (1978), *Do Kamo*, New York: Arno Press.

Lévi-Strauss, Claude (1969), *Conversations with Claude Lévi-Strauss* (ed. G. Charbonnier, trans. John and Doreen Weightman), London: Jonathan Cape.

Lewis, L.J., ed. (1962), *Phelps-Stokes Reports on Education in Africa*, London: Oxford.

Locke, John (1690), *Two Treatises of Government* (introd. Peter Laslett), Cambridge: Cambridge University Press [1964].

London, Norrel A. (2003), "Entrenching the English Language in a British Colony: Curriculum Policy and Practice in Trinidad and Tobago", *International Journal of Educational Development*, 23: 97–112.

Lotherington, Heather (1998), "Language Choices and Social Reality: Education in Post-Colonial Fiji", *Journal of Intercultural Studies*, 19 (1): 57–68.

Macaulay, Thomas Babbington (1835), "Minute of the 2nd February, 1835", in G.M. Young (ed.) *Speeches*, London: Oxford University Press [1935].

McClintock, Anne, Aamir Mufti and Ella Shohat, eds. (1997), *Dangerous Liaisons: Gender, Nation and Postcolonial Perspectives*, Minneapolis: University of Minnesota Press.

McGuire, James (1992), "Forked Tongues, Marginal Bodies: Writing as Translation in Khatibi (Moroccan Bilingual Writer Abdelkebir Khatibi)", *Research in African Literatures*, 23 (1): 107–10.

McHoul, Alec and Wendy Grace (1993), *A Foucault Primer*, Melbourne: Melbourne University Press.

Mackenzie, D.F. (1985), *Oral Culture, Literacy & Print in Early New Zealand: the Treaty of Waitangi*, Wellington: Victoria University Press.

Mair, Christian, ed. (2003), *The Politics of English as a World Language*, Amsterdam: Rodopi.

Malouf, David (1978), *An Imaginary Life*, Sydney: Picador [1990].

Mandelbaum, D. (1949), *Selected Writings of Edward Sapir*, Berkeley: University of California Press.

Mannoni, Octave (1950), *Prospero and Caliban: the Psychology of Colonization*, Ann Arbor: University of Michigan [1990].

Marshall, Paule (1969), *The Chosen Place, the Timeless People*, New York: Vintage [1992].

Mazrui, Ali A. (1975), *The Political Sociology of the English Language*, The Hague: Mouton.

Mazrui, Ali A. and Mazrui Alamin M. (1998), *The Power of Babel: Language and Governance in the African Experience*, Oxford: James Curry.

Moore, Bruce, ed. (2001), *Who's Centric Now? The Present State of Post-Colonial Englishes*, Melbourne: Oxford University Press.

Morris, Mervyn, ed. (1973), "Introduction" to Vic Reid's *New Day* [Reid 1949].

Mukherjee, Tuntun (2002), "Translation, Communication, Utopia: Rediscovering *Gora*", in Rahman 2002: 145–57.

Müller, Max (1859), *A History of the Ancient Sanskrit Literature so Far as it Illustrates the Primitive Religion of the Brahmas*, Allahabad, India: The Panini Office Bhuvaneshwari Ashrama.

Müller, Max (1881), *Selected Essays on Language, Mythology and Religion*, London: Longmans Green & Co.

Müller, Max (1882), *Lectures on the Science of Language*, London: Longmans Green & Co.

Müller, Max (1891), *Physical Religion: the Gifford Lectures Delivered Before the University of Glasgow*, London: Longmans Green & Co.

Müller, Max (1898), *Collected Works*, London: Longmans Green & Co.

Naik, M.K., ed. (1979), *Aspects of Indian Writing in English: Essays in Honour of Professor Srinivasa Iyengar*, Madras: Macmillan.

Naipaul, V.S. (1957), *The Mystic Masseur*, Harmondsworth: Penguin [1985].

Naipaul, V.S. (1962), *The Middle Passage*, London: André Deutsch.

Naipaul, V.S. (1971), *In a Free State*, London: André Deutsch.

Narasimhaiah, C.D., ed. (1978), *Awakened Conscience*, New Delhi: Sterling.

Narayan, R.K. (1979), "English in India: Some Notes on English Indian Writing", in M.K. Naik (ed.) 1979.

Nash, R. (1982), *Wilderness and the American Mind*, New Haven, CT: Yale University Press.

Nemser, W. (1971), "Approximative Systems of Foreign Language Learners", *IRAL* (*International Review of Applied Linguistics*), 9 (2): 115–23.

Neumann, R.P. (1996), "Dukes, Earls and Ersatz Edens: Aristocratic Nature Preservationists in Africa", *Environment and Planning D: Society and Space*, 14: 79–98.

Newbolt, Henry (1921), *The Teaching of English in England: Report of the Departmental Committee appointed by the President of the Board of Education to Inquire into the Position of English in the Educational System of England*, London: HM Stationery Office.

Ngugi wa Thiongo (1967), *A Grain of Wheat*, London: Heinemann.

Ngugi wa Thiongo (1981), *Decolonizing the Mind: the Politics of Language in African Literature*, London: James Curry.

Nichols, Grace (1983), *I is a Long Memoried Woman*, London: Karnak House.

Okara, Gabriel (1964), *The Voice*, "African Writers Series", London: Heinemann [1970].

Olmsted, Jane (1997), "The Pull to Memory and the Language of Place in Paule Marshall's *The Chosen Place, the Timeless People* and *Praisesong for the Widow*", *African American Review*, 31 (2): 249.

Olwig, Kenneth R. (2002), "The Duplicity of Space: Germanic 'Raum' and Swedish 'Rum' in English Language Geographical Discourse", *Geografisker Annaler*, 84 B: 1–17.

Ong, Walter J. (1982), *Orality and Literacy: the Technologising of the Word*, London: Methuen.

Ooi Boo Eng (1987), "Malaysia and Singapore", *Journal of Commonwealth Literature*, 22: 83–9.

Oyewùmí, Oyèrónké (1997), *The Invention of Women: Making an African Sense of Western Gender Discourses*, Minneapolis: University of Minnesota Press.

Parakrama, A. (1995), *De-Hegemonizing Language Standards: Learning From (Post)Colonial Englishes about "English"*, Basingstoke, Hampshire: Macmillan; New York: St. Martin's Press.

Pennycook, Alistair (1994), *The Cultural Politics of English as an International Language*, London: Longman.

Pennycook, Alistair (1998), *English and the Discourses of Colonialism*, London: Routledge.

Phillipson, R. (1992), *Linguistic Imperialism*, Oxford: Oxford University Press.

Pindell, Terry (1995), *A Good Place to Live: America's Last Migration*, New York: Henry Holt.

Poliakov, Leon (1977), *The Aryan Myth: a History of Racist and Nationalist Ideas in Europe* (trans. Edmund Howard), New York: New American Library.

Prasad, G.J.V. (1999), "Writing Translation: the Strange Case of the Indian English Novel", in Bassnett and Trivedi 1999: 41–57.

Prasad, G.J.V. (2002), "Creating Indian Novels in English: R.K. Narayan as a Fellow Translator", in Rahman 2002: 44–54.

Pratt, Mary Louise (1992), *Imperial Eyes: Travel Writing and Transculturation*, London: Routledge.

Rahman, Anisur, ed. (2002), *Translation: Poetics and Practice*, New Delhi: Creative Books.

Ramakrishna, S. (1997), *Translation and Multilingualism: Post-Colonial Contexts*, Delhi: Pencraft International.

Rao, Raja (1938), *Kanthapura*, New York: New Directions [1963].

Ray, Mohit, K. (2002), "Translation as Interpretation", in Rahman 2002: 80–90.

Reid, V.S. (1949), *New Day*, London: Heinemann [1973].

Reinecke, John and Aiko Tokimasa (1934), "The English Dialect of Hawaii", *American Speech*, 9 (1): 48–58.

Rénan, Ernest (1848), *Future of Science*, Boston: Roberts Bros [1891].

Rénan, Ernest (1855), *Histoire Générale et Systéme Comparé des Langues Sémetiques*, in *Oeuvres complétes*, Paris: Calmann-Lévy [1947–1961] Vol. 1: 69–97.

Rénan, Ernest (1856), "Lettre a Gobineau" (June 26 1856), in *Oeuvres complétes*, Paris: Calmann-Lévy [1947–1961], Vol. 1: 437–48.

Rénan, Ernest (1858), *De l'Origine du langage*, in *Oeuvres complétes*, Paris: Calmann-Lévy [1947–1961], Vol. 8: 9–23, 109–10.

Rénan, Ernest (1887), *Histoire du Peuple Israël*, *in Oeuvres Complétes*, Paris: Calmann-Lévy [1947–1961], Vol. 6.

Rénan, Ernest (1888), "Islamism and Science", in *The Poetry of the Celtic Races and Other Studies* (trans. William G. Hutchinson), Port Washington, NY: Kennikat Press [1970]: 84–108.

Rénan, Ernest (1891), *The Future of Science*, London: Chapman and Hall.

Rénan, Ernest (1896), *Caliban: a Philosophical Drama Continuing "The Tempest" of William Shakespeare* (trans. Eleanor Grant Vickery), New York: AMS [1971].

Retamar, Roberto Fernández (1971), "Caliban", in Retamar 1989.

Retamar, Roberto Fernández (1986), "Caliban Revisited", in Retamar [1989].

Retamar, Roberto Fernández (1989), *Caliban and Other Essays* (trans. Edward Baker), Minneapolis: University of Minnesota Press.

Roberts, P.A. (1997), *From Oral to Literate Culture: Colonial Experience in the English West Indies*, Kingston, Jamaica: The Press, University of the West Indies.

Rousseau, Jean Jacques (1755), *A Discourse on Inequality* (trans. Maurice Cranston), London: Penguin [1988].

Rushdie, Salman (1991), *Imaginary Homelands: Essays and Criticism 1981–91*, London: Granta.

Russel, William P. (1801), *Multum in Parvo; or A Brief Display of More than a Thousand Errors in Each of the Undermentioned Writers: Johnson, Sheridan, Walker, Nares, Perry, Entick (and in the Works of Other Philologists)*, London: Barrett (1801): 93–5; quoted in Richard W. Bailey, *Images of English*, Ann Arbor: University of Michigan Press [1991], 106–7.

Ryden, Kent C. (1993), *Mapping the Invisible Landscape: Folklore, Writing and the Sense of Place*, Iowa City: University of Iowa Press.

Said, Edward (1978), *Orientalism*, New York: Vintage.

Said, Edward (1983), *The World, the Text and the Critic*, Cambridge, MA: Harvard University Press.

Said, Edward (1993), *Culture and Imperialism*, London: Chatto & Windus.

Salter, John (1989), *The Poetry of Judith Wright*, unpublished thesis, University of NSW, Sydney.

Sartre, Jean Paul (1972), *Black Orpheus*, in Léopold Sédar Senghor (ed.) *Anthologie de La Nouvelle Poésie Nègre et Malgache de Langue Française*, Paris: Presses Universitaires de France [1948].

Saussure, Ferdinand de (1916), *Course in General Linguistics* (trans. W. Baskin), Glasgow: Collins [1974].

Schama, Simon (1995), *Landscape and Memory*, London: HarperCollins.

Schmidt, Nancy J. (1985), "Review of Gerhard Fritschi, *Africa and Gutenberg: Exploring Oral Structures in the Modern African Novel* ", in *Research in African Literatures* 16 (4).

Sebald, W.G. (2001), *Austerlitz* (trans. Anthea Bell), New York: Random House.

Sebald, W.G. (2002), *The Rings of Saturn*, London: Vintage.

Seligman, C.G. (1957), *Races of Africa*, Oxford: Oxford Universtiy Press.

Selinker, Larry (1972), "Interlanguage", *IRAL* (*International Review of Applied Linguistics*), 10 (2): 209–31.

Selvon, Samuel (1975), *Moses Ascending*, London: Davis-Pointer.

Simmons, Marlise (1994), "Bar English? French Bicker on Barricades", *The New York Times* 15 March 1994, A1 and A14.

Simon, Sherry (1992), "The Language of Cultural Difference: Figures of Alterity in Canadian Translation", in L. Venuti (ed.) *Rethinking Translation: Discourse, Subjectivity, Ideology*, London: Routledge.

Simon, Sherry (1996), *Gender in Translation: Cultural Politics and the Politics of Transmission*, London: Routledge.

Simon, Sherry (1999), "Translating and Interlingual Creation in the Contact Zone: Border Writing in Quebec", in Bassnett and Trivedi 1999: 58–74.

Simon, Sherry (2000), *Changing the Terms: Translating in the Postcolonial Era*, Ottawa: University of Ottawa Press.

Singer, P. (2003), "Practical Ethics", in S. Armstrong and R. Botzler (eds.) *The Animal Ethics Reader*, London: Routledge.

Skinner, John (1998), *The Stepmother Tongue: an Introduction to New Anglophone Fiction*, London: Macmillan.

Soaba, Russel (1979), *Maiba*, Washington: Three Continents.

Sobusobu, Akainsi (1980), *The Taboo*, in Albert Wendt (ed.) *Lali: a Pacific Anthology*, Auckland: Longman Paul.

Soyinka, Wole (1975), "Neo Tarzanism: the Poetics of Pseudo Tradition", *Transition*, 48: 38–44.

Soyinka, Wole (1988), *Art, Dialogue and Outrage: Essays on Literature and Culture*, New York: Pantheon.

Spivak, Gayatri Chakravorty (1985), "The Rani of Simur", in Francis Barker *et al.* (eds.) *Europe and Its Others* 1, Proceedings of the Essex Conference on the Sociology of Literature July 1984, Colchester: University of Essex.

Sridhar, M. (2002), "How Cultures Meet: Translation from English to Telegu", in Rahman 2002: 107–12.

Stepan, Nancy (1982), *The Idea of Race in Science: Great Britain, 1800–1960*, London: Macmillan.

Stocking, George, ed. (1996), *Volksgeist as Method and Ethic: Essays on Boasian Ethnography and the German Anthropological Tradition*, Madison: University of Wisconsin Press.

Stubbs, William (1900), *Lectures in Early English History*, ed. A. Hassall, London: Longmans Green and Co.

Tagore, Rabindranath (1916), "Interview", *Portland Me Press*, 23 October 1916.

Talib, Ismail S. (2002), *The Language of Postcolonial Literatures*, London: Routledge.

Tawali, Kumula (1972), *Manki Masta*, in *Five New Guinea Plays*, Brisbane: Jacaranda.

Terdiman, Richard (1985), *Discourse/Counter Discourse: the Theory and Practice of Symbolic Resistance in Nineteenth-century France*, Ithaca, NY: Cornell University Press.

Thieme, John (1996), *The Arnold Anthology of Post-colonial Literatures in English*, London: Edward Arnold.

Thompson, Edgar and E.C Hughes, eds. (1965), *Race: Individual and Collective Behavior*, New York: Free Press.

Tiffen, Brian (1968), "Language and Education in Commonwealth Africa", in Julian Dakin, Brian Tiffen and H.G. Widdowson, *Language in Education*, London: Oxford.

Todorov, Tzvetan (1993), *On Human Diversity: Nationalism, Racism, and Exoticism in French Thought* (trans. Catherine Porter), Cambridge, MA: Harvard University Press.

Tonkinson, Robert (1974), *Aboriginal Victors of the Desert Crusade*, Menlo Park, CA: Cummings.

Traynor, Joanne (1997), *Sister Josephine*, London: Bloomsbury.

Tuan, Yi-Fu (1991), "Language and the Making of Place: a Narrative-Descriptive Approach", *Annals of the American Association of Geographers*, 8 (14): 684–96.

Tutuola, Amos (1952), *The Palm-wine Drinkard*, London: Faber.

Tuwhare, Hone (1993), *Deep River Talk: Collected Poems*, Auckland: Godwit Press.

Tymoczko, Maria (1999), "Post-Colonial Writing and Literary Translation", in Bassnett and Trivedi 1999: 19–40.

Uma, Alladi (2002), "Can a Translator be Self-effacing?", in Rahman 2002: 91–7.

Vaughan, Alden T. and Virginia Mason Vaughan (1991), *Shakespeare's Caliban: a Cultural History*, Cambridge: Cambridge University Press.

Vavrus, F. (2002), "Postcoloniality and English: Exploring Language Policy and the Politics of Development in Tanzania", *Tesol Quarterly*, 36 (3): 373–97.

Verhovek, Sam Howe (1995), "Mother Scolded by Judge for Speaking Spanish", *The New York Times*, 30 August 1995.

Vickers, N., P. Stallybrass *et al.* (1997), *Language Machines: Technologies of Literary and Cultural Production*, New York: Routledge.

Vico, G. (1968), *The New Science of Giambattista Vico* (trans. T.G. Bergin and Max Fisch), cited in Northrop Frye (1982), *The Great Code: the Bible and Literature*, New York: Harcourt, Brace Jovanovich.

Viswanatha, Vanamala and Sherry Simon (1999), "Shifting Grounds of Exchange: B.M. Srikantaiah and Kannada Translation", in Bassnett and Trivedi 1999: 162–81.

Viswanathan, Gauri (1987), "The Beginnings of English Literary Study in British India", *Oxford Literary Review*, 9 (1–2): 2–25.

Viswanathan, Gauri (1989), *Masks of Conquest: Literary Study and British Rule in India*, New York: Columbia University Press.

Walcott, Derek (1965), *The Castaway and Other Poems*, London: Jonathan Cape.

Walcott, Derek (1977), *The Star-apple Kingdom*, New York: Farrar, Straus and Giraux [1979].

Walcott, Derek (1986), *Collected Poems 1948–1984*, New York: Noonday Press.

Walcott, Derek (1996), *Conversations with Derek Walcott*, W. Baer (ed.), Jackson: University of Mississippi Press.

Watson, Maureen (1982a), Personal Interview, cited in Adam Shoemaker, *Black Words White Page: Aboriginal Literature 1929–1988*, Canberra: ANUE Press: 130.

Watson, Maureen (1982b), 'Walk Tall', in *Black Reflections*, Wattle Park: Education Information Retrieval Service.

Watts, R. and P. Trudgill, eds. (2002), *Alternative Histories of English*, London: Routledge.

Wechselblatt, Martin (1996), "The Pathos of Example: Professionalism and Colonialization in Johnson's 'Preface' to the Dictionary", *The Yale Journal of Criticism*, 9 (2): 381–403.

Wendt, Albert (1986), *The Birth and Death of the Miracle Man*, Harmondsworth: Penguin.

White, Patrick (1958), *The Tree of Man*, London: Eyre and Spottiswood.

Whitman, James (1984), "From Philology to Anthropology in Mid-nineteenth Century Germany", in George W. Stocking (ed.) *Functionalism Historicized: Essays on British Social Anthropology*, Madison: University of Wisconsin Press.

Whorf, Benjamin Lee (1952), *Collected Papers on Metalinguistics*, Washington, DC: Foreign Service Institute, Department of State.

Williams, Raymond (1989), *Resources of Hope: Culture, Democracy, Socialism*, London: Verso.

Wittgenstein, Ludwig (1961), *Blue and Brown Books*, Oxford: Blackwell.

Wittgenstein, Ludwig (1975), *Philosophical Investigations* (trans. G.E.M. Anscombe), Oxford: Blackwell.

Wittgenstein, Ludwig (1979), "Remarks on Frazer's *Golden Bough*" (ed. Ruch Rees, trans. A.C. Miles), Retford, UK: Brynmill.

Wolfe, Cary (2003), *Animal Rites: American Culture, the Discourse of Species and Posthumanist Theory*, Chicago: University of Chicago Press.

Wright, Alexis (2006), *Carpentaria*, Sydney: Giramondo.

Zabus, Chantal (1985), "A Calibanic Tempest in Anglophone and Francophone New World Writing", *Canadian Literature*, 104: 35–50.

Zabus, Chantal (1993), *The African Palimpsest*, Amsterdam: Rodopi.

Zabus, Chantal (2002), *Tempests After Shakespeare*, Basingstoke: Palgrave Macmillan.

Index